Helion & Company Limited
Unit 8 Amherst Business Centre
Budbrooke Road
Warwick
CV34 5WE
England
Tel. 01926 499 619
Email: info@helion.co.uk
Website: www.helion.co.uk
Twitter: @helionbooks
Visit our blog: https://helionbooks.wordpress.com/

Published by Helion & Company 2025
Designed and typeset by Farr out Publications, Wokingham, Berkshire
Cover designed by Paul Hewitt, Battlefield Design (www.battlefield-design.co.uk)

Text © Antonio Luis Sapienza Fracchia 2025
Illustrations © as individually credited
Colour profiles © David Bocquelet, Luca Canossa, Tom Cooper, Renato Dalmaso. 2025
Maps drawn by author 2025

Every reasonable effort has been made to trace copyright holders and to obtain their permission for the use of copyright material. The author and publisher apologise for any errors or omissions in this work, and would be grateful if notified of any corrections that should be incorporated in future reprints or editions of this book.

ISBN 978-1-804515-77-8

British Library Cataloguing-in-Publication Data
A catalogue record for this book is available from the British Library

All rights reserved. No part of this publication may be reproduced, stored in a retrieval system, or transmitted, in any form, or by any means, electronic, mechanical, photocopying, recording or otherwise, without the express written consent of Helion & Company Limited.

We always welcome receiving book proposals from prospective authors.

CONTENTS

Abbreviations and acronyms		2
Acknowledgements		3
Introduction		3
1	Brief History of Bolivia	3
2	Ernesto Che Guevara (1928–1967)	11
3	Bolivia's National Liberation Army (ELN)	16
4	General René Emilio Barrientos Ortuño (1919–1969)	22
5	Bolivian Armed Forces in the mid-1960s	32
6	US Military Training in Bolivia	44
7	The Ñancahuazú Guerrilla in 1967	48
The Aftermath		77
Epilogue		81
Appendices		86
Sources		93
Notes		94
About the Author		96

ABBREVIATIONS AND ACRONYMS

AFB	Air Force Base
BI	*Batallón de Infantería* – Infantry Battalion (Bolivian Army)
CIOS	*Centro de Operaciones de Selva* – Jungle Operation Centre (Bolivian Army)
CITE	*Centro de Instrucción de Tropas Especiales* – Special Troops Training Centre (Bolivian Army)
COB	*Confederación Obrera Boliviana* – Bolivian Workers Confederation
COIN	Counterinsurgency
CP	Letters assigned to Bolivia to register civil aircraft, followed by digits
DIC	*Departamento de Investigación Criminal* – Criminal Investigation Department (Bolivian Police)
ELN	*Ejército de Liberación Nacional* – National Liberation Army (Bolivia)
ETA	*Escuadrón de Transportes* Aéreos – Air Transport Squadron (Bolivian Air Force)
FAB	*Fuerza Aérea Boliviana* – Bolivian Air Force
KIA	Killed in action
LAB	*Lloyd Aéreo Boliviano*
MG	Machine gun
MILGP	US Military Groups
MIR	*Movimiento de Izquierda Revolucionaria* – Revolutionary Left Movement (Bolivia)
MNR	*Movimiento Nacionalista Revolucionario* – Revolutionary Nationalist Movement (Bolivia)
MPC	*Movimiento Popular Cristiano* – Christian Popular Movement (Bolivia)
M-26-7	*Movimiento 26 de Julio* (Cuba)
MTT	Mobile Training Team (US Army)
NCO	Non-Commissioned Officer
PCB	*Partido Comunista Boliviano* – Bolivian Communist Party
PRA	*Partido Revolucionario Auténtico* – Authentic Revolutionary Party (Bolivia)
PSD	*Partido Social Demócrata* – Social Democratic Party (Bolivia)
RA	*Regimiento de Artillería* – Artillery Regiment (Bolivian Army)
RC	*Regimiento de Caballería* – Cavalry Regiment (Bolivian Army)
RI	*Regimiento de Infantería* – Infantry Regiment (Bolivian Army)
RP	*Región Policial* – Police Region
SOUTHCOM	United States Southern Command
TAM	*Transporte Aéreo Militar* – Military Air Transport (Bolivian Air Force)
UDP	*Unión Democrática y Popular* – Popular and Democratic Union (Bolivia)
YPFB	*Yacimientos Petrolíferos Fiscales Bolivianos* – Bolivian Fiscal Oil Fields

ACKNOWLEDGEMENTS

The author wishes to express his deep gratitude to Bolivian historians Jorge Cornejo and Rodrigo Rosa Larserna for the data provided for this volume. Regarding the photographs, those of the guerrilla were seized by either the Bolivian Army or police and have been widely published ever since. Those of the FAB are from its historical archives, some of them through Jorge Cornejo, as are those of the Bolivian Army. Regarding the MTT pictures in Bolivia, they belong to the US Army Archives.

INTRODUCTION

Bolivia is a country with a very peculiar history, since in different conflicts with neighbouring countries it has lost large tracts of land and even its sovereign access to the Pacific Ocean. In this country, an immense number of aborigines of ancestral origin who normally inhabit the highlands of the country, and the descendants of Europeans, who inhabit the lowest and most productive areas of Bolivia, have long cohabited.

For a long time, the European descendants have been part of the ruling class in Bolivia, relegating the original inhabitants to a situation of extreme poverty. It is not for nothing that it is precisely among these aborigines that revolutionary movements arose to demand those rights that had been curtailed by the white ruling class for centuries. In this context, the so-called *Ejército de Liberación Nacional* (National Liberation Army/ELN) arose, which would be led by the Argentine-Cuban Ernesto 'Che' Guevara in 1966–67. However, the guerrilla uprising came at the wrong time since by the time it was instigated in Bolivia, the aborigines had already obtained many social achievements due to the 1952 Revolution.

The revolutionary figure of Che has generated a polarisation of opinions: admired by leftist movements across the planet and equally hated as a vulgar bloodthirsty murderer by many. The bibliography on Che and the Bolivian Ñancahuazú guerrilla is very extensive and this polarisation is reflected in it, depending on the political orientation of the authors. That is why this volume is an attempt to present a balanced panorama between both political orientations, presenting above all objective facts that have actually happened, leaving subjective opinions aside.

This volume is divided in eight chapters, including first a brief history of Bolivia, followed by a short biography of Ernesto Che Guevara. Then, a chapter is dedicated to Bolivia's National Liberation Army (ELN). Due to its historical importance in the leadership of the Bolivian government at that time, a biography of Air Force General René Barrientos Ortuño, constitutional President of Bolivia, is also included. One chapter is devoted exclusively to describing the Bolivian Armed and Police Forces, followed by another chapter describing the training of Bolivian Army Rangers by Green Beret instructors of the US Army. The penultimate chapter describes month by month the guerrilla actions of the ELN led by Che Guevara as well as the response of the Bolivian Armed Forces until the capture and execution of the main guerrilla leader. The final chapter is devoted to the two subsequent attempts by the ELN to restart guerrilla actions in Bolivia that were also repressed by the Bolivian Army. And finally, an epilogue where the failure of Che Guevara in his Bolivian adventure is analysed.

1
BRIEF HISTORY OF BOLIVIA

In Bolivia there are remains of human occupation from 12,000–10,000BC at the Viscachani site, Sud Lípez (10,000BC), and Altiplano de Sama (10,000–6000BC). Until 1600BC, sedentary cultures developed in the highlands, including the Chiripa and Wankarani.

The Tiwanaku (also spelled Tiahaunaco) culture, near Lake Titicaca, marked a moment of cultural flourishing in the altiplanic zone, extending its influence throughout the Andean area. Around 1,100AD, the Tiwanaku disappeared and there was a fight between the different groups that inhabited the region: Aymaras, Collas, Lupacas, and Pacajes. The Aymaras established a domain that encompassed Arequipa and Puno in Peru, and La Paz, Oruro and Cochabamba in present Bolivian territory, which lasted until Pachacuti Inca defeated the last Colla sovereign, Chunqui Cápac, in 1438 incorporating the Bolivian highlands into Tahuantinsuyo, as part of the province of Collasuyo, and imposing Quechua as the official language, although Aymara continued to be spoken regularly. The conquest of the Inca Empire by Francisco Pizarro paved the way for the subjugation of present-day Bolivia in the year 1535 and the establishment of the *Real Audiencia de Charcas* (Royal Audience of Charcas), an essential part of the Viceroyalty of Peru, which encompassed all of Bolivian territory today. The history of Bolivia in the Vice Regal period has been closely linked to Peru, being known by the name of Alto Peru (Upper Peru).

On the other side, the conquering current of the Río de La Plata expanded into the territory of what is now Bolivia, with the founding of Santa Cruz de la Sierra in 1561. A group of Spaniards from Asunción del Paraguay and Buenos Aires led by Ñuflo de Chaves together with Itatine allies conquered the region. The former founded Santa Cruz on the banks of the Sutó mountain range and the latter settled themselves in the north, in the region today known as Guarayos. The continental subtropical climate, the lack of indigenous labour, the absence of mines and great wealth, and the constant attack by the Guaranies made Santa Cruz of little interest

The Tiwanaku ruins of the Kalasasayao Temple of the Standing Stones in the south shores of Lake Titicaca in Bolivia (left). The Sun Gate of the Tiwanaku civilization (right). (Open source).

A drawing representing the *Cerro Rico de Potosí* (Rich Hill of Potosí) in the 16th century, called that way because of its deposits of silver. (Open source).

The *Real Audiencia de Charcas*, established in 1559 in the city of La Plata (present Sucre) in Bolivia. (Open source).

to Spanish migration, though. However, Santa Cruz remained an agricultural, cattle-raising culture isolated from the mining boom of Upper Peru, but it grew in population and its inhabitants founded other important towns and cities throughout the Chaco-Beniana plain and the southwestern valleys such as Vallegrande, Portachuelo, Trinidad, Charagua, Cuevo, Samaipata, San Ignacio, Riberalta and others.

For its part, Upper Peru was characterised by its mining-agricultural base. The city of Potosí, the most populous city in America in 1574 with 120,000 inhabitants, became a great mining centre due to the exploitation of the silver mines of Cerro Rico de Potosí and in 1611, it was the largest producer of silver in the world. King Carlos I had granted this city the title of Imperial Villa after its foundation.

As an additional cushion for the Spanish presence before the Portuguese advance, the crown allowed the establishment of Jesuit missions to the north and east of Santa Cruz in the Moxos and Chiquitos regions. These missions were very successful and important and advanced centres were established both culturally and economically.

One of the most important institutions in the history of Bolivia was the so-called Royal Audience of Charcas which was created by Decree of King Felipe II on 18 September 1559. It had five *oidores* (hearers), a president and some junior officials. The president of the Royal Audience of Charcas was also Captain General of La Plata, a position equivalent to that of a governor, and therefore also had administrative powers.

For more than 200 years, the territory of present-day Bolivia constituted the Royal Audience of Charcas, one of the most prosperous and densely populated centres of the Spanish Viceroyalties. In the last decades of the eighteenth century, Potosí, the most important city in the western hemisphere of the Spanish Empire, began to decline into oblivion as the richest veins of silver dried up and the economy diversified.

In 1776 the Royal Court of Charcas, which belonged to the Viceroyalty of Peru, became dependent on the new Viceroyalty of the Río de la Plata, based in Buenos Aires.

Between 1810 and 1826, Upper Peru was the scene of endless fighting and battles between the royalist Peruvians and Upper Peruvians and the Argentine and Upper Peruvian patriots, who would try to extend independence in the territories that would remain under royalist control until after the battle of Ayacucho. The independence movement in Upper Peru was impacted by the Rebellion of Pedro Antonio Olañeta, who commanded the entire royalist Army of Upper Peru on 22 January 1824 against the authority of the Viceroy of Peru, José de la Serna. The war came to an end with

On 6 August 1825, the National Assembly, meeting in the *Aula magna* of the historic University of San Francisco Xavier (today the Independence Hall) of the city of Chuquisaca (present Sucre), approved the proposal to form a free and sovereign country, signing the act of independence of Upper Peru, as it was known then. (Open source).

Portraits of the Liberator Simón Bolívar (left) and Marshal Antonio José de Sucre (right). Upper Peru adopted the name of the Republic of Bolívar first and then Bolivia in homage to the liberator and its capital received the name of Sucre. (Martín Tovar y Tovar).

without a resolution from the Deliberative Assembly, upon accepting the argument proposed by the deputy from Potosí, Presbyter Manuel Martín Cruz, who said the following: '...If from Romulus, Rome; from Bolívar, Bolivia...'[1] The new republic officially adopted the name of Bolivia on 3 October 1825. The capital of the country and seat of the state administration was established in the city of Chuquisaca. In Spanish colonial times, this city was known as La Plata or Villa de la Plata de la Nueva Toledo. It was not until 1839 that it received the official name of Sucre, in honour of the Venezuelan Hero Marshal Antonio José de Sucre.

After its emancipation, Bolivia plunged into a chronic state of revolutions, military uprisings, terrible internal struggles, and bloody civil wars for a long period of 55 years, which resulted in the political instability that lasted practically until the year 1880. But it would be in the first 16 years of the republic where the young nation was truly in danger due to constant external threats that put its own independence, sovereignty and territorial integrity at risk.

After the Battle of Ayacucho that took place in December 1824 in Peru, where the pro-independence forces defeated the last Spanish troops settled in South America, the Venezuelan Liberator Simón Bolívar entered Bolivian territory on 14 August 1825, crossing the Desaguadero River with his troops. It is worth mentioning that during the short time that his government lasted for just four months, Bolívar spent his time travelling throughout the country on a grand tour of all the main cities of Bolivia at that time.

Bolivar abolished the indigenous tribute and prohibited the aborigines from being forced to work against their will. Bolívar delegated command of the nation to the young Marshal Antonio José de Sucre on 29 December 1825. The first measure of Marshal Sucre was the economic revival of the young nation, since the long war of independence had decimated public funds, so he created a Ministry of

the Sucre Campaign, which ended up killing the royalist general Pedro Antonio Olañeta in the Combat of Tumusla on 1 April 1825.

After the proclamation of independence from the Spanish Empire on 6 August 1825, the Deliberative Assembly approved on the 11th of the same month the law of awards and honours to the liberators. The first article of that law indicated that the new state would receive the name of 'Republic of Bolívar'. Months later, the name was modified,

Portraits of Presidents Marshals Andrés de Santa Cruz (left) and José Ballivián (right). (Open source).

Finance. He also reorganised the army through a ministry established for that purpose. Sucre was also concerned about education and health, establishing several schools, colleges and hospitals as well as prisons. He eliminated the old colonial demarcation and made a new territorial organisation of Bolivia, dividing it into departments, provinces and cantons.

In 1828, Peru wanted to recover its ancestral territory of Upper Peru and began a military expedition against Bolivia, whose head of state at that time was General José María Pérez de Urdininea. The Peruvian Army invaded Bolivia, occupying several cities and when it was approaching the capital Sucre, it was decided to sign a treaty that stipulated the departure of the Colombian troops from Bolivia, who had been in the country since its independence, the definitive separation from power of Marshal Sucre and his departure from the country and the abolition of the Bolivian Constitution. Once the Bolivian assembly was formed, it decided on 2 August 1828 to accept the resignation of Marshal Sucre and proceeded to elect Marshal Andrés de Santa Cruz y Calahumana as President of Bolivia, and General José Miguel de Velasco as Vice President.

Bolivia's time of greatest splendour was during the presidency of Marshal Andrés de Santa Cruz. This period was characterised by great economic development and political and social progress, the greatest in Bolivian history. A Peru-Bolivian Confederation was then founded that would face the Argentine Confederation and Chile in a war, in which it would be victorious in a first stage, but then in 1839, a Unified Army of Peruvians and Chileans defeated the Bolivian forces and consequently, the Peru-Bolivian Confederation disappeared and Marshal Santa Cruz was overthrown. Taking advantage of the existing chaos in Bolivia with the dissolution of the confederation, Peru once again tried to annex that country and in the interim, Marshal José Ballivián assumed the presidency, leading the Bolivian troops defeating the Peruvian Army in the Battle of Ingavi.

Map of the Bolivian coastline on the Pacific Ocean before the war against Chile (left) (Map by author). Bolivian President Hilarión Daza in 1879 (right). (Open source).

Ballivián ruled until 1847. Between 1848 and 1879 there were nine presidents: Manuel Isidoro Belzú (1848–

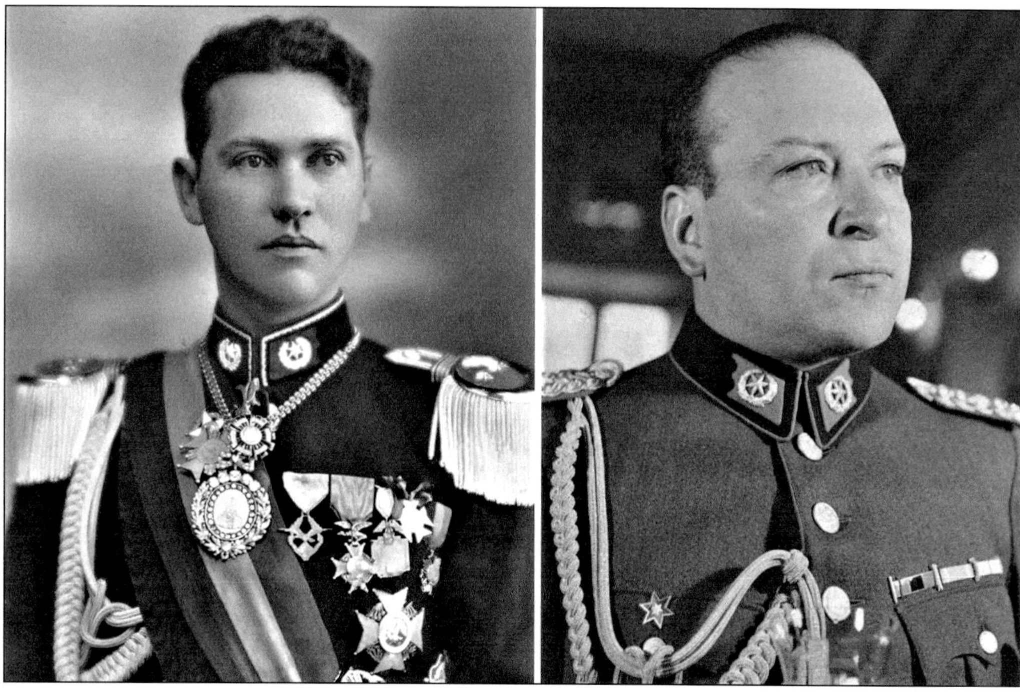

Two socialist Bolivian military presidents, both veterans of the Chaco War, who implemented social conquests for the population, Germán Busch (left) and Gualberto Villaroel (right). They both died tragically. The first committed suicide in 1939 and the second was lynched by mobs in 1946. (Open source).

Four historical leaders of the MNR foundation. From left to right: Walter Guevara Arze, Víctor Paz Estenssoro, Juan Lechín Oquendo and Hernán Siles Suazo. Guevara, Paz Estenssoro and Siles Suazo were presidents of Bolivia and Lechín was vice president. (Open source).

1855), Jorge Córdova (1855–1857), José María Linares (1857–1861), José María Achá (1861–1864), Mariano Melgarejo (1864–1871), Agustín Morales (1871–1872), Adolfo Ballivián (1873–1874), Tomás Frías (1874–1876) and Hilarión Daza (1876–1879). All these governments were characterised by political instability, military uprisings and coups, as well as border conflicts with neighbouring countries. Also during this period, the mines were nationalised and the silver, guano and saltpetre mining industry grew considerably, injecting money into the ailing state finances.

In 1878, President Hilarión Daza introduced a tax on saltpetre. This produced a diplomatic crisis since the Boundary Treaty with Chile of 1874 demanded that Chilean capital would not be taxed for the first 25 years after the treaty. Within the diplomatic conflict, the Bolivian government confiscated the assets of these concessions, which the neighbouring country of Chile interpreted as the breach of the boundary treaty, and they proceeded to take control of the new disputed territory. Despite mediation attempts, this led Bolivia, Chile and Peru to the *Guerra del Pacífico* (War of the Pacific), which would mean for Bolivia the loss of both these new deposits and the loss of its sovereign access to the Pacific Ocean.

In 1879, the War of the Pacific broke out, pitting Chile against the alliance between Bolivia and Peru. The conflict was originated by the interests of exploitation of guano and saltpetre, which is why it is also known as the *Guerra del Salitre* (Saltpetre War) and had as a final consequence the loss of the sovereign access to the sea for Bolivia, when Chile took possession of Antofagasta, and for Peru the loss of its territories of Tarapacá and Arica. After that, Bolivia became a landlocked country, like Paraguay, which would generate another international war, that of the Chaco, to try to obtain an exit to the Atlantic Ocean via the Paraguay River.

Between 1880 and 1899 there were five governments that were characterised by conservatism, followed with five liberal governments between 1899 and 1920. It was in the liberal era that the presidency of the republic moved from Sucre to La Paz and the era of tin exploitation began with the businessman Simón I. Patiño, who became one of the richest and most powerful men in the world.

The rise of elastic rubber led in the years 1903–1904 to a conflict known as *Guerra del Acre* (Acre War) with Brazil over control of the Beni-Pando axis, a major producer of the aforementioned material. After that war, Bolivia ceded an approximate area of 191,000 square kilometres to Brazil, through the Petrópolis Treaty that was signed on 7 November 1903. Additionally, in 1904, Bolivia signed a peace treaty with Chile, through which it ceded the territories won by it in the War of the Pacific in exchange for the construction of the Arica-La Paz railway.

A milestone in the history of Bolivia was undoubtedly the creation of an airline, *Lloyd Aéreo Boliviano* (LAB) in 1925, just when the country was celebrating 100 years of independent life. It began its flights with a Junkers F.13 donated by the German community residing in Bolivia and over the years it acquired other German aircraft (Junkers F.13, A.50, W.34, K.43 and Ju.52/3m), connecting the main cities in the country. It had pilots and mechanics of German and Bolivian nationality and it proved to be extremely useful in a country whose roads were very precarious and where there were not enough railway lines to transport people, freight and mail.

The next political era in Bolivia was dominated by republican governments between 1920 and 1936. It was precisely during the government of Dr Daniel Salamanca (1931–1934) that the *Guerra del Chaco* (Chaco War) against Paraguay broke out. Bolivia had been occupying, at first peacefully and stealthily, large areas of the Chaco since the beginning of the 20th century, a territory considered by the Paraguayan government as its own. By 1932, Bolivia already occupied 143,450 square kilometres of the Chaco when the war broke out. The war lasted three years and Bolivia had to withdraw from that territory before the unstoppable advance of

Two PCB leaders, Mario Monje Molina (left) and Jorge Kolle Cueto (centre). The PCB logo on the right. (Open source).

the Paraguayan Army, which even started the invasion of Bolivian territory but it was contained with a strong counteroffensive. In the midst of this war, President Salamanca was overthrown, and Vice President José Luis Tejada assumed the presidency. The definitive treaty of peace and borders was signed in 1938 through which Bolivia had to cede 10,000 square kilometres and Paraguay about 17,225 square kilometres, but almost the entire Chaco remained in the definitive ownership of Paraguay.

After the Chaco War, as was traditional in the history of Bolivia, a series of military governments that acceded to the presidency via coups d'état began, starting the era of socialist military and old order governments between 1936 and 1952 with the presidencies of David Toro (1936–37), German Busch (1937–39), Carlos Quintanilla (1939–40), Enrique Peñaranda (1940–43), Gualberto Villaroel (1943–46), Néstor Guillén (1946), Tomás Monje (1946–47), Enrique Hertzog (1947–49), Mamerto Urriolagoitia (1949–51) and Hugo Ballivián (1951–1952).

The *Movimiento Nacionalista Revolucionario* (Revolutionary Nationalist Movement/MNR) was founded by Víctor Paz Estenssoro together with a group of politicians and intellectuals as a centre left-wing political party in 1942 during the government of General Peñaranda. The MNR forged an alliance between the middle class and working class sectors and elaborated a nationalist plan that would unleash the seizure of power, either by democratic means or through a bourgeois revolution, to end the prevailing political system and mode of production.

In 1950, the Bolivian Communist Party (PCB) was founded and would incredibly support the MNR in the 1952 revolution.

Between 9 and 11 April 1952 the so-called *Revolución Boliviana* (Bolivian Revolution) broke out organised by the MNR, which brought together radical middle-class intellectuals. The Carabineros and Police Corps had an outstanding participation in starting the revolt that later had the support of the population, the workers of Villa Victoria and the miners who arrived from the Milluni mine.

On Wednesday 9 April, the Carabineros and Police Corps were mobilised by the Minister of the Interior, General Seleme, and they seized strategic institutions, such as prefectures and radio stations, to spread the news. The police regiments *Captain Zeballos* and *21 de Julio*, the Departmental Police Brigade, cadets from the School of Police and Carabineros, and the General Directorate of Police and Carabineros, all with weapons and ammunition, were also mobilised to take strategic areas. The MNR civilians who participated in the revolt, as well as the many volunteers, workers above all, received guns and ammunition from the Departmental Brigade, the General Directorate and the Carabineros regiments. The arsenal in the Antofagasta square, seized by Army Captain Israel Téllez, had already been distributed to civilian combatants. But General Torres Ortiz, involved in the uprising, distanced himself at the

Scenes from the 1952 Revolution led by the MNR. Above, from left to right: protests by students and workers in the cities; peasants armed with Mauser rifles from the Chaco War; anti-aircraft and heavy machine guns confiscated from the Army in the hands of civilians. Below, from left to right: Víctor Paz Estenssoro (centre with a police officer) poses with armed miners; the militia formed with armed peasants; a police officer with civilians carrying weapons stolen from the Army. (Open source).

last minute and had the Army quartered and he prepared to repel the revolutionaries. Dr Siles Suazo took refuge in the Nunciature that same day. Seeing the uncontrollable popular overflow, General Seleme resigned from the leadership of the 'Revolutionary Government'. Lechín Oquendo, top leader of the Miners' Federation, remained, leading the uprising in the streets with the slogans 'Agrarian reform' and 'Nationalisation of mines.'

On Thursday 10 April, the fighting continued. Juan Lechin Oquendo, leading the Milluni miners, took over the Bolivian Military Aviation Fighter Air Group and from there sent planes to drop leaflets over the Miraflores Great Barracks, inducing them to surrender. MRN supporters assaulted the checkpoint of the Garita de Lima, took out weapons and ammunition and continued fighting.

On Friday 11 April, Lechín, together with Rolando Requena, went to take the Great Barracks of Miraflores. Later, supported by the revolutionaries, they seized the Government Palace called *Palacio Quemado*, with which the revolutionary victory took place. The defeat of the army claimed a balance of 490 dead. Hernán Siles Zuazo and Juan Lechín Oquendo assumed the temporary command of the government until a few days later Víctor Paz Estenssoro returned, having been in exile in Buenos Aires, and he assumed the presidency.

The *Palacio Quemado* (Burnt Palace) in La Paz, so named because it suffered a great fire in 1875, has been the seat of the Executive Branch since 1853. (Open source).

The so-called 'Tin Barons' in Bolivia (from left to right): Simón Iturri Patiño, Moritz Hochschild and Carlos Víctor Aramayo. Its mines were expropriated by the Bolivian State in 1952. (Open source).

During the first government of Paz Estenssoro, universal voting was implemented, so that illiterates, indigenous people and women could vote for the first time in Bolivia. There was also the founding of the *Central Obrera Boliviana* (Bolivian Workers' Confederation/ COB) on 17 April 1952 with the objective of integrating the unions of miners, manufacturers, railways, banks, graphics, industry and commerce employees, builders, bakers and peasants. Its first executive secretary was Juan Lechín Oquendo. The MNR reduced the size of the army from approximately 20,000 to 5,000 effectives between April 1952 and January 1953 mainly by discharging conscripts. In addition, it is estimated that the government retired around 300 officers. The army's budget was cut from 20 percent of the general budget in 1953 and to 6.7 percent in 1957. In replacement of the army, the MNR formed urban and rural militias with workers and peasants. Between 1952 and 1956, the police and popular militias predominated in internal security and public order. From 1956 to

President Víctor Paz Estenssoro (centre in a civilian suit) posing with Vice President General René Barrientos Ortuño (second from the right) in 1964. (Open source).

1964, the legitimacy of the militias and the importance of the police were reduced as the army was reconstituted, which predominated in internal security and public order. This would be of vital importance for the fight against the guerrillas a few years later.

Meanwhile, the mines were nationalised from the three main mining business groups (Patiño, Hochschild and Aramayo) and an agrarian reform was carried out, since 70 percent of the agricultural land was owned by only 4.5 percent of the population. Thousands of acres were expropriated from the landowners, who received compensation from the state and these lands passed to the aborigines through the unions.

The educational reform process also began, since at the beginning of the 1950s, 60.9 percent of the population was illiterate. In 1955 the Bolivian Education Code was promulgated which divided the educational system into an urban area, under the Ministry of Education, and another for rural education under the then recently created Ministry of Rural Affairs. The Code sought to extend education to the majority and redirect education towards technical instruction. The vast majority of the indigenous population only spoke Quechua and Aymará, without command of Spanish, which also made it difficult for them to access to formal education. The educational code provided for the teaching of Spanish to that population and the transfer of knowledge to turn them into farmers or cattle breeders.

The National Revolution in Bolivia had the help of the American government. Such help came in the form of food first and was key to coping with the food shortage resulting from the disorganisation of the first effects of the agrarian reform. US aid grew from $1.5 million in 1952 to $79 million in 1964. Of this total amount, military aid rose from $0.1 million in 1952 to $3.2 million in 1964. It is estimated that the total amount of aid received between 1953 and 1964 was $368 million or about $35 million annually.

But of course not everything was positive. The MNR established strict political control and even set up several concentration camps for political opponents, mainly communists. Those camps were placed in cold towns of the Bolivian Andes, such as Catavi, Uncía, Corocoro and Curahuara de Carangas.

During the reorganisation of the military forces, the Bolivian Air Force (FAB) was founded on 26 September 1957 as an independent force. Its Military Aviation School (EAM) had been created on 12 October 1923 and the Military Aviation participated in several military coups and uprisings as well as in the Chaco War.

In 1960 Paz Estenssoro was elected for the second time as president and in August 1964 he was again elected. Shortly after, on 5 November, he was overthrown by a military coup led by his vice president, Air Force General René Barrientos. From 1964 to 1982, a series of military governments followed one another. It was precisely during the military government of General Barrientos that the Marxist-oriented National Liberation Army emerged, leading to the Ñancahuazú guerrilla uprising in 1967. The year before, the PCB supported the formation of the National Liberation Army (ELN) guerrilla that Ernesto Che Guevara intended to install in Bolivia. In the beginning, the Bolivian Communist Party sent militants to train in Cuba and they actively participated in the guerrilla columns: the brothers Inti and Coco Peredo, Loro Vázquez Viana, Rodolfo Saldaña, Ñato Méndez Korné and Benjamín Coronado Córdova, all members of the Bolivian Communist Youth. The PCB wanted to assume the command of the ELN but it was not allowed, therefore the former withdrew its support.

When Bolivia became an independent state in 1825 it had a territorial extent of 2,220,319 square kilometres, but it lost more than half of its territory due to a series of diplomatic conflicts or wars during the 19th and 20th centuries. After all the territorial losses, Bolivia has been left with a territorial extent of 1,098,581 square kilometres. The territory is divided into nine departments: Beni, Cochabamba, Chuquisaca, La Paz, Oruro, Pando, Potosí, Tarija and Santa Cruz. It has borders with Peru, Brazil, Paraguay, Argentina and Chile. The city of Sucre is the constitutional capital and headquarters of the judiciary power. The headquarters of government is the city of La Paz, where the executive power and the legislative power function. The main cities are La Paz, Sucre, Cochabamba, Potosí, Santa Cruz de la Sierra, Oruro, Tarija, Trinidad, Cobija, and so on. The population of the country in 1964 was 4,029,472 inhabitants and La Paz had a population of 600,000 inhabitants then. Its population was made up of white descendants of Europeans (20 percent), mestizos (30 percent) and indigenous people (50 percent). The languages spoken in Bolivia are: Spanish, Quechua, Aymará, Chiquitano, Guaraní, Mojeño, Guarayo and Uru.

Table 1: Territories ceded by Bolivia due to diplomatic conflicts or wars.[2]

Country	Territory	Years
Brazil (Acre War and others)	490,430 km^2	1860–1958
Peru	250,000 km^2	1909
Paraguay (Chaco War)[3]	126,225 km^2	1932–1935[4]
Argentina	170,758 km^2	1839–1897
Chile (Pacific War)	120,000 km^2	1879–1883
TOTAL	1,157,413 km^2	1839–1958

The Bolivian nation has three well-defined geographical zones from west to east:

- **The mountainous zone**, with the Andes mountain range, with an average height of 3,500 metres, whose economy is merely mining. The main cities are La Paz, Oruro and Potosí.
- **The zone of the temperate valleys**, with an average height of 2,000 metres, very rich in agricultural crops. Its main cities are Sucre, Cochabamba and Tarija.
- **The warm plains**, with an average height of 500 metres, characterised by innumerable ranches where various types of cattle are raised. The biggest cities are Santa Cruz de la Sierra, Trinidad and Cobija.

Seventy percent of the Bolivian economy was based on mineral exploitation (tin, copper, zinc, lead, wolfram, silver, bismuth and antinomy) and the extraction of oil and gas. The remaining 30 percent had to do with the manufacturing industry, and agricultural activity including raising cattle.

Regarding the political parties, the first ones were the centre-right *Partido Liberal* (PL), founded in 1883 which disappeared in 1978 and the other traditional party, the *Partido Conservador or Constitucional* (PC) founded in 1880, basically anti-liberal, which disappeared in the early 20th century. The parties that were still active in politics in the 1960s were:

- The Trotskyist *Partido Obrero Revolucionario* (POR) founded in 1935.

- The extreme-right *Falange Socialista Boliviana* (FSB) founded in 1937.
- The extreme-left *Partido de Izquierda Revolucionaria* (PIR) founded in 1940.
- The centre-left *Movimiento Nacionalista Revolucionario* (MNR), founded in 1942.
- The centre-left *Partido de la Unión Republicana Socialista* (PURS) founded in 1946.
- The extreme-left *Partido Comunista de Bolivia* (PCB) founded in 1950. The PCB had split into two antagonistic factions in 1964, a pro-Soviet group led by Jorge Kolle Cueto and a pro-Chinese group led by Oscar Zamora. This internal situation in the PCB led to the foundation of the *Partido Comunista Marxista-Leninista* (PCML) in 1965.
- The extreme right *Partido Demócrata Cristiano* (PDC) founded in 1954.
- The centre-right *Partido Revolucionario Auténtico* (PRA), founded in 1959.
- The left *Partido Revolucionario de la Izquierda Nacionalista* (PRIN), founded in 1963.

2

ERNESTO CHE GUEVARA (1928–1967)

Ernesto Guevara de la Serna was born in the city of Rosario, Province of Santa Fe, Argentina on 14 June 1928, the eldest of the five children of Ernesto Guevara Lynch (1900–1987) and Celia de la Serna (1906–1965). Both parents belonged to families of the upper class and of the so-called Argentine aristocracy.

His father, in addition to receiving income from rents that he had inherited, had acquired a large yerba mate plantation in the Caraguatay area, in the Province of Misiones, located about 200 kilometres north of Posadas, on the Paraná River. He also owned, along with his brothers, a shipyard in the San Fernando area, which also produced income. His mother belonged to a traditional family of Buenos Aires ranchers. After Ernesto, the family had four more children: Celia (1929–2023), Roberto (1932–2018), Ana María (1934–1988) and Juan Martín (b. 1943).

One characteristic of Ernesto's parents that considerably influenced his childhood and youth was their constant moving. Besides this, the Guevara-de la Serna house was completely disorganised and dirty, despite having servants. All these situations were forging the character and personality of little Ernesto. Until leaving Argentina definitively in 1953, Ernesto's family had lived in at least twelve houses in Buenos Aires, Caraguatay, San Isidro, Alta Gracia and Córdoba. The first years of Ernesto's life were spent between the houses his family owned in Buenos Aires and Caraguatay, constantly travelling by river in steamers. In Buenos Aires they settled in the typical areas of the upper class: first in the Palermo neighbourhood, then in the San Isidro district and finally in the Recoleta neighbourhood.

When Ernesto was two years old, he had his first asthma attack, due to poorly cured bronchitis, a disease that would accompany him all his life. It was due to this disease and on medical recommendation that the family moved to the city of Córdoba, where Ernesto spent his childhood and adolescence. He went to elementary school in Alta Gracia and high school in Córdoba. Due to his frequent asthma attacks, he missed classes a lot and could not play sports, so he devoted himself to reading and playing chess.

From left to right: baby Ernesto Guevara in 1929; a neat little boy in the mid-1930s; the Guevara-de la Serna family in the 1940s; Ernesto is first from left, posing with his parents and his three siblings; as a teenager in 1943. (Open source).

Despite his chronic asthma, Ernesto (first from the right) practiced rugby, a sport for the wealthy classes in Argentina. Here he is seen as a young adult towards the end of the 1940s. (Open source).

During his childhood, Ernesto was educated very strictly, especially by his father, while due to his illness, he was overprotected by his mother. These events forged the child's character, so that he became determined, arrogant and daring, and his asthma was not an impediment. This type of behaviour would repeat throughout his short life and could have been the main cause of his failures.

Ernesto Guevara stood out throughout his childhood and adolescence for his rebellion. He was a typical *enfant terrible*. Extremely mischievous, disobedient and reckless with fierce arguments with his parents and teachers, dishevelled to the point of being called *Chancho Guevara* (Pig Guevara), a nickname he gladly adopted, which was also quite appropriate, since he was prone to not grooming himself properly. He did not bathe regularly and wore unwashed clothes for weeks. In fact, Che himself wrote in his diary that in the 11 months that his Bolivian adventure lasted, he only bathed twice and it was not necessarily due to lack of water, since he always wandered through areas of mighty rivers in Bolivia. He used to perform daredevil acts at great personal risk, and demonstrated a very bad character, often coming to blows in discussions, making provocative and scandalous comments, habitually seeking to defend the opposite position of the interlocutors.

Two other facets of Ernesto's pre-revolutionary life: his motorcycle trips, and as a student at the School of Medicine in Buenos Aires. (Open source).

Ernesto Guevara with Hilda Gadea in Guatemala in 1954. She was Ernesto's first wife (left). Ernesto, Hilda and their daughter Hilda Beatriz in Mexico in 1956. (Open source).

Although Ernesto's parents were openly anti-Peronists, like all of the upper and upper middle classes, Ernesto nonetheless admired Perón. Ernesto grew up in a family where his father hated American imperialism and his mother hated the Catholic Church. The entire family was anti-American and anti-clerical. In his adolescence, he hated communism for its sectarianism, although he began to be openly against the American imperialist policy.

After the economic collapse of the Guevara family and the separation of his parents, they moved to the federal capital, where Ernesto went to the Medicine School of the University of Buenos Aires (UBA) in 1948. He graduated as a doctor in 1953 and began to work as an assistant in an allergy clinic that was dedicated to asthma research, directed by Dr Salvador Pisani. It was also then that he began to play rugby, despite his asthma.

Also at that time he began to read Karl Marx, a character who fascinated him. While in Buenos Aires, Ernesto Guevara began to travel precariously, hitchhiking, by bicycle or motorbike, with little money, further and further away. Guevara's trips gave him social and human experience, which would put him in contact with the workers and the popular sectors of Argentina and Latin America, and would finally lead him to join the guerrilla group that would carry out the Cuban Revolution later. On 1 January 1950, he made his first solo trip, on a Cucciolo motorised bicycle, visiting his friend Alberto Granado in San Francisco del Chañar, Córdoba, then continuing to the northwest to get to know the poorest and most backward provinces in the country; Santiago del Estero, Tucumán, Salta, Jujuy, Catamarca, La Rioja, before returning through San Juan, Mendoza, San Luis. In total he travelled 4,500 kilometres.

In 1951 Guevara was hired as a paramedic on board a ship of the Argentine state oil company *Yacimientos Petrolíferos Fiscales* (YPF). On 9 February, he embarked for the first time. On these trips he toured the Atlantic coast of South America, from the Patagonian port of Comodoro Rivadavia to the then British colony of Trinidad and Tobago, passing through Curaçao, British Guyana, Venezuela, and various ports in Brazil. The following year, with his friend Alberto Granado, he made his first Latin American trip with a Norton motorcycle starting from San Francisco in the province of Córdoba and visiting Buenos Aires, Miramar, Bariloche in Argentina, Osorno, Valdivia, Temuco, Santiago, Valparaiso, Antofagasta and Chuquicamata in Chile, Taraca, Titicaca, Cuzco, Macchu Picchu, Abancay and Lima in Peru. In Lima, Ernesto met Dr Hugo Pesce, member of the Peruvian Communist Party, who greatly influenced the young Argentine. The trip then proceeded to Pucallpa, Iquitos and San Pablo in Peru, Leticia and Bogotá in Colombia on a hydroplane, and finally Caracas in Venezuela by bus. His friend Granado remained in Venezuela and Ernesto flew to Miami and finally returned to Buenos Aires by plane. The whole trip took seven months.

In July 1953, Ernesto began his second Latin American trip, this time with his friend Carlos Ferrer. The trip started in Buenos Aires and they went to La Paz, Bolivia by train. From there they continued to Lima. From Lima they went to Guayaquil by bus. While Ferrer continued his trip to Caracas, Ernesto embarked for Panama. He then went hitchhiking to Costa Rica and Nicaragua. The last stage of the trip was made by car passing through Honduras and El Salvador until finally arriving in Guatemala. He stayed in Guatemala for several months to experience the revolution that Colonel Jacobo Arbenz was leading there. He wanted to work as a doctor in that country but it was not possible, so he experienced serious financial problems. There he established friendships with a series of exiles from the progressive left from various countries and began a clear sympathy for the communism that he had hated in his adolescence. However, when the communist-leaning Guatemalan Workers Party (*Partido Guatemalteco de Trabajadores*, PGT) told him that if he wanted to work as a doctor in Guatemala he had to join that party, Ernesto flatly rejected the proposal.

It was in Guatemala that the nickname *Che* was given to Ernesto Guevara by his friend Ñico López in 1954. As an Argentine, that

Ernesto Che Guevara posing in both photos with members of the 26 July Movement (M-26-7) in Mexico in the mid-50s, with the Castro brothers and other members. (Open source).

Fidel Castro (left) and Che Guevara (right) in Sierra Maestra, Cuba in 1958. (Open source).

interjection, meaning *Hey!* was repeatedly used by Ernesto so everybody started calling him that. The interjection *Che* is used in countries like Argentina, Uruguay and Paraguay to get someone's attention.

In June 1954, the army overthrew Arbenz and established a new government in Guatemala. Ernesto took refuge in the Argentine Embassy and obtained a safe-conduct to leave Guatemala, travelling to Mexico, where he lived for a couple of years. There he got married to the Peruvian economist Hilda Gadea Acosta (1925–1974) whom he had met in Guatemala and they had a daughter, Hilda Beatriz Guevara (1956–1995).

It was in Mexico that he defined his political ideas and in 1955 joined Fidel Castro's *Movimiento 26 de Julio* also known as M-26-7. This movement was named in commemoration of the failed assault by revolutionaries on the Moncada barracks of the Batista Army in Cuba. The plan was to form a guerrilla group in Cuba to overthrow the Batista's regime and start a social revolution. That movement initially had an anti-imperialist-democratic ideology founded on the ideas of José Martí and mainly anti-communist. It was Fidel Castro himself who invited Ernesto Guevara to join the movement to work as a doctor.

Many of Che's close friends and relatives in Argentina as well as Cuban acquaintances and other nationalities, although politically sympathetic to the left, defined Ernesto Guevara as racist, arrogant and even homophobic, the latter due to his contempt for homosexuals. In fact, Che considered Mexicans, Bolivians, black people and aborigines as 'inferior' human beings.

In February 1956, a group of about 20 people who belonged to M-26-7 began training in guerrilla warfare under the command of retired Spanish Colonel Alberto Bayo Giroud in Guadalajara, Mexico. Che, who hid his asthma, 'excelled' in military training, and became one of the leaders of the group. After being arrested by the Mexican police along with Fidel Castro and released, on 25 November 1956, from the Port of Tuxpan, 82 men, including Ernesto Guevara, left for Cuba on an old, leaky yacht called *Granma,* carrying weapons and supplies.

Upon arriving in Cuba, the long revolution against the regime of Fulgencio Batista began, which would culminate only in 1959. The development of the revolutionary actions of Fidel Castro and his group is beyond the scope of this volume, which is why only Che's actions will be described. The revolutionary group established itself in Sierra Maestra and from there the actions against the prevailing regime began. Che Guevara acted as a doctor and a combatant. Despite suffering severe asthma attacks in a country that due to its climate has one of the highest rates of asthma in the world, he quickly stood out for his 'reckless courage', tactical vision and ability to command. Guevara also imposed his personality by being strict against acts of indiscipline, treason and criminals, not only in the revolutionary troops themselves, but also with respect to the enemy soldiers and the peasants who inhabited the area. He did not hesitate for a second to put those he considered traitors or deserters to death and it would be his trademark until 1967. Many of the executions were carried out by Che himself, with impressive coldness and no doubt. Che, in addition to his medical role, was commander of one of the combatant columns of the revolution and by order of Fidel Castro, he took charge of the Guerrilla Military School for the training of newcomers.

After an arduous military campaign throughout 1958, the revolutionary forces finally took full control of the country in the face of the disbandment of Batista's army and their flight from the country. Guevara's troops proceeded to arrest former members of the

The infamous San Carlos de la Cabaña Fortress, where mass executions were carried out after 1959 (left). Che himself, commander of that fortress, gave frequent orders for execution and several times he carried out the executions himself (centre and right). (Open source).

Che at the United Nations General Assembly in New York in 1964, speaking about executions in Cuba (left). Che in an office in Havana as Minister (right). (Centro de Estudios Che Guevara).

production fell to the point of shortage. Had it not been for the help of the Soviet Union, the Cuban people would have suffered excruciating hunger. In fact, the Soviet Union disapproved of many of Che's policies and this was made known to Prime Minister Fidel Castro, which caused constant friction with Che. What was more, Che bitterly criticised the Soviet Union's trade policy with undeveloped countries, which was described as the same as 'Yankee imperialism'.

The confrontation between Che and Fidel arose after the former's disastrous management as minister, his speeches which contained veiled criticism of the Soviet Union, and the failed guerrilla adventure in the Congo. (Open source).

Batista regime and shot those considered war criminals in summary trials. A revolutionary government was then established, of which Che was a part in various functions. First, he was first appointed head of the San Carlos de La Cabaña Fortress, which was converted into a prison where he presided over 'revolutionary tribunals' of 'war criminals' until June 1959. Several thousand people were tried at La Cabaña. They were either sentenced to prison or executed. Former government officials, police, and army personnel who had served Batista were rounded up. Che was known as the 'La Cabaña butcher'. It has been possible to document the cold-blooded murders of Che, committed without prior trial: 14 in Sierra Maestra, 23 in Santa Clara, and 175 in La Cabaña in a period of only three years. These numbers reflect the murders committed directly by Che, but there were also the firing squad orders that reached around 1,500 people under his command at La Cabaña. And above all, Che was proud of what he did. So much so that in the UN General Assembly on 11 December 1964, Che himself confessed that: '...Executions, yes, we have executed, we execute and we will continue executing...'[5]

Che later held various key functions, including director of the Department of Industrialisation of the National Institute of Agrarian Reform (INRA) and Minister of Industry and President of the National Bank, all without any knowledge of finance and economics. Che himself once commented that when Fidel asked for a good economist, he raised his hand, believing that Fidel had asked for a 'good communist' and thus he arrived at the Central Bank of Cuba. In those key positions, Che committed huge errors that brought the already delicate Cuban economy to the brink of collapse, only saved by the multi-million-dollar Soviet subsidy. Just to mention one example, he tried to replace the monetary incentives of highly productive workers with 'moral' incentives, and

Although Che and Fidel Castro were seen in public smiling and even embracing, in private there was an open rivalry. Che said that Fidel was a great leader but a failure as a military leader, while Fidel admired Che's intelligence but was repulsed by his dogmatism and arrogance. In fact, many think that Fidel agreed to Che's proposed Bolivian adventure as a way of getting him off his back. Che was creating serious relationship problems with the Soviet Union, and Cuba desperately needed Soviet money to survive as a nation. Besides, Fidel knew very well that Che would not leave Bolivia alive. Che distanced himself from the Soviet Union in the last years of his life, blaming Moscow for being too soft ideologically and diplomatically, unlike China, which Guevara said was the haven of communist orthodoxy. Che had become a major obstacle in Fidel Castro's policy of rapprochement with the USSR.

From the moment the Cuban Revolution took power, Che began to organise and promote guerrilla experiences in Latin America, highlighting those that were opened in Guatemala, Nicaragua, Peru, Colombia, Venezuela and Argentina. All of them failed, but in some cases they laid the foundations for future guerrilla movements, such as the Sandinista National Liberation Front (FSLN) in Nicaragua and the Tupamaros in Uruguay. This position led to a strong confrontation between Che Guevara and the communist parties of Latin America, which in general did not approve of the strategy of generalised armed struggle that he proposed. The Soviet Union did not agree with this procedure either, since at that time the Soviet leadership already favoured the model of 'peaceful coexistence' with capitalism. In fact, Fidel tried to keep Che away by sending him on endless trips to various parts of the world on diplomatic missions.

His second marriage was to Aleida March Torres (born 1936) on 9 June 1959, in Havana. March was a Cuban militant from the M-26-7 from the province of Las Villas whom Guevara met in 1958 when he was carrying out his final offensive against the Batista regime, shortly before the battle of Santa Clara. Together they had four children: Aleida Guevara March (born 1960), Camilo Guevara March (1962–2022), Celia Guevara March (born 1963) and Ernesto Guevara March (born 1965).

Che Guevara wanted to start the armed struggle in his native country. In 1963, after extensive training in Cuba, he sent a guerrilla group to Argentina. It was directed by Jorge Masetti, the Peronist journalist who had directed the Prensa Latina agency and who had to resign from his position due to his confrontation with the Cuban communist party (*Partido Comunista de Cuba*/PCC). The group settled in the province of Salta, under the name of the People's Guerrilla Army (EGP), with support in Bolivia, Córdoba and Buenos Aires. Masetti held the rank of second commander,

Che with Aleida March Torres in December 1958 in Cuba (left). Ernesto Che Guevara with his second wife Aleida and their four Cuban children in 1965 (right). (Centro de Estudios Che Guevara).

Che in the Congo in 1965, a failed experience. (Centro de Estudios Che Guevara).

Fidel Castro visiting the guerrilla training camp in Cuba in 1966. Che already wears his middle-aged bald man disguise with which he would legally enter Bolivia (third from right). The photo shows 11 of those who would accompany him on his Bolivian adventure. (Centro de Estudios Che Guevara).

reserving the rank of first commander for Guevara. After sending a letter to the democratic president Arturo Illia announcing his decision to start the armed struggle, the group suffered different complications that led to its complete collapse in 1964. Some of its members died in combat, such as the Cuban Hermes Peña, one of the men in Guevara's inner circle; others were arrested and Masetti disappeared into the jungle without a trace. In this context, in 1964, Che Guevara got in touch with Juan Domingo Perón in the utmost secrecy. Some even believe that Che and Perón actually met in Madrid, although this has never been proven. Che sent Perón funds to support his return to Argentina, an attempt that was prevented by the Brazilian government that same year. Perón promised to support the guerrilla initiatives against the Latin American dictatorships, which he did until 1973.

The guerrilla failure in Argentina led him to evaluate the possibility of participating in places other than his country and even other continents. In that sense, Africa began to appear as a suitable possibility. In 1965, Che showed up to fight in the Congo without prior notice to any of the rebel leaders, an act that was poorly received by them, due to the international implications. Guevara settled in the combat zone, while the Congolese military leaders hardly went to the frontlines and stayed most of the time in the city of Dar es Salaam, in Tanzania. Malaria, acute gastroenteritis due to the terrible hygiene conditions, the absence of military training of the local guerrillas and, above all, indiscipline led the guerrillas to total chaos. The Cuban participation headed by Che in the Congolese rebellion was a disastrous experience.

After the African experience, he spent a few months in Prague, Czechoslovakia, time that served him to meditate on all the failures he had accumulated. But he did not resign himself to no longer being a 'revolutionary', and he began to form the idea of a communist revolution in Bolivia which would then spread to neighbouring countries. He communicated the idea to Fidel Castro and the latter replied that he should return to Cuba to organise that guerrilla uprising.

On 21 July 1966, Che secretly returned to Cuba. There he met with Fidel Castro, his wife Aleida March, Orlando Borrego and the group of guerrillas who would accompany him to Bolivia. The physical and strategic preparation was carried out in a period of four months, from July to October 1966, where both Che and some 15 Cuban guerrillas meticulously selected by himself underwent rigorous training, which lasted 13 hours a day, consisting of combat practices, shooting and long walks with backpacks of more than 20 kilos.

Shortly after, in late October 1966, Che Guevara asked Perón for Peronism's support for his guerrilla project in Bolivia. Perón promised not to prevent those Peronists who wanted to accompany Guevara from doing so, but he did not agree to involve the Peronist movement as such in a guerrilla action in Bolivia, although he did commit Peronism's support when Che's guerrillas transferred their action to Argentine territory. On 2 November, he saw his children for the last time and then he travelled to Bolivia disguised as a bald, middle-aged Uruguayan citizen.

In less than a year later, Che would be killed during his last 'revolutionary' adventure in Bolivia after the resounding failure of his guerrilla uprising in that country, which is described in the corresponding chapter in this volume.

3
BOLIVIA'S NATIONAL LIBERATION ARMY (ELN)

During 1966, Che Guevara planned in detail the establishment of a guerrilla movement in Bolivia, which at that time was under the military government of Air Force General René Barrientos Ortuño. Ortuño had come to power in November 1964 after overthrowing the historical leader and constitutional president Víctor Paz Estenssoro which thus put an end to the nationalist-popular revolution that began in April 1952. The population was mainly peasant and indigenous.

The powerful Central Obrera Boliviana (COB), based on mine workers, conducted a fierce opposition to the regime that in 1965 expelled its general secretary, Juan Lechín Oquendo, from the country, a fact that in turn generated widespread riots throughout the country and established a state of siege. Thus, as Che had thought, the perfect situation was created for the instigation of a guerrilla uprising in Bolivia, which, due to general discontent, would have the support of the neediest classes. But as will be seen in the following chapters of this volume, the supposed popular support never materialised and, added to other circumstances, led Che's project to total failure.

The possibility of a guerrilla action in Bolivia, with the objective of expanding it to Argentina, had been being prepared directly by Ernesto Guevara for several years before. Already in 1964 Guevara had sent the Argentine-East German citizen Haydée Tamara Bunke Bider, *aka* (known as) Tania, under the false name of Laura Gutiérrez Bauer, as an agent in charge of infiltrating the military government in La Paz. In her cover as a researcher of indigenous folk music and as a German tutor for wealthy children, she began collecting strategic and tactical information.

Besides this, the Argentine Ciro Bustos had to organise a support network in Argentina, based on different dissident groups of the Communist Party. In mid-1966, Che sent two of his trusted men to Bolivia: Harry Villegas *aka* Pombo and Carlos Coello *aka* Tuma, to meet José María Martínez Tamayo *aka* Ricardo in order to organise the contacts and analyse the situation in that country. Tania was a triple agent who also worked for the Soviet KGB and the East German secret police, the Stasi. Another foreigner who strongly supported Che's guerrillas was the French philosopher Jules Régis Debray, a devoted communist admirer of Fidel Castro, who entered Bolivia under the false identity of Sergio Debrú as a 'journalist'.

Che's intelligence regarding Bolivian social conditions in 1967 was highly inaccurate. Two Bolivian communists, Roberto Peredo Liegue *aka* Coco and Guido Peredo Liegue *aka* Inti, were his primary sources of misperception. They reinforced his earlier analysis during visits to Cuba in 1962 and again in 1965. They, like many other Bolivian communists, related stories of widespread dissent with the regime of President General Rene Barrientos ignoring that he had won democratic elections with more than 60 percent of the votes, and he was also very loved by the peasantry. But Guevara was right in one thing – the Bolivian military was one of the most poorly organised in Latin America. Another misconception of Che was that Bolivia, being a poor country, did not interest the United States and that when the revolution broke out, it would not support its military. All of these elements convinced Che that Bolivia was the 'best' candidate for a guerrilla movement.

On the other hand, the PCB, which at that time was led by Mario Monje *aka* Estanislao from La Paz, maintained an ambiguous position regarding the armed struggle. Monje himself and other party militants had received military training in Cuba but they had expressed their opposition and rejection of a guerrilla-type action in Bolivia.

On 3 November 1966, Che Guevara arrived in Bolivia under the false identity of a Uruguayan economist named Adolfo Mena González, disguised as a bald middle-aged man with large glasses, an Organisation of American States researcher. Of the 17 Cubans who accompanied him on the Bolivian mission, five were 'commandants' in the Cuban Army, seven others were officers of lesser rank, and

COB union march on 31 October 1964, repressed by the forces of order. The banner reads: *'Long live the march for life. Workers to Power.'* On the right, the general secretary of the COB and former Vice President Juan Lechín Oquendo. (Open source).

The organisers of the guerrilla action in Bolivia: From left to right: Ciro Roberto Bustos, Harry Villegas, Carlos Coello and José María Martínez Tamayo. (Open source).

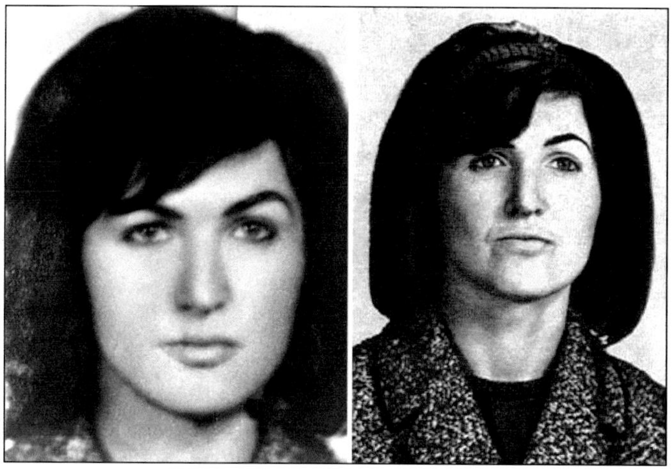

The Argentine-East German spy in the service of the KGB and the Stasi, Haydée Tamara Bunke Bider, *aka* Tania. In her role as a spy in Bolivia, she used the name of Laura Gutiérrez Bauer. (Policía Boliviana).

The Bolivian brothers Inti and Coco Peredo Liegue were in charge of the intelligence work prior to Che's arrival in Bolivia. (Open source).

The Uruguayan passport photo that Che used under the name of Adolfo Mena González to enter Bolivia on 3 November 1966 (left). Che in his disguise poses with Tuma in front of the Toyota Jeep that took them to Lagunillas in southeastern Bolivia (right). (Policía Boliviana).

one was the chief of the Border Police. In order not to arouse suspicion in the Bolivian authorities, they entered Bolivia little by little, usually in pairs, with false identities and through different means. The guerrilla Tania, who also worked for Che, had received instructions from the Soviet KGB through the East German Stasi to spy on him.

Some days later on 7 November, the day Che started writing his *Diario de Bolivia* (*Bolivian Diary*), he settled in the Ñancahuazú Camp with just three other guerrillas, Pacho, Pombo and Tuma. The rest would be joining the following days, normally in couples in order to ensure security. Very soon they started digging a series of tunnels and caves in order to hide food and medical supplies, clothes, documents, ammunition and weapons. Besides this, they also built an open-air classroom, a kitchen, and a dispensary.

The Ñancahuazú guerrilla camp was a large farm of 1,227 hectares that had been purchased by Roberto Peredo Leigue *aka* Coco in July of that year, paying 30,000 Bolivian pesos (around 2,500 US dollars), in the southeastern part of the country, 80 kilometres from Camiri and 225 kilometres from Santa Cruz de la Sierra, right on the border of the Departments of Santa Cruz and Chuquisaca, where the last foothills of the Andes Mountains meet the Gran Chaco region. The property was crossed by the Ñancahuazú River, a seasonal tributary of the Grande River, in an indigenous area of the Guarani culture. This camp had belonged to a farmer named Remberto Villa and was later known by the name of *Casa de Calamina* (the 'tin roof house' for its shiny metal roof) but the main guerrilla camp was established two kilometres northeast of it. That farmer had a property next to the one sold to Coco. In order not to arouse suspicion, the residents of the property were informed that a farm would be established to raise pigs. The place was not good. It was located in an almost uninhabited area, too far from the border with Argentina and was bought with virtually no strategic analysis and no clear awareness of its location. Che Guevara thought the struggle in Bolivia could last seven to 10 years, and prepared for that eventuality. The guerrilla support organisation smuggled supplies, ammunition, and weapons into the camp from La Paz, over 400 miles away. Guevara's account of the following four months detailed the many reconnaissance missions undertaken by his group, the arrival of new personnel and the preparations on the three guerrilla camps built, during the First Phase of Operations.

The second guerrilla camp was called *Cueva del Oso* (bear's cave), so named because the Frenchman Debray had hunted a bear in that area, and it was located about four hours' walk north of the other secondary camp called *Clínica* (clinic), which just functioned as a medical aid post. Three observation posts were also built, one on the banks of the Ñancahuazú River with a heavy machine gun and

The famous *Casa de la Calamina* on the farm bought by Coco Peredo for the guerrilla base in Ñancahuazú, already seized by army troops (left). Part of the central guerrilla camp in Ñancahuazú. (AP).

a mortar; the second observation post had a portable radio device installed some 300 metres from the central camp; and the third was in the camp Oso. The observation posts dominated the entire area including the Lagunillas-Camiri road.

The guerrillas settled into a daily routine. Supplies were carried up from the farm. Che instituted a robust education program for the guerrillas that included history, political economy, mathematics, Spanish, French, and Quechua. Only then did he realise that although Quechua was the dominant aborigine language, it was spoken in the Bolivian highlands to the south and west. The local population in the Ñancahuazú region spoke Guaraní. Incredibly, the veteran guerrillas committed numerous security violations: photographs were taken, diaries were kept, and radio messages were sent almost daily and they also allowed visitors to the place. When they carried out long training walks, they left visible traces, so it was easy to track them down.

From left to right: Joaquín, Braulio, Rolando, Urbano, Alejandro, Marcos, Benigno, Antonio, Ramón (Che still wears traces of his initial disguise), Miguel and El Rubio guerrillas at *Ñancahuazú* camp in December 1966. (Centro de Estudios Che Guevara).

The general secretary of the PCB Mario Monje (left) in a very tense meeting with Che in Ñancahuazú on 31 December 1966. (Open source).

The Cuban Orlando Pantoja Tamayo (left) and the Bolivian Maoist Moisés Guevara (not related to Che). (Centro de Estudios Che Guevara).

The guerrilla group took the name of *Ejército de Liberación Nacional* (National Liberation Army/ELN) and had the support of units located in Argentina, Chile and Peru.

During the month of December 1966, a total of 24 guerrillas were already in the Ñancahuazú camp. On 31 December, Mario Monje, the general secretary of the PCB, arrived at the Ñancahuazú guerrilla camp. The interview between Monje and Guevara had a negative result, since Monje claimed for himself the leadership of the guerrilla group, in the face of Che Guevara's strict opposition. Monje asked the Bolivian effectives from his party to leave the guerrilla group, but he received a resounding refusal. Before leaving the camp, Monje, in an almost prophetic manner, said, 'When the Bolivian people find out that this guerrilla is led by a foreigner, they will turn their backs on you and they will deny the support you need. I am sure that your guerrilla will fail because of that. You all will die very heroically, but you have no prospect of success.'[6] Every word said by the PCB leader was inexorably fulfilled. The PCB resented the Cubans' intrusion in Bolivia but also the Castro-Che decision to make Bolivia the scene of a revolutionary war without consulting them. This is why the PCB did not give any institutional support to the ELN, although individual members of that party did.

Monje finally left Ñancahuazú and tried by all means to decimate the support of the communist youth for Guevara's project. As an example, when the leader of the Communist Youth Loyola Guzmán visited Ñancahuazú to support Che, she was dismissed by the PCB. Inti Peredo, Coco's brother, would become the leader of the Bolivian guerrillas within the ELN. Shortly afterwards, Moisés Guevara, leader of a dissident Maoist group of the Bolivian Communist Party, also joined the ELN with several men. Che himself organised a support network for the guerrillas that would be installed in La Paz, Cochabamba, Santa Cruz, Sucre and Camiri, with chiefs in each city, who would lead a group that would be in charge of supplies, information (intelligence), finances, urban action and attention to supporters. In theory, it would function like clockwork, but in practice it did not work out, since very few people wanted to get involved in this adventure, despite their political orientations.

Recruitment to join the guerrilla group was a serious problem, since Che found himself facing the reality that the vast majority of the peasants were not interested in this adventure and even repudiated them, denouncing the guerrillas to the authorities. They could not gather more than 50 troops in total for 'his' revolution. The guerrillas experienced further problems, since several effectives became ill because of the new field diet and the hostile environment. The area was plagued with biting pests, thorny vegetation, frequent rains and swollen rivers which were difficult to cross. The guerrillas had to cut their way through the thick jungle with machetes and their boots were not suitable for the terrain. All this resulted in very low morale in the guerrillas and fights began among them. The Cubans gave the Bolivian recruits menial tasks and resentment soon developed. However, Che settled the issues and the group slowly began somehow to coalesce. But Che himself was also a point of conflict, since he very frequently mistreated his troops for small offenses committed. In fact, Che had little military training and many of the Cubans were already trained because they were officers of the Cuban Army. But Che was arrogant and did not consult anyone.

A neighbour of the *Casa de Calamina* farm, Ciro Algarañaz, informed the police about strange movements and activities in the area. On 19 January 1967, the local police showed up unexpectedly at the farmhouse and confiscated some guns, believing that they

Guerrilla camp in *Ñancahuazú*. From left to right: Coco Peredo, Loyola Guzmán, Inti Peredo and the Cuban Gustavo Machín (left). Loyola Guzmán with Che (right). (Centro de Estudios Che Guevara)

Another image in Ñancahuazú at the end of 1966. From left to right, Arturo, Tuma, an unrecognizable Che still without a beard and moustache, Loro and Pombo. (Centro de Estudios Che Guevara).

were cocaine manufacturers but did not find anything else, so they left the place. It was only in March that the Security Forces identified the guerrilla group in the area.

During the months of December and January, the guerrillas worked in the camp digging defensive trenches, preparing the stores for weapons and canned food, and conducting local reconnaissances in the area.

Guevara quickly realised that no one was familiar with the local terrain and the maps provided by Debray were inaccurate. He decided that a conditioning march was needed to accomplish his three goals:

- First, to harden them, teaching them how to adapt themselves to the rigours of guerrilla life such as hunger, thirst, long marches and little rest.
- Second, to get to know the peasantry, and start winning them over, to establish a base of popular support in the region.
- Third, to have a complete knowledge of the land where they would start their operations.

Their equipment had come from Cuba or been bought in Bolivia. A high-powered short wave radio – although obsolete – packed on a mule was the communications link with Havana via coded messages. Their weapons consisted of a mix of civilian rifles, US-made M 1 Garand rifles and carbines, Bolivian Mausers, and Czech ZB-30 light machine guns.

Regarding the internal organisation of the guerrilla group, the Supreme Commander was Che, while the Chief of Staff and Second Commander was Joaquín. Rolando was S-1 (Personnel Administration), Antonio S-2 (Intelligence), Alejandro S-3 (Plans, Operations and Training) and Pombo S-4 (Logistics).

The total group of guerrillas was organised in four platoons:

- Vanguard: Commander Marcos with 10 troops, who was substituted by Miguel in March.
- Centre: Commander Ramón (Che) with 18 troops.
- Rear guard: Commander Joaquín with 18 troops.
- Services: Commander Pombo with six to eight troops as needed.

A column of guerrillas crossing one of the many rivers In southeastern Bolivia during the long reconnaissance march led by Che in February 1967. (Centro de Estudios Che Guevara)

For the first reconnaissance mission, some effectives were left behind in order to take care of the camps. On 1 February, Che Guevara set out with most of the group in order to reconnoitre the surrounding terrain and carry out training. The marching column was organised into three groups:

- The vanguard, led by Marcos, with five men.
- The central column, led by Che himself, with 18 men.
- The rear guard, led by Joaquín, with six men.
- Total: 29 guerrillas (15 Cubans and 14 Bolivians).

A hierarchy was established within the patrol. Joaquín was appointed as Second Commander; the Chief of Operations was Alejandro, while the Political Commissioners were Rolando and Inti. Antonio was in charge of information, data collection and organisation of the troops; the head of supply was Camba and the head of all services was Pombo.

The group was attacked by insects and bad weather. Four of the Cubans suffered from bouts of malaria, including the doctor. It quickly became apparent that no one was physically ready for the rigors of guerrilla combat, including their leader. The physical stamina of the 38-year-old asthmatic revolutionary had diminished considerably since his days in the Sierra Maestra 10 years earlier. The group regularly became separated and radio communications failed in the canyons. On 29 February, disaster struck while crossing the rain swollen Grande River. Benjamín drowned, and valuable supplies and weapons were lost. To add further misery to the march, it rained heavily and frequently. The lack of food weakened them further. Scavenging for edible plants and hunting animals for food became a daily routine as they slowly wandered through the area. Everything from small birds, monkeys, sparrowhawks, and finally their own mules and horses made up the menu. Rather than unite them, the hardships of the march increased stress and caused dissension and daily arguments between guerrillas. The guerrillas failed to gain any support from the local population. The few Bolivian guerrillas from the Altiplano (Bolivia's high lands) had difficulty understanding the Guaraní language spoken in that area. The peasants were curious, but they did not want to join that strange band of foreigners, whom they feared because they were armed. Many of the peasants were there because government land reforms had given 10-hectare homesteads to 16,000 families.

The terrain in which the guerrilla mobilised was rough and impenetrable: jungle, mountains, mighty rivers. Each guerrilla carried backpacks of up to 20 kilos, in addition to their weapons. On the left, Manuel Hernández and Inti Peredo. On the right, two unidentified guerrillas, one Cuban on the left and the other Bolivian. (Centro de Estudios Che Guevara).

On 16 March, the second fatality occurred, Carlos, also due to drowning. In addition, backpacks with ammunition, one Brno MG, two M-1 and three Mauser rifles were lost in the attempt to cross the Rio Grande with a raft, which was dragged by the strong current and capsized.

After much suffering and privation, the demoralised guerrillas returned to the central camp on 20 March. By then, the number of guerrillas reached 51 and no more additions would be achieved for the rest of the campaign.

At the beginning of March, when Guevara had not yet returned to the base, Haydée Tamara Bunke *aka* Tania, the Frenchman Régis Debray, the Argentinean Ciro Roberto Bustos *aka* Pelado and the Peruvian Juan Pablo Chang arrived in Ñancahuazú. Shortly after, on 11 March, two men from Moisés Guevara's group, Vicente Rocabado and Pastor Barrera, deserted and were arrested three days later by the police. Rocabado confessed that there was a guerrilla group led by Che Guevara, in which there was also a woman. That same day, the Bolivian Constitutional President General Barrientos requested the cooperation of the United States and organised a coordinated intelligence system with the military regimes of Argentina, Brazil, and Paraguay, and the democratic governments of Chile and Peru.

Three visitors in Ñancahuazú. From left to right: the Frenchman Régis Debray; the Argentine-East German Tamara Bunke; and the Argentine Ciro Bustos. Debray and Bustos were able to leave the camp but were captured by the Bolivian Army. Tamara had to stay and was killed in Vado del Yeso months later. None of the three were combatants. (Open source).

The Peruvian guerrilla Juan Pablo Chang Navarro *aka* El Chino, next to Che in Ñancahuazú. El Chino wore thick glasses, without which he was practically blind. (Centro de Estudios Che Guevara)

ERNESTO CHE GUEVARA DE LA SERNA
(RAMÓN)

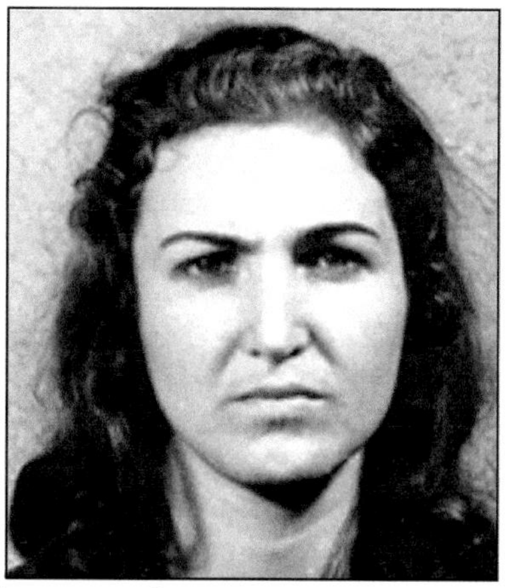

HAYDÉE TAMARA BUNKE BIDER
(TANIA)

CIRO ROBERTO BUSTOS
(EL PELAO)

The three Argentine guerrillas. Only Che was a combatant. (Open source)

JUAN PABLO CHANG NAVARRO (EL CHINO)

RESTITUTO JOSÉ CABRERA FLORES (EL NEGRO)

LUCIO EDILBERTO GALVÁN HIDALGO (EUSTAQUIO)

The three Peruvian guerrillas, all of them combatants. (Open source).

JULES RÉGIS DEBRAY
(DANTÓN or EL FRANCÉS)

The only French guerrilla but he was not a combatant. (Open source).

Debray and Bustos left again a few days later to organise support groups, but Tania, whose secret identity had been exposed, had to remain as a combatant. Tania's decision to go to Ñancahuazú did not have a clear explanation since she was in charge of organising the logistics of the guerrilla group in La Paz and establishing contacts with Argentina, which was why Guevara had ordered her not to go to Ñancahuazú for any reason. When he returned to the camp and saw her, he became really angry. She had also made a gross mistake on her way to Ñancahuazú by leaving behind certain documents in a grey Toyota Jeep that she abandoned in a garage on a deserted street in Camiri. The Jeep had La Paz licence plates and that raised suspicions among the local police, who thoroughly checked it and found the documents. There was a wealth of information about the guerrilla group since four of Tania's notebooks listing the entire Bolivian network of urban contacts, friendly communists outside of Bolivia, and secret money accounts were found. Within the week, communist safe houses throughout Bolivia were raided and many of the contacts arrested by the police DIC, a sort of Bolivian FBI. Whether by negligence or stupidity, Tania, the experienced operative with East German, Soviet, and Cuban training, had compromised the operation through her actions. Che was infuriated since all the spy work Tania had done during two years was lost.

By the time that Che and his guerrilla group got to their main camp, the Bolivian government already knew of their presence and began to organise a broad repressive operation. An emergency zone was established which was called *Zona Roja* (Red Zone) that comprised of five provinces in the southeastern Departments of Chuquisaca and Santa Cruz; this would be the theatre of war. In fact, a small army patrol had approached the *Casa de Calamina* by chance and the lookout, Jorge Vásquez Viana *aka* Loro, opened fire, wounding a soldier who would later die in the Camiri hospital. Faced with this situation and the absence of Che, it was decided to withdraw and dismantle the main camp, fearing a strong incursion by the army. While they were doing this, Che arrived and revoked the withdrawal order, setting up an ambush in the Ñancahuazú canyon in case army troops showed up.

Regardless, despite the harsh conditions of the terrain and the scant support obtained up to that moment, the ELN led by Che was about to enter into combat against the armed forces of the Bolivian state.

The ELN preparations consisted on the accumulation of ammunition, arms, food and clothing. Some items were acquired in excess, with the hopes of enlisting local men. A secondary camp called *Cueva del Oso* was established near the town of Lagunillas, where a store of weapons, ammunition and canned food was prepared.

The final guerrilla group consisted of 29 Bolivians, 16 Cubans, three Argentines, three Peruvians and one French. With the exceptions of Regis Debray *aka* Danton, Ciro Roberto Bustos *aka* El Pelao and Tamara Bunke *aka* Tania, all were combatants, although with varying degrees of efficiency and expertise. The Cubans were seasoned troops

The 16 Cuban guerrillas, all combatants and occupying the most responsible positions within Che's guerrilla force. (Open source).

26 of the 29 Bolivian guerrillas, all combatants although some of them were not fit for combat. (Open source).

since they had either fought in Sierra Maestra in Cuba or in Congo, being regular officers of the Cuban Revolutionary Army (FAR), while the Bolivians did not have any combat training. Che came to belittle Bolivians on many occasions in his diary, comparing them to 'little animals' that moved and behaved with great fear, including his own Bolivian guerrillas. Some of the latter were described as *resacas* (hangovers or drags), unfit for combat, for being fearful and physically weak.

Che's basic idea was not to seize power in Bolivia but to create a guerrilla focus with continental influence, a sort of new Vietnam against 'Yankee imperialism'. He followed the *foquista* model of rural guerrilla similar to the Cuban experience in Sierra Maestra, but he did not have the support of the Bolivian Communist Party and he was also unable to recruit Bolivian peasants for his campaign, as will be seen in the following chapters in this volume.

4

GENERAL RENÉ EMILIO BARRIENTOS ORTUÑO (1919–1969)

René Emilio Barrientos Ortuño was born in Tarata, Department of Cochabamba, on 30 May 1919. His parents were Dr César Barrientos, a prominent lawyer and Ercilia Ortuño, a distinguished lady of a wealthy family. René was the third child, preceded by César and Elena; years later the fourth child, Corina, was born.

The childhood and adolescence of René and his siblings were quite tragic. The father passed away in 1928 from a painful illness while the children were still young. Years later, the eldest of the brothers, César, would enlist in the army to fight in the Chaco War, where he was killed in combat in the area of Fortín Gondra with the rank of sergeant. When René was 15 years old, his mother died from an accidental shot from a gun she was cleaning, thus leaving all the children orphans.

He went to elementary school in his hometown and later he was sent to the Franciscan Convent of Tarata in order to continue his studies, but he soon left there as his philosophy of life did not coincide with staying locked up and praying. In 1934, at the age of 15, after a discussion with the principal of the convent, he decided to leave with the idea of dedicating himself to a military career. He travelled to the city of La Paz. With the help of an uncle who was a colonel in the army, he was accepted as a cadet at the Army Military School in La Paz when he was 16.

He graduated as a sub lieutenant in 1943. In that same year he joined the successful revolution led by Colonel Alberto Villaroel who overthrew General Peñaranda. He then got into Boquerón Military Aviation School in La Paz and then to Capitán Valle Military Aviation School in Santa Cruz de la Sierra where he received flight training. In 1944 he got a scholarship to study at the US Army Air Force Enid Army Flying School in Oklahoma first, and then at Moore Field and Randolph Field, both in Texas, in the United States where he finally got his military pilot wings on 30 April 1945. He also completed the Command and Staff Course in the United States. Once in Bolivia in 1946, he joined the Army Air Force and made the Higher Military Studies Course at Coronel Eduardo Avaroa School of Higher Military Studies.

From a political point of view, he was an admirer of President Villaroel but in 1946, Villaroel was overthrown and killed during a violent coup. Lieutenant Barrientos and many other officers tried to defend the regime but the rebels took over the government and all the officers who tried to defend the deposed president were discharged. Barrientos was arrested and spent long months in various prisons.

René Barrientos on a pony in 1923 when he was just four years old (left). Barrientos' hometown, Tarata, in the Department of Cochabamba (right). (Open source).

Sub Lieutenant René Barrientos posing next to a Curtiss-Wright CW-14 Osprey fighter-bomber, a veteran of the Chaco War, and a Curtiss-Wright CW-22 at the Military Aviation School in Santa Cruz de la Sierra in 1944. (FAB).

When the persecutions stopped and a truce was given, Barrientos was able to obtain his freedom. He soon found employment as a pilot at *Lloyd Aéreo Boliviano* (LAB), the national airline of Bolivia, like eight of his comrades in arms who had belonged to the Military Aviation.

Barrientos later joined the ranks of the *Movimiento Nacionalista Revolucionario* (MNR) led by Victor Paz Estenssoro and Hernán Siles Suazo. During the government of President Mamerto Urriolagoitia Harriague, the 1949 Civil War led by the MNR broke out. Barrientos joined the Revolutionary Command made up of former army officers in Cochabamba and the first action was to seize the Military Aviation airbase. He flew over La Paz to drop leaflets supporting the revolution. As the revolution was put down by the government, many revolutionaries just fled to neighbouring countries but Barrientos hid in the mountainous area, where he wandered for several months until he finally reached Tarata, his hometown, where he remained hidden and supported by the inhabitants.

At the end of 1951, during the de facto government of General Hugo Ballivián Rojas, Barrientos and his companions were reincorporated into active service in the Military Aviation, and he was promoted to the rank of captain.

At the beginning of the 1952 Revolution led by the MNR, the military aviators received orders from the government to attack the revolutionaries, but Captain Barrientos, leading a group of military pilots, refused, remaining inactive inside the El Alto Air Base.

Once the MNR came to power, and Vitor Paz Estenssoro assumed the presidency, Captain Barrientos was able to continue with his military career due to the strong support for the MNR cause.

On 16 January 1953, Barrientos was promoted to the rank of major. He competed and obtained a scholarship from Italy to carry out his General Staff Course at the Air Warfare School of the Italian Air Force. He also took specialisation courses in the air transport industry at the American University in Washington, DC in 1955.

With the creation of the Bolivian Air Force in 1957, he was transferred to the FAB and was promoted to the rank of lieutenant colonel. During his service in the FAB, he held the following positions:

- Flight Instructor at Boquerón Military Aviation School.
- Commander of Air Base No. 2
- Aeronautical Attaché at the Bolivian Embassy in the United Kingdom.
- Commander of Teniente General Germán Busch Military Aviation School.
- Commander of Military Air Transport (TAM).
- General Director of Production of the Air Force.
- Professor at Mariscal Andrés de Santa Cruz Command and General Staff School.
- Chief of the General Staff of the Air Force.

The family after the death of the father in 1928. The widow and the girls are in rigorous mourning with black clothes. Behind to the left, nine-year-old René, together with his brother César, who would be killed in the Chaco War. Seated in front, from left to right, his mother Ercilia and his sisters Elena and Corina. (Open source).

A teenage René posing in a square in Cochabamba with his mother Ercilia Ortuño in the mid-1930s. (Open source).

A very young cadet René Barrientos from the Military School in La Paz in the early 1940s. (Open source).

Sub Lieutenant René Barrientos upon his return from the United States, wearing the Bolivian and USAAF pilot wings in 1946. (FAB).

When Barrientos was dismissed from the army, he found a job as a pilot for *Lloyd Aéreo Boliviano* (LAB) airlines. (*Lloyd Aéreo Boliviano*/LAB Archives).

Captain René Barrientos (fifth from the left in the back row) posing with a group of pilot officers and mechanics of the Bolivian Military Aviation in the United States next to a USAF North American T-28 Trojan. (FAB).

- Professor at Coronel Eduardo Avaroa School of Advanced Military Studies.
- Commander of the Air Force. (His last position in the FAB).

General Barrientos (centre in the back row) posing with a group of FAB pilot officers who were on training courses in the USAF in the early 1960s with a North American F-100 Super Sabre in the background. (FAB).

On 17 December 1958, Barrientos was promoted to colonel and was first appointed as chief of the general staff of the FAB. In 1960 he was promoted to major general and appointed commander-in-chief of the Air Force. His final rank in the FAB was general of the Air Force.

During his command at the FAB, the Air Application School in Cochabamba, the Air Combat Group in El Alto, the Tactical Support Air Group in Riberalta and the Agricultural Group in Caranavi and Santa Ana de Yacuma, Air Detachments 1 (Cochabamba), 2 (Tarija) and 3 (Caranaví) were created and organised. Furthermore, TAM was completely reorganised so as to fly more efficiently and the construction of an Air Terminal for its flights was built. The Military Parachuting School was also started at El Alto Air Base and airfields were built in rural border areas.

Also during his command, he achieved the acquisition of six North American P-51D Mustang fighters from the Uruguayan Air Force in 1960, 12 North American T-28 Trojan advanced trainers (which arrived in 1967), two Douglas C-47s and the donation of spare engines for the fleet of the T-6 Texan from the United States.

On 24 February 1964, General Barrientos suffered an attempt on his life while leaving a family reunion, from which he only emerged bruised, despite the fact that the attacker shot him in the chest, causing him to fall to the ground. To his surprise, he would later see that the bullet had been deflected by his pilot's wings, which were made of thick metal. The attacker would never be caught, but he was almost certainly a hitman sent by political adversaries, since the general had involved himself in politics through the MNR.

Due to his charisma as an officer and as a person, General Barrientos enjoyed a lot of popular support. This meant that the MNR candidate Víctor Paz Estenssoro decided that he should accompany him in his presidential campaign for the 1964 elections. The presidential elections were held on 31 May of that year and the MNR won by a large majority with 98.8 percent of the votes for the period 1964 to 1968.

Barrientos took office as vice president on 6 August 1964. But soon the relations between the two began to deteriorate as Paz Estenssoro moved away from those postulates of the MNR of 1952,

The main types of FAB aircraft during the command of General Barrientos: North American P-51D Mustang fighters (top left), North American T-6G Texan advanced trainers (top right), Douglas C-47 (bottom left) and Douglas C-54 transport aircraft (bottom right). (FAB).

Major General René Barrientos as Commander of the Bolivian Air Force in 1960. On the right, General Barrientos shaking hands with United States President John F. Kennedy in 1961 along with commanders of other Latin American Air Forces. (FAB).

establishing a police state, mercilessly persecuting his opponents. Basic consumer products became scarce and unemployment increased, and there were also numerous cases of government corruption in illicit enrichment. Protests by students, workers, peasants and miners were breaking out all over the country and government forces were sent in to violently suppress them. Once again, General Barrientos, together with Army Commander General Alfredo Ovando and senior military commanders decided that it was necessary to interrupt these actions and thus planned a coup. In fact, Paz Estenssoro wanted to modify the constitution in order to remain in power indefinitely and that triggered the coup on 4 November 1964 led by General Barrientos.

The above mentioned coup was known as the *Revolución Restauradora* (Restorative Revolution). On the following day, he was appointed President of the Military Junta. All the heads of the ministries and main state institutions were high-ranking military officers. Barrientos created the so-called *Frente de la Revolución Boliviana* (Front of the Bolivian Revolution), which was made up of the PRA, PSD and MPC, all political parties with a small number of affiliates.

On 15 May 1965, General Barrientos dismissed all the mining leaders from their posts and dissolved the Bolivian Mining Workers Union Federation (FSTMB). The mining union leader Juan Lechín Oquendo was arrested, which led to a general miners' strike, which was violently repressed by the government, causing several deaths and many injuries. Nine days later, through Decree Law No. 7188, the salaries of Comibol miners were reduced by an average of 26 percent. The persecution of communist leaders began. Due to this crisis, General Barrientos had to accept a co-president, Army Major General Alfredo Ovando Candia, with whom he had to share power. General Ovando had been appointed as Commander-in-Chief of the Bolivian Armed Forces in 1964.

On 16 January 1966, he resigned from the presidency to participate as a candidate in the general elections of that year. Major General Alfredo Ovando Candia took over as provisional president.

During his electoral campaign, he travelled more than 22,000 kilometres visiting some 1,300 towns and cities, most by air, mobilising large numbers of people. He spoke vehemently and presented his great projects for the country.

It was expected to be the perfect presidential pairing. Victor Paz Estenssoro was the most popular politician in 1964 and General René Barrientos Ortuño was the most charismatic military figure and was loved by the people, so he joined the former as vice president. The government just lasted three months and Barrientos, with the help of the armed forces, overthrew Paz Estenssoro in November of that year. (Open source).

Army General Alfredo Ovando (left) with Air Force General René Barrientos (right). Both governed together as co-presidents between 1964 and 1966. (Open source).

On 3 July 1966 in free elections, General Barrientos was elected Constitutional President of the Republic with 61.81 percent of the votes for the presidential term 1966–1970. He was sworn in on 6 August of that year. His Vice President was Luis Adolfo Siles Salinas from the PSD. He led a government of economic development in which he favoured the peasants but faced off against workers and miners. As Commander in Chief of the Armed Forces, he held the rank of captain general, which corresponded to the President of the Republic.

During his constitutional government, his main achievements included:

- Congress sanctioned the 18th Political Constitution of the State in 1967, which was in force for 42 years until 2009.
- Construction of road projects 1 and 4 began; some routes connecting major cities were improved.
- Construction of the Corani and Santa Isabel hydroelectric projects in Cochabamba.
- The new International Airport at El Alto, serving the capital La Paz.
- The Bolivian National Radio and Television Company was created on 19 June 1968 and the contract was signed with the Spanish company INELEC for the installation of the State

Luis Adolfo Siles Salinas (second from the left) and René Barrientos Ortuño during the presidential campaign in 1966. (Open source).

The Constitutional Vice President of Bolivia Luis Adolfo Siles Salinas (left) and the President of Bolivia for the period 1966–1970 General René Barrientos Ortuño (right). (FAB).

Television Channel (TV7) which was inaugurated on 30 August 1969.
- Through the Law of 14 February 1967, the lease of the Matilde Mine was granted to the American Company United States Still and Phillips Company for the exploitation of zinc.
- The contract with the Gulf Oil Company for the supply of oil was renewed.
- He transferred all the weapons that the Public Security and Transit Guard (Police) had to the armed forces.
- The Executive Branch and the Municipal Mayors installed new drinking water service, electric lighting. Sewerage, paving and urban decoration works were undertaken in the departmental and provincial capitals.
- The railway network was improved and expanded thanks to credits from Japan and Germany, with which 20 new diesel locomotives were purchased, as well as passenger and freight wagons.
- The international reserves of the country reached the sum of 37,082,455,316 million dollars.
- Agricultural production increased notably, mainly wheat, coffee and rice. A great boost was also given to cattle farming.
- Yellow fever and malaria were eradicated.

Barrientos, who was appropriately called *El General del Pueblo* (The People's General), had broad popular peasant support.

Clear examples of the popularity of President Barrientos: peasants, children, and the elderly acclaimed him wherever he went. In fact, there was no corner of Bolivian territory that he had not visited. (Open source).

The infamous Nazi war criminal Klaus Barbie, refugee in Bolivia under the name of Klaus Altmann (left) (Gendarmerie Nationale de Lyon). SS-Hauptsturmführer Klaus Barbie in Germany in 1937 with the Gestapo uniform (right). (Bundesarchiv).

During his presidential trip to the United States in 1968, Barrientos visited USAF Randolph Field AFB where he had been trained more than 20 years before. He had the opportunity to sit in the cockpit of a Northrop T-38 Talon advanced jet trainer. (AP).

René Barrientos with his third wife Rose Marie Galindo de Ugarte (left) and the presidential couple with four of their children at home during Christmas (right). Barrientos had a total of nine children but he also helped hundreds of orphans throughout Bolivia. (Open source).

Barrientos spoke Quechua fluently, which helped the Military-Peasant Pact to become a hallmark of his government, and this allowed him to have the support of the peasants. However, during his term in office, he dedicated himself more to politics and travelling weekly to all the districts of the country, especially to the Department of Cochabamba. Barrientos was one of the few presidents of Bolivia who travelled almost all over the country. He was also known as *Tata Barrientos* (a Latin word meaning *father* but also a word in Greek, Quechua, Guaraní and others with the same meaning) since he adopted many poor orphans throughout Bolivia. Although he did not take them to his house to live, he made sure to send funds for their food, health and education.

During the period between November 1966 and October 1967, his government led the determined repressive struggle against Che Guevara's Marxist National Liberation Army (ELN) in the Ñancahuazú area, with the support of the US government through the mission of the US Army Green Berets, which trained the Bolivian Ranger troops. This subject is dealt with in more detail in this volume in the corresponding chapter.

President Barrientos faced various problems with the mining leaders from 1965. In 1967 he ordered the military occupation of the mines and armed confrontations took place between the army and the miners with the tragic outcome of 20 deaths. The main headlines state: 'Law and order will be maintained at any cost' and '"I am solely responsible for the entry of troops into the mines," President Barrientos said.' (Diario Presencia).

In 1967, during his constitutional government he declared the mining centres 'military zones' in order to apply the Triangular Plan, which consisted of reducing the influence of the Bolivian Mining Corporation (Comibol). Furthermore, the mining sector was heavily influenced by communist leaders who frequently boycotted the government through strikes. These leaders declared that the Catavi and Siglo XX mines were free territories and urged the population to overthrow the military government. In addition, there were street protests in La Paz, which caused damage to the YPFB (*Yacimientos Petrolíferos Fiscales Bolivianos*/Bolivian Fiscal Oil Fields) building and the TAM offices. To counter these riots, Barrientos militarised the mining camps and outlawed the unions. In response, the mining movement organised the 'mining-university-student pact' to resist the military regime and its privatisation measures. Thus, in the early morning of 24 June, army troops of the Rangers and Camacho Regiments from Oruro were deployed by train to the Siglo XX mining camp, located in the town of Catavi, Department of Potosi. Once there, the troops surrounded the place and seized it. Faced with the resistance of the miners who were armed with rifles and submachine guns, the troops opened fire which led to 20 fatalities and around 72 wounded, although it was estimated that the victims were around 200.

During his administration, Barrientos appointed Nazi war criminal Klaus Barbie, who called himself Klaus Altmann, as president of the State Shipping Society *Compañía Transmarítima Boliviana*, which at the time had only one ship. According to confidential information, he was engaged in the illegal international arms trade. Barbie was also appointed by Barrientos as an advisor to the Bolivian intelligence services.

General Barrientos got married three times. Firstly, with Carmen Porro Castillo, then with Marta Cuéllar Landívar with whom he had three children, Claudia Alejandra, María Renée and René Antonio, and finally with Rose Marie Galindo de Ugarte, with whom he had six children: Walter René, Sandra Rose, María Ximena, César Fernando, Germán Pablo and Paula Cecilia.

In December 1968, a group of technicians, intellectuals and professionals founded the *Partido de la Revolución Boliviana* (Bolivian Revolution Party/PRB) and President Barrientos assumed its leadership.

In his last speech delivered on 19 January 1969, President Barrientos highlighted that private sector investment had increased from 19.5 million dollars in 1966 to almost 41 million dollars in 1968. In three years of government, there was an investment of 74 million dollars.

On 22 March, through the Supreme Decree No. 8703, a special force was created to fight urban guerrillas under the name of the *General Esteban Arze* Battalion. This force was known as Command of United Mobile Forces to preserve Order and Development (FURMOD). President Barrientos, prophetically, was aware that other guerrilla adventures would take place in Bolivian territory (as indeed is seen in the last chapter of this volume). He never thought that with the disappearance of the Ñancahuazú Guerrilla, the subversive problem would be solved.

Many of his friends, military comrades, government ministers, and advisers had told him on several occasions to take care of himself on his many flights for presidential visits throughout the country. That did not intimidate General Barrientos and he said that

General Barrientos in one of his flights around the country, arriving on a FAB Hiller UH-12SL4 helicopter at a town in a remote area. (FAB).

if he died in a plane crash, it would be a glorious death for an aviator – again, prophetic words.

In one of his many trips to the interior of the country, on Sunday 27 April 1969, President Barrientos visited the town of Arque on board the Air Force Hiller SL4 helicopter, serial FAB-602, nicknamed *Holofernes*. The President was accompanied by his aide-de-camp, Army Artillery Lieutenant Leovigildo Orellana and Air Force Pilot Lieutenant Carlos Estivariz Cardozo. When it took off at 0140 hours to return to Cochabamba, the pilot decided to take the route through a canyon, flying low, not seeing that there was a taut

President Barrientos's coffin being unloaded from a TAM Douglas C-47 at El Alto Airport for the state funeral after his tragic death. Vice President Siles is at the front of the coffin. (UPI).

Hiller SL4 FAB 602 taking off from Arque on its fatal flight that 27 April 1969 (left). President Barrientos decorating his aide-de-camp Lieutenant Leovigildo Orellana López. Both would die together in the accident, along with the pilot Lieutenant Carlos Estivariz Cardozo (right). (FAB vía Jorge Cornejo).

steel telegraph cable, with which the helicopter collided, wrapping itself in the Hiller's main rotor. As a consequence it fell to the ground on a river bank and caught fire. The fall was from a low altitude and the three occupants could have survived the accident but they had a jerrycan of aviation fuel on board and when they crashed, fuel spilled and started a large fire.

Although some peasants, witnesses of the accident, ran towards the remains of the Hiller to rescue the passengers, nothing could be done. For a long time, there was a rumour that the Hiller was shot down by bursts of machine gunfire, but autopsy of the bodies did not reveal any gunshot wounds nor were any bullet holes found in the wreckage of the Hiller. Both lieutenants who accompanied President Barrientos were posthumously promoted to captain.

The commander of the FAB, General León Kolle Cueto, gave orders to the commander of Air Base No. 2 of Cochabamba, Lieutenant Colonel Víctor Lora Ríos, that the mortal remains of President Barrientos were flown to La Paz aboard an Air Force Douglas C-47 in order to receive all the corresponding honours at the state funeral. Thousands of people, mostly peasants, attended

General Barrientos's coffin is being carried on top of an Army FMC M113A1 personnel carrier which was escorted by the Military School Cadets in La Paz. (FAB).

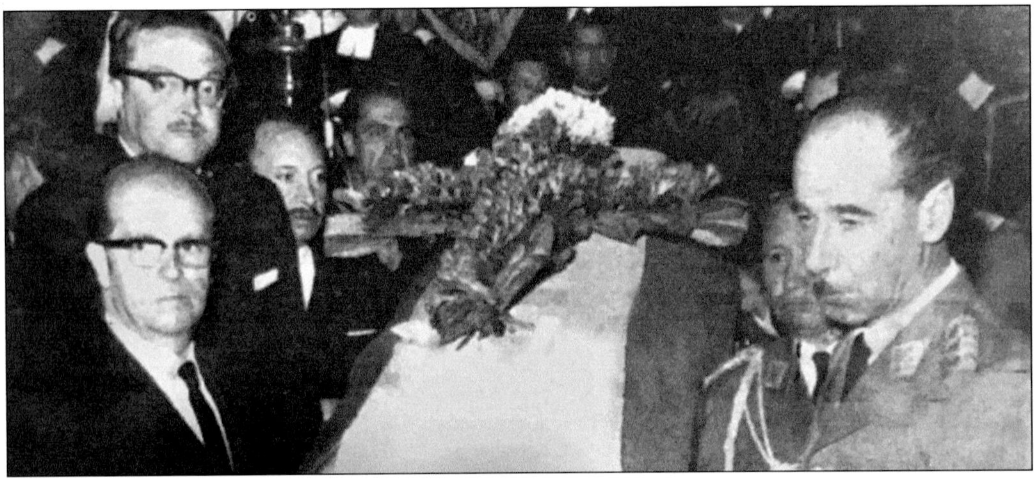

State funeral for President Barrientos in La Paz. To the left of the coffin, Vice President Siles and to the right is General Ovando, Commander of the Armed Forces. (Open source).

René Barrientos's tomb at Cochabamba Cemetery. (Open source).

General Barrientos's funeral. He was finally buried in Cochabamba on 2 May 1969.

During his lifetime, General Barrientos had received the following awards:

Bolivian decorations:

Constancia Militar (Military Constancy) 3rd and 2nd Class.

Condor de los Andes in the rank of Grand Officer.

Foreign decorations:

Abdón Calderón of the Republic of Ecuador.

Santos Dumont Mérito Aeronáutico of Brazil.

Legion of Merit of the United States.

Légion d'honneur in the degree of Grand Cross, of France.

Immediately after Barrientos's death, his Vice President Luis Adolfo Siles Salinas took over the presidency of Bolivia, but he did not stay in the presidency very long. He was overthrown five months later by a new military coup led by General Alfredo Ovando Candía who ruled for a year.

5

BOLIVIAN ARMED FORCES IN THE MID-1960s

Ejército de Bolivia (Bolivian Army)

The Bolivian Army was created with the proclamation of the country's Independence on 6 August 1825. The army had an active participation in the country's history, not only in international wars against Chile, Peru, Argentina, Paraguay and Brazil, but also in uprisings, revolutions, civil wars and coups. Among these conflicts, it is worth highlighting the following:

- The Peruvian invasion of Bolivia in 1828.
- The formation of the Peru-Bolivian Confederate Army in 1836.
- The war against the Argentine Confederation (also called Tarija War) in 1837–38
- The Peruvian-Bolivian War in 1841–42.
- The Pacific War in 1879–1883, in alliance with Peru against Chile, which led to the loss of the Antofagasta area and the maritime coast for Bolivia.
- The Federal War (also known as the Bolivian Civil War) in 1898–99.
- The Acre War against Brazil in 1899–1903, which entailed a great territorial loss.
- The Chaco War against Paraguay in 1932–1935, where Bolivia lost its claim to possess that territory when its army was expelled from the Chaco by the Paraguayan Armed Forces.
- The Civil War of 1949.

- During the Popular Revolution of 1952, the MNR practically dismantled the armed forces, ostensibly reducing its personnel and weapons, empowering the popular militias and the security forces (police and carabineros).
- After the 1964 coup in which the military assumed power, all the fighting capability returned to the army, which three years later, in 1967, would successfully confront the Marxist guerrilla led by Che Guevara in Ñancahuazú.

During the 20th century, the Bolivian Army was shaped by German military missions and in fact, during the Chaco War, its commander, Hans Kundt, was a First World War German general. Faced with heavy defeats on the battlefield in the Chaco, a Czech military mission was hired. The German influence in the Bolivian Army continued until the end of the Second World War, when the American influence began, as seen in uniforms, helmets, weapons and organisation.

On 20 December 1963, the Bolivian Congress, with the approval of President Víctor Paz Estenssoro, sanctioned the Organic Law of the Armed Forces that reorganised them. That law regulated the constitution and dependency of the armed forces, the Ministry of National Defence, the territorial organisation of the three forces, compulsory military service, pre-military training, military justice, the use of the armed forces in the maintenance of public order, the command in chief, the military institutes, the specific organisation of the army, air force and naval force, civilian employees of the armed forces, the ranks, and many other things.

The Bolivian Army had a commander-in-chief, a general staff and a number of large units. Geographically, the army had six military zones and within them 10 divisions (see Tables 3 and 4), each one with infantry, cavalry, artillery, communications and logistics regiments, which in turn were subdivided into brigades, battalions and groups. At that time, the army did not have its own aviation, so for the air transport of troops and other services it collaborated with the Bolivian Air Force.

The Bolivian Army used three British Vickers Mark E (one Type A and two Type Bs) tanks and three Carden-Lloyd Mark VI tankettes during the Chaco War without much success. One Vickers Type B tank and one Carden-Lloyd tankette were destroyed in the Second Battle of Nanawa in July 1933 and the other two Vickers were captured intact in the Battle of Campo Vía in December 1933 by Paraguayan troops. Towards the end of the Chaco conflict, the Bolivian Army received 14 Fiat-Ansaldo Carro Veloce L3/35 (CV-35) tankettes, which arrived too late to participate in the Chaco War. Right after World War II, the Bolivian Army received 12 M3A1 Stuart light tanks and 24 M3 Half-tracks through the American government's Lend-Lease Program, which remained in service long into the 1970s. Starting in 1966, FMC M113A1 armoured personnel carriers began to be used and in 1977 sixty of them were in service. In 1967, 24 Mowag Roland armoured personnel carriers were purchased from Switzerland to be used by the Army Military Police, which are still operational nowadays. That year also, the army acquired 14 M706 Cadillac Gage Commando V-100 armoured vehicles. Given the characteristics of the terrain in the anti-guerrilla fight, neither armoured vehicles nor tanks were used, and not even heavy artillery.

Regarding other vehicles, the army had a good number of REO M35A2 and Dodge M37 3⁄4 ton 4x4 cargo trucks that began to be acquired in the late 1950s and during the 1960s, and also several dozens of Willys Jeep M38A1 four-wheel drive vehicles that were donated by the United States in the 1950s and 1960s.

In 1964 Major General Alfredo Ovando Candia was appointed commander of the army and in 1967 commander-in-chief of the armed forces. He led a deep reorganisation of the armed forces but still the army was not yet prepared to fight when the guerrilla appeared on the scene. In 1967, Army General David Lafuente Soto was appointed as the army commander. The main military authorities were the chief of staff of the army, General Marcos Vásquez Sempérteguie, Colonels Joaquín Zenteno Anaya, commander of the VIII Army Division, Luis Reque Terán, commander of the IV Army Division and Juan Lechín Suárez, President of Comibol. In the mid-1960s, the armed forces had a total of 20,000 effectives, of which 16,000 belonged to the army. The officers and NCOs studied in Military Schools but the troops were composed of conscripts for the Compulsory Military Service (*Servicio Militar Obligatorio*/SMO).

As for the combat uniform, although the Bolivian Army used the regular khaki uniform for troops, non-commissioned officers and officers during the Chaco War, it would later change to olive green uniforms. Regarding weapons, the 7.65mm Mauser rifles from the Chaco conflict were still used, as well as 7.65mm Vickers and Colt heavy machine guns, 7.92mm Czech ZB-30 light machine guns, 82mm mortars and some 75mm howitzers. Beginning in 1959, the army received from the United States .30 calibre Garand M-1 rifles and M-1/M-2 carbines, Browning Automatic Rifles (BARs), M-1919A6 light machine guns, 60mm mortars, 57mm recoilless rifles, and 3.5-inch rocket launchers. In 1964 M-1 metal helmets

Army troops mobilised in trucks to put down the miners' rebellion in 1965. The photo gives an idea of the poor road infrastructure of the time. (AP)

Bolivian Army troops during a parade at the end of the 60s, wearing American M-1 helmets. M-1 and M-2 carbines were used as standard weapons for troops. (AP).

were introduced, which began to replace the German *Stahlhelm* M35 helmets that the Bolivian Army had acquired from the German *Polizei* in the 1950s. The United States provided over 12 million dollars through the Military Assistance Program to Bolivia by 1967. There were also FAL 7.62mm calibre assault rifles made in Argentina, which began to be incorporated into some army companies involved in the fight against the guerrillas in 1967. As for communication equipment, the Bolivian Army had AN/GRC-9 radios, as well as the PRC-10 and PRC-6 tactical radios, which had been donated by the United States.

Bolivian Army Rangers

The Second Company of Rangers of the Infantry Regiment RI.12 *Manchego*, known as Ranger-2, of the Bolivian Army was an elite unit and depended on the VIII Army Division. Its headquarters were in Santa Cruz de la Sierra. It would be chosen by the High Command to receive anti-guerrilla training from the Green Berets of the US Army in 1967. Its commander was Lieutenant Colonel José Gallardo and the deputy commander was Major Miguel Ayoroa. There was also a Ranger Company, Ranger-1, which belonged to the Infantry Regiment RI.24 *Mendez Arcos*, which was based in Challapata, Department of Oruro. It depended on the II Army Division. This company was not involved in the Mobile Training Team (MTT) program in La Esperanza, although they had been trained by the Bolivian Army as assault troops. Both Ranger companies would be involved in the fight against the guerrilla. Ranger troops debuted a camouflaged combat uniform and used either green berets or camouflaged caps. Their armament consisted of M-1 Garand rifles, M-1/M-2 carbines and also FN FAL assault rifles.

Table 2: Organisation of the Bolivian Army.

Military Region/ Headquarters	Army Units	City
1 (La Paz)	I Army Division Anti-aircraft Artillery Defence Group GADA.91 Military Police Battalion Saavedra Military Hospital 1 Orihuela Army Military School Cnel. Gualberto Villarroel Horseback-riding School Military Intelligence School General Zenteno Anaya Military School of Engineering Mariscal Sucre Military Communications School Military Police School Armoured Vehicle School Military School of Music TCnel. Patiño Army Engineering Regiment Cap. Felipe Ochoa I Mechanised Division	Viacha La Paz La Paz La Paz La Paz La Paz La Paz La Paz La Paz La Paz Patacamaya Viacha El Alto Viacha
2 (Oruro)	II Army Division Mountain Warfare School	Oruro Carangas
3 (Potosí)	X Army Division III Army Division	Tupiza Villamontes
4 (Cochabamba)	VII Army Division IX Army Division Central Arsenal Logistics Battalion 2 Transport Battalion 3 Military Hospital 2 Military Police Battalion BPM.272 Command and General Staff School Mariscal Andrés de Santa Cruz Army Sergeants Military School Maximiliano Paredes NCO & Sergeants Training School Guido Pradel V. Army Artillery School Weapons Application School Mariscal Ballivián Special Troops Training Centre (CITE) Jungle Operations Training Centre II (CIOS II) Military High School Teniente Edmundo Andrade	Cochabamba Villa Tunari Cochabamba Cochabamba Cochabamba Cochabamba Cotapachi Cochabamba Cochabamba Cochabamba Cochabamba Cochabamba Cochabamba Chapare Chuquisaca
5 (Beni)	VI Army Division IX Army Division	Trinidad Apolo
6 (Santa Cruz)	IV Army Division V Army Division VIII Army Division School of Bolivian Condors (Special Forces)	Camiri Roboré Santa Cruz Sanandita

Armoured vehicles of the Bolivian Army in the 1960s: Mowag Roland (top left), M3A1 Stuart light tank (top right), M706 Cadillac Gage Commando V-100 (bottom left) and FMC M113A1 personnel carrier (bottom right). (Ejército Boliviano).

A motorised column of Rangers led by a Willys Jeep M38A1 and followed by Dodge M37 3⁄4 ton 4x4 trucks from the Bolivian Army (top left). An M3 half-track on military manoeuvres (top right). Army troops being transported in REO M35A2 trucks (bottom). (Ejército Boliviano).

A key element in the history of the Rangers was the addition of Captain Gary Prado Salmón as a company commander. He was the son of a retired Bolivian army general who had fought in the Chaco War and later became a diplomat. In fact, Gary was born in Rome in 1938. In 1954 he entered the Military School, earning the rank of sub lieutenant in the Cavalry in 1958. He was an instructor in the Ingavi and Toledo Regiments, a staff officer at the NCO School and the Army Military School. The Prado Salmón family settled in Santa Cruz de la Sierra. He received military training in Panama, at Fort Gulick. He completed the Command and General Staff School in the Brazilian Army. He was commander of the Tarapacá Armoured Regiment and later of the VIII Division. He was already an expert in military tactics before being assigned to the Rangers.

In 1978 he was appointed Minister of Planning and Coordination of the government of General Padilla. In 1981, as commander of the VIII Division, during a military operation to recover an oil field taken over by insurgents, he was wounded by an accidental shot from a firearm by a sub lieutenant under his command. The shot injured his spine and left him confined to a wheelchair for the rest of his life. However, he continued as an active officer and was finally promoted to the rank of major general in 1985. He concluded his military career as Head of the Bolivian Military Delegation to the Inter-American Defence Board, in Washington DC. From 1990 to 1993, he was Bolivia's Ambassador to Great Britain, and from 2000 to 2002, he was Ambassador to Mexico. Upon his return to Bolivia, he obtained his master's degree in Security and Defence at the School of Higher National Studies. He dedicated himself to university teaching and wrote some books on his experience fighting the guerrillas and other historical topics. He passed away in May 2023.

Fuerza Aérea Boliviana (Bolivian Air Force)

The Bolivian Military Aviation was born as the *Escuela Militar de Aviación* (Military Aviation School/EMA) on 12 October 1923 by supreme decree of the government of President Bautista Saavedra Mallea. This school was located in the town of El Alto, near La Paz. In the first 10 years of existence, a total of 24 trainers (Caudron C.97, Morane Saulnier M.S.35, Vickers 155 Vendace III, Junkers A.50fe

Army General Alfredo Ovando Candia, Commander-in-Chief of the Bolivian Armed Forces (left). Major General David Lafuente Soto, Commander of the army. (Ejército Boliviano).

Table 3: Bolivian Army tanks and armoured vehicles in the mid-1960s.		
Vehicle	**Quantity**	**Years of service**
M3A1 Stuart light tank	12	1946–1979
M3 Half-track	24	1946–1979
FMC M113A1 personnel carrier (*)	4	1966–present
Mowag Roland	24	1967–present
M706 Cadillac Gage Commando V-100	14	1967–present
(*) Between 1966 and 1977 60 M113A1 carriers were acquired by the Bolivian Army.		

Junior and Curtiss-Wright CW-16E Trainer); 71 combat aircraft (Fokker CVb, De Havilland DH.9, Breguet XIX, Vickers 143 Scout, Vickers 149 Vespa III, Curtiss-Wright CW-14R Osprey, Curtiss-Wright 35A/65 Hawk II, Curtiss-Wright Cyclone Falcon and Junkers K.43b); and 15 transport aircraft (Junkers F.13L/W, Junkers W.34ci, Junkers Ju.52/3m, Ford 5-AT-D Trimotor and Sikorsky S.38B) were acquired, most of the latter belonging to *Lloyd Aéreo Boliviano* (LAB), an airline that cooperated closely with the Military Aviation. A further twelve 20mm Semag-Becker and 16 Oerlikon anti-aircraft

Table 4: Bolivian Army Divisions.	
Army Division/HQ	**Military Units (Headquarters)**
Army General Command (La Paz)	Infantry Regiment RI.1 Colorados de Bolivia (La Paz) Communications Battalion 1 Coronel Vidaurre (La Paz) Transport Battalion 1 (La Paz) Military Police Battalion 1 Capitán Saavedra (La Paz) Anti-aircraft Artillery Regiment 6 General Bernardino Bilbao Rioja (Viacha) Cavalry Regiment RC.4 Ingavi (El Alto) Cavalry Regiment RC.5 General José Miguel Lanza (Guaqui)
I Division(Cobija)	Infantry Regiment RI.8 Ayacucho (Achacachi) Infantry Regiment RI.23 Max Toledo (Viacha) Infantry Regiment RI.30 Murillo (Apolo) Infantry Regiment RI.35 Bruno Racua (Puerto Rico) Infantry Regiment RI.36 Soldado Santos Parramo (Rurrenabaque) Artillery Regiment RA.2 Libertador Simón Bolívar (Viacha) Engineering Battalion 6 Riosinho (Cobija) Engineering Battalion 2 General Federico Román (Caranavi) Military Police Battalion IV Soldado Rodolfo Siles (Cobija) Command and Services Battalion XI (Viacha)
II Division(Oruro)	Special Forces Regiment 1 Teniente General Germán Busch (Challapata) Infantry Regiment RI.21 Illimani (Uncía) Infantry Regiment RI.22 Mejillones (Huachacalla) Infantry Regiment RI.24 Méndes Arcos (Challapata) Infantry Regiment RI.25 Tocopilla (Curahuara de Carangas) Artillery Regiment RA.1 Camacho (Oruro) Cavalry Regiment RC.8 Braun (Oruro) Engineering Battalion 7 Sajama (Corque) Air Defense Artillery Group GADA.202 (Oruro) Logistics Battalion 1 Heroicas Rabonas del Pacífico (Oruro) Command and Services Battalion II (Oruro)
III Division(Villamontes)	Infantry Regiment RI.5 Campero (Ibibobo) Infantry Regiment RI.20 Padilla (Tarija) Cavalry Regiment RC.3 Aroma (Yacuiba) Artillery Regiment RA.3 Pisagua (Villamontes) Engineering Battalion 1 Eustaquio Méndez (Tarija)
IV Division(Camiri)	Infantry Regiment RI.6 Campos (Boyuibé) Infantry Regiment RI.11 Boquerón (Charagua) Cavalry Regiment RC.1 Avaroa (Choreti) Artillery Regiment RA.4 Bullain (Cuevo)

V Division(Roboré)	Infantry Regiment RI.13 Montes (San José Chiquitos) Infantry Regiment RI.14 Florida (San Matías) Infantry Regiment RI.15 Junín (Roboré) Cavalry Regiment RC.6 Castrillo (Puerto Suárez) Artillery Regiment RA.5 Vergara (Santiago de Chiquitos) Engineering Battalion 3 General Pando (Roboré)
VI Division(Trinidad)	Jungle Infantry Regiment RI.16 Teniente Coronel Jordán (Riberalta) Infantry Regiment RI.17 Independencia (Guayaramerín) Infantry Regiment RI.29 Echevarria (Trinidad) Cavalry Regiment RC.2 Ballivián (San Joaquín) Artillery Regiment RA.8 Teniente Coronel Félix Aguirre (Santa Cruz)
VII Division(Cochabamba)	Command and Services Battalion VII (Cochabamba) Infantry Regiment RI.18 Victoria (Cochabamba) Infantry Regiment RI.26 Juana Azurduy (Colomi) Artillery Regiment RA.7 Tumusla (Cotapachi) Military Police Regiment 3 General Esteban Arce (Cotapachi) Transport Battalion 3 Suboficial Raúl Cornejo (Cochabamba)
VIII Division(Santa Cruz)	Infantry Regiment RI.6 Campos (Boiyubé) Infantry Regiment RI.7 Marzana (Cabezas) Infantry Regiment RI.10 Warnes (San Ignacio de Velazco) Jungle Infantry Regiment RI.12 Coronel Manchego Rangers (Montero) Cavalry Regiment RC.10 General José Manuel Mercado (Buena Vista) Cavalry Regiment RC.1 Avaroa (Camiri – Choreti) Air Defense Artillery Group GADA.93 (Santa Cruz) Military Police Regiment School 2 Teniente Rubén Amezaga (Santa Cruz) Command and Services Battalion VIII (Santa Cruz) Transport Battalion 4 (Santa Cruz) Logistics Battalion 3 (Santa Cruz)
IX Division(Villa Tunari)	Infantry Regiment RI.31 Coronel Epifanio Rios (Villa Tunari) Infantry Regiment RI.32 General Idelfonso Murguia (Villa Tunari) Infantry Regiment RI.33 Ladislao Cabrera (Rio Blanco)
X Division(Tupiza)	Infantry Regiment RI.2 Mariscal Antonio José de Sucre/Amarillos (Sucre) Infantry Regiment RI.3 General Juan José Pérez/Verdes (Potosí) Infantry Regiment RI.4 Loa (Uyuni) Infantry Regiment RI.27 Antofagasta (Colcha) Cavalry Regiment RC.7 Chichas (Tupiza) Artillery Regiment RA.12 Ayohuma (Tupiza) Engineering Battalion 5 Teniente Coronel Napoleón Ovando Rojas (Sucre)

guns were also purchased. During that period of time, 104 military pilots, 38 air observer-gunners and 67 aviation mechanics were trained. By the time the Chaco War broke out against Paraguay, the Bolivian Military Aviation had all the necessary tools and human resources to establish air superiority, but unfortunately for Bolivia, its senior army commanders did not know how to use their powerful military aviation either tactically or strategically. They were never able to prevent offensive air raids by the Paraguayan Military Aviation. Both belligerent Air Forces engaged in 21 dogfights and carried out numerous reconnaissance missions and bombing raids during the three years of war.[7]

In the immediate post-war years, the Military Aviation acquired a total of 23 aircraft including Klemm Kl.25 and Breda Ba.25 trainers, Curtiss-Wright CW-19R All Metal fighters and Junkers Ju.86E/Z transport/bombers, the latter jointly used with LAB. In the 40s and when the Bolivian government supported the Allied cause in World War II, the Military Aviation received American aircraft through the Lend-Lease Program. Between 1941 and 1945, the Bolivian Military Aviation received 111 aircraft of different types: Lockheed 18 Lodestar (which went to the LAB), Interstate L-8A Cadet, Stinson L-9A Voyager, Boeing-Stearman PT-17, Vultee BT-13A, North American AT-6C and AT-6D Texan, Curtiss-Wright CW-22B Falcon, Grumman JRF-6B Goose, Beechcraft AT-7 and AT-11, and Douglas C-47A.[85] Since the years of World War II, numerous pilot officers and maintenance non-commissioned officers received training at air bases of the United States Air Force through the USAF Mission in Bolivia.

Bolivia signed the Rio de Janeiro Inter-American Treaty of Reciprocal Assistance (TIAR) in 1947 and the US Military Assistance Program followed with various deliveries: Initially Curtiss CW-22B Falcon and AT-6C/D Texan were delivered, followed by North American P-51D Mustang fighters purchased from the US in 1954, Uruguay in 1960 and Nicaragua in 1966, some of them modified as Cavalier F-51D Mustang in the US financed under the Peace Condor Plan in the mid-1960s. A single Republic P-47D Thunderbolt was also acquired but it was of very limited use. In addition, the FAB bought North American T-28D Trojan advanced trainers which arrived in 1967.

Regarding transport aviation, with the acquisition of the first Douglas C-47A, the Military Aviation created the *Escuadrón de Transporte Aéreo* (Air Transport Squadron/ETA) in 1945, but a milestone was the creation of the *Transporte Aéreo Militar* (Military Air Transport/TAM) in 1955. Douglas C-47 aircraft had been acquired starting in 1945 and C-54 in 1960, in addition to Curtiss C-46 in 1964.

The Rangers of the Manchego Infantry Regiment RI.12, considered elite troops in the Bolivian Army. Captain Gary Prado Salmón in front, with his officers in the second row and behind the Rangers troops. These were the troops trained by the Green Berets of the US Army in 1967. (Ejército Boliviano).

The then-Captain Gary Prado Salmón, Commander of the Rangers' B Company. (Ejército Boliviano).

Flight line of some North American AT-6C/D Texans received through the Lend-Lease Program in 1945. (FAB)

FAB Curtiss C-46 serial TAM 61 (left) and Douglas C-47 serial TAM 25 (right). (FAB).

Before the creation of the FAB, during the Chaco War, the Military Aviation was known as *Fuerzas Aéreas en Campaña* (Air Forces in Campaign) but later the name changed to *Cuerpo de Aviación del Ejército de Bolivia* (Bolivian Army Aviation Corps). In 1949, the MNR led an uprising against the government. Part of the Military Aviation joined the revolution and another part remained loyal to the government. Rebel forces seized all the LAB fleet plus nine AT-6 Texans, nine BT-13s, one Curtiss CW-22B fighter, a PT-17 Kaydet and a Grumman JRF-6B Goose. Meanwhile, the loyal Military Aviation had six AT-6s, five BT-13s, some C-47s, at least two C-46s, and also some Curtiss CW-22B Falcon fighters. Although there were no dogfights, both air factions bombed enemy targets using C-47 aircraft, which came to cause the destruction of several aircraft on the ground, and armed T-6s were also involved in strafing enemy troops. It was during this revolution that forces loyal to the government managed to acquire the first Lockheed P-38J Lightning on the civilian market, which upon arrival in Bolivia was properly armed and used against the rebels. Finally, the loyal forces managed to subdue the rebels and many aviation officers were forced to leave the Military Aviation, among them young Lieutenant René Barrientos. A second P-38 was purchased in the United States in 1949 but it was destroyed when it collided with an Eastern Airlines DC-4 while attempting to land in Washington. Finally, a third Lightning was acquired, an F-5G for aerial mapping in 1964.

Seven modified Boeing B-17G Flying Fortresses were purchased in 1956 as transport aircraft for the LAB but three examples saw service in the FAB for some years. By 1965, TAM had a fleet of 20 transport aircraft, flying an average of 400

A Bolivian Air Force North American P-51D Mustang fighter at El Alto Air Base in the 1960s. Note the large shark mouth and eyes painted on the front fuselage. (FAB).

A C-47 of the Military Air Transport flying over the mighty Andean peaks. Inserted in the lower part, the emblems of ETA and TAM. (FAB).

One of the three modified Boeing B-17G Flying Fortresses that saw brief service in the FAB as cargo aircraft. (FAB).

Clockwise, a pair of Cavalier TF-51D Mustang of the GAC, a trio of Harvard IIs in an overall yellow colour scheme, one of the last Stearman PT-17 in flying conditions in an overall red colour scheme and a North American T-28D Trojan. (FAB and Trevor Bartlett).

hours per month, connecting by air the main cities and towns of Bolivia. Through the 1960s, the FAB received many transport aircraft, specially C-47s, through the US Military Assistance Program.

During the government of General Hugo Ballivián Rojas, the Aviation Chief of Staff was created on 31 August 1951. Then, through Supreme Decree No. 04743 of 26 September 1957 of the government of Dr Hernán Siles Suazo, the Bolivian Air Force was created, thus becoming independent from the army. In the mid-1960s, the FAB had a total of 2,500 effectives, including officers, NCOs and conscripts. The commanders of the FAB between 1957 and 1970 are shown in Table 5.

Aircraft types in use by the Bolivian Air Force in the mid-1960s are shown in Table 6.

In the mid-1960s, the FAB flight training program started with the Brazilian-built version of the Fairchild PT-19 primary trainer, the Galeão PT-3FG and the Boeing-Stearman PT-17. Then, the advanced training was carried out with either the North American T-6 Texan or T-28 Trojan. Once the pilot officers got their wings, they were destined for combat aviation with the armed T-6D/G Texan attack aircraft and the North American P-51D Mustang fighters, or for transport aviation, first with the Cessna U-17 and later with the Douglas C-47, Curtiss C-46 and Douglas C-54. It was not until the mid-60s that the FAB incorporated its first helicopters, the Hiller UH-12SL4, Hiller OH-23 and Sikorsky H-19B Chickasaw.

In 1967, the FAB pilots assigned to the *Grupo Aéreo de Caza* (Fighter Air Group) were the following: Major Juan Pereda Asbún (Commander); Captains Jaime Zegada and Juan Muñoz Rebollo; Lieutenants Alberto Gómez, Ernesto Mendoza, Rogelio Maldonado,

Air Force General René Barrientos Ortuño was the commander of the FAB between 1960 and 1964. (AP)

Aerial view of the Military Aviation School (COLMILAV) in the 50s in Santa Cruz. (FAB).

A group of pilot officers and some aviation mechanics from the *Grupo Aéreo de Combate* (GAC) pose with FAB Commander General René Barrientos and Major León Kolle Cueto (both in the centre of the group) at the El Alto Air Base with a T-6 Texan in the early 1960s. (FAB)

Beechcraft AT-7 Navigator serial FAB 830. The title on the fuselage says *Posta Aérea Militar de las Américas* (Military Air Post of the Americas). (FAB via Jorge Cornejo).

Commanders of the FAB between 1957 and 1970: From left to right, Major Generals Walter Arze and Javier Cerruto, Air Force General René Barrientos, Major General Jorge Belmonte, Brigadier Generals León Kolle Cueto and Fernando Sattori. (FAB).

Military manoeuvres in 1962 at the El Alto Air Base, near La Paz. President Víctor Paz Estenssoro (in civilian clothes with binoculars) poses with General René Barrientos and other high-ranking commanders of the Air Force. (FAB).

Grover Rojas and Edgar Salas; Sub Lieutenants Gonzalo Dalence, Dardo Gómez, José Pantoja, Fernando Sanjinés, Roberto Taboada and Oscar Vargas. The first helicopter pilots were Major Jaime Niño de Guzmán, Lieutenants Carlos Estivariz Cardozo and Rolando Arévalo Dorado, and Sub Lieutenants Roberto Taboada Barriga and Gonzalo Dalence Ugarte. The first helicopter technician was NCO Orlando Requera Soriano.

Table 5: Bolivian Air Force Commanders 1957–1970.‡

Commander	Years
Air Force Major General Walter Arze Rojas	1957–1958
Air Force Major General Javier Cerruto Calderón	1958–1960
Air Force General René Barrientos Ortuño	1960–1964
Air Force Major General Javier Cerruto Calderón	1964
Air Force Major General Jorge Belmonte Ardiles	1965–1967
Air Force Brigadier General León Kolle Cueto	1968–1969
Air Force Brigadier General Fernando Sattori Ribera	1969–197t0

‡ *Fuerza Aérea Boliviana: Resumen Histórico de de las Brigadas Aéreas, Institutos y Unidades de la Aviación Militar* (La Paz: Editorial Aeronáutica, 2001.

Regarding the Air Force serial system, all aircraft had the title FAB + three digits (except the transport aircraft, which used the title TAM + two digits) as follows:

- **Primary and Basic Trainers**: From FAB 001 onwards (PT-17), from FAB 051 onwards (PT-19) and from FAB 101 onwards (BT-13).
- **Light Transport aircraft**: From FAB 201 onwards (U-17).
- **Advanced Trainers/Light Attack aircraft**: From FAB 301 onwards (T-6) and from FAB 401 onwards (T-28).
- **Fighters**: From FAB 501 onwards (P-51).
- **Helicopters**: From FAB 601 onwards (OH-23, H-19).
- **Transport aircraft**: From TAM 01 onwards (C-46, C-47, C-54).

The serials of some FAB aircraft were outside the named system, such as the Cessna 195 with serial FAB 372, the Cessna 180C with serial FAB 001 and the Beechcraft C-45 with serial FAB 830.

The FAB had a total of five air bases, as follows:

Base Aérea No. 1: As mentioned before, El Alto Airport ('The High One', so called that way because it is located at an altitude of 4,097 metres/13,442 feet above sea level) was not only La Paz International Airport but also the headquarters of the Military Aviation School and Air Force Base No. 1 Teniente Carlos Lazo de la Vega. This base was the headquarters of the *General Jorge Jordán Mercado Grupo Aéreo de Combate* (Air Combat Group, later GAC-31), with four squadrons, with NA P-51D Mustang fighters and armed NA AT-6C/D Texan attack aircraft. There was also an Air Transport Group with two squadrons as well as an Anti-Aircraft Artillery Squadron.

Base Aérea No. 2: In 1943, Air Force Base No. 2 Teniente Coronel Rafael Pabón was created in Cochabamba. In 1958, this base was the headquarters of Air Detachment No. 1 and already in 1967 the name was changed to *Grupo Aéreo Mixto* (Mixed Air Group/GAMX), with four squadrons, including NA T-6 Texan aircraft. There was also a helicopter squadron with Hiller SL4/OH-23s and Sikorsky H-19s.

Base Aérea No. 3: In 1943, Air Force Base No. 3 Teniente Alberto Montaño was created in Santa Cruz de la Sierra where Boquerón Military Aviation School operated and then Teniente General Germán Busch Military Aviation School (COLMILAV), with two squadrons, with PT-17/PT-

Table 6: Bolivian Air Force aircraft types between 1957 and 1970.[1]

Aircraft Type/Years in service	Number of aircraft	Role
North American P-51D/TP-51D Mustang (1954–1977)	12/3	Fighter/Advanced Trainer
Cavalier F-51D/TF-51D Mustang (1967–1977)	6/3	Fighter/Advanced Trainer
Lockheed P-38J/P-38L/F-5G Lightning (1949–1964)	1/1/1	Fighter-Bomber/Aerial mapping
Republic P-47D Razorback Thunderbolt (1949–1965)	1	Fighter trainer
North American AT-6B/C/D/G Texan (1941–1992) (1)	30	COIN/Attack/Advanced Trainer
North American T-28D Trojan (1965–1988)	12	COIN/Attack/Advanced Trainer
Vultee BT-13A (1942–1962)	37	Basic Trainer
Fairchild PT-19/Galeão PT-3FG (1941–1974)	11	Primary Trainer
Boeing-Stearman PT-17 Kaydet (1942–1965)	26	Primary Trainer
Beechcraft AT-11 Kansan (1943–1972)	2	Transport
Beechcraft AT-7 Navigator (1943–1975)	2	Transport/Aerial Photography
Douglas C-47A (1945–1997) (2)	17	Transport
Curtiss C-46 Commando (1964–1977)	4	Transport
Douglas C-54 Skymaster (1960–1991)	5	Transport
Boeing B-17G Flying Fortress (1956–1958) (3)	3	Transport
Grumman JRF-6B/G-21A Goose (1942–1966)	1	Light Transport
Cessna 195/U.20A (1957–1969)	1	Light Transport
Cessna A185E/A185F/U-17A (1963–1992)	7/8/7	Liaison/Reconnaissance/FAC
Cessna 180C (1960–1973)	1	Light Transport
Hiller UH-12SL4/OH-23 (1966–1976)	1/2	Utility helicopter
Sikorsky H-19B Chickasaw (1967–1974)	2	Utility helicopter

(1) A total of 82 T-6 aircraft saw service in the FAB from 1941 to 1992. They were acquired from the US, Brazil, Argentina and Peru.
(2) Nearly 50 C-47s were in service in the FAB between 1945 and 1997.
(3) Three B-17G were briefly used by the FAB and then transferred to the LAB.

19 primary trainers and T-28 advanced trainers.

Base Aérea No. 4: This base was created in the 1950s in the city of Trinidad but at that time, there were no squadrons assigned to this base.

Base Aérea No. 5: This base was also created in the 1950s but in Tarija. In 1958, the Air Base in Tarija became the headquarters of Air Detachment No. 2.

In 1954 the former School of Mechanics and Aviation Specialists became the Military Aeronautics Polytechnic (PMA) Sub Teniente José Max Ardiles Monroy. Alongside this, Air Detachment No. 3 was created in 1964 in Caranavi. Other Air Groups were *Grupo Aéreo No. 1* (Air Group No. 1) in Villa Montes and *Grupo Aéreo No.2* (Air Group No. 2) in Cuevo. There was also a *Grupo Aéreo de Cobertura* (Tactical Support Air Group) in Riberalta. During the Ñancahuazú campaign, FAB aircraft used a temporary air base in that area, in the town of Choretí-Camiri, but the main base was Santa Cruz de la Sierra. In addition to the aforementioned air bases, there were also landing strips that have been used by the FAB in Cobija, San Borja, Santa Ana, San Joaquín, Oruro, Ascensión, Potosí, Sucre, San José de Chiquitos, and Puerto Suarez.

During the anti-guerrilla campaign in 1967, several Mustangs and T-6Ds received tactical camouflage. In the case of the F-51Ds it was a three-tone South East Asia type camouflage in dark green, medium green and tan. In the case of the T-6Ds the camouflage was in two tones, dark green and tan. (FAB).

From left to right: El Alto International Airport where FAB Air Base 1 is located. Cochabamba Airport where FAB Air Base 2 is located. Major General Jorge Belmonte Ardiles, FAB Commander and Brigadier General León Kolle Cueto, FAB Chief of Staff in 1967. (FAB).

The two types of helicopters in service with the FAB in the 1960s: one of the two Sikorsky H-19 Chickasaw of the *Grupo Aéreo Mixto* (GAMX) still without camouflage (left). A camouflaged Hiller OH-23 Raven also from GAMX (right). (FAB via Jorge Cornejo).

Given the possibility of the formation of a guerilla movement on Bolivian soil, between 1964 and 1965, the military personnel belonging to the FAB counterinsurgency (COIN) training. In the mid-1960s, the FAB had some 4,000 effectives, including officers, NCOs, and troops. At that time, the commander of the FAB was Major General Jorge Belmonte Ardiles, and the Chief of Staff was Brigadier General León Kolle Cueto.

Once the presence of guerrillas on Bolivian soil was known, President Barrientos requested, among other things, napalm bombs from the United States, but was denied. However, the government of Lieutenant General Juan Carlos Onganía of Argentina, faced with

Fighter pilots of the FAB Combat Air Group in 1967. On the right, the GAC emblem. (FAB).

the possibility of guerillas operating in Argentina, provided 100 aviation napalm bombs, in addition to various types of ammunition that was sent by train to Bolivia.

Fuerza Naval Boliviana (Bolivian Naval Force)

On 19 November 1826, the Bolivian Navy was born under the name of Escuadra Naval (Naval Squadron), whose main base was in the Port of Cobija, on the Pacific Ocean, in the Antofagasta region. The first acquisitions were the warships *Yanacocha* and *Confederación*, brigantines *La Fállete* and *Congreso* and corvette *Libertad,* which all belonged to the Peru-Bolivian Confederation. Later the Coast Guard *General Sucre*, the brigantine *Maria Luisa*, the gunboat *El Morro* and other minor vessels were purchased.

Because the squadron lacked an organisational structure, it was disbanded before the War of the Pacific (1879–1883). The Chilean invasion of 1879 and the loss of all maritime coasts abruptly interrupted the development of the Bolivian Navy, until 1897, the year in which the government, by Supreme Decree, created the Military Shipyard in Cobija, which was later moved to the town of Bahía, in Riberalta. The shipyard did an outstanding job building steam-powered vessels such as *Beni, Madre de Dios, Castro Rojas, Manu, Fortaleza, Manoa,* and *Pando,* among others.

During the Acre War (1899–1903), given the lack of adequate roads to mobilise war material and soldiers, the Bolivian government found it necessary to establish a fluvial-lacustrine branch within the Bolivian Army. During the Acre Campaign, the naval forces were present with the above mentioned vessels and others such as the *Tahuamanu,* a surface unit manufactured in Germany for the transport of troops, war materiel and equipment.

In 1939, the Bolivian Army created the School of Mechanics and Navigation in the city of Riberalta, on the banks of the Beni and Madre de Dios rivers. By 1951, the Military Shipyard No. 1, in addition to still having the ship *Tahuamanu*, had eight speedboats, *Beni, Castro Rojas, Manu, Fortaleza, Manoa, Pando, Heath* and *Madre de Dios*, which patrolled the main Bolivian rivers and lakes.

On 4 January 1963, the Bolivian Army's VI Division reorganised its naval branch as the *Fuerza Fluvial Lacustre* (Lacustrine Fluvial Force). It was in that year that the American government donated four 12-ton PBR Mk. I patrol boats (Patrol Boat Riverine Mk I) that received the names of *Presidente Paz Estenssoro, Presidente Kennedy, Comandante Arandia* and *Doctor By.* By then, the naval force had 1,500 effectives including officers, NCOs and sailors. Its first commander was Rear Admiral Ronald Monje Roca.

Finally, on 8 January 1966, the *Fuerza Naval Boliviana* (Bolivian Naval Force) was created by Supreme Decree No. 7469 as the third component of the Bolivian Armed Forces, completely independent of the army. Despite the fact that Bolivia is a landlocked country, without maritime coasts, it is furrowed by numerous and mighty rivers, the main ones being Acre, Beni, Madre de Dios, Mamoré, Parapetí, Blanco, Grande, Piraí, Pilcomayo, Sajama, Chapare, and Madera, and so on. It also has large lakes like the Titicaca, Poopó, and Huaytunas, just to mention the largest, whose protection has been under the Bolivian Naval Force.

By the mid-1960s, the Bolivian Naval Force had an endowment of fast armed patrol boats, ferry boats, and river vessels that were deployed jointly with their personnel during the campaign against the Ñancahuazú guerrillas, acting as logistical support for the army in transporting troops and war material to the conflict zone. At that time, the following vessels were in service: *Mariscal Santa Cruz, Almirante Grau, Nicolás Suárez, Topater, Mapiri, Tahuamanu, Iténez, Bruno Racua, Presidente Kennedy, Toribio, Muchula, Litoral, Rio Madera, Chapare* and *Ibare.*

The Commander of the Bolivian Naval Force in the mid-1960s was Rear Admiral Horacio Ugarteche. The Bolivian Naval Force was organised in Naval Areas and Naval Districts, as shown in Table 7.

The Bolivian Naval Force collaborated in the fight against the guerrillas with a company of 120 marines in the Abapó sector, Department of Santa Cruz.

Cuerpo de Aviación Naval (Naval Aviation Corps)

Created in 1968, its first aircraft was a Cessna 182. That Cessna operated from its base in Santa Ana de Yacuma, for Medevac missions. In 1969, the Argentine Naval Aviation donated two North American SNJ-5 Texans for advanced training, although another source indicated that both SNJ-5s were actually donated to the FAB. Years later it would incorporate Cessna U206 and 402C aircraft. Back then the military serials used the letters FNB (*Fuerza Naval Boliviana*) followed by three digits were used.

Table 7: Bolivian Navy organisation

Naval Area	Location (*)	Naval District	Location
A.N.1	Cochabamba	D.N.1	Beni
A.N.2	Santa Cruz	D.N.2	Mamoré
A.N.3	Bermejo	D.N.3	Madera
A.N.4	La Paz	D.N.4	Titicaca
-	-	D.N.5	Santa Cruz de la Sierra
-	-	D.N.6	Cobija

(*) Note that the names of these Naval Areas (AN) and Naval Districts (DN) derived from the river basin or region in which they were located.

Policía Boliviana (Bolivian Police)

During the government of Marshal Antonio José de Sucre, the Police Regulatory Law was instituted on 24 June 1826, which then created this internal security body. Over time, the population identified police officers with different names such as sheriffs, wardens, watchmen, gendarmes, commissioners, mayors, guards, order agents, carabineros and police.

On 28 July 1930, the government instructed the unification of the police units under the command of the General Directorate of Police and Carabineros. During the Chaco War against Paraguay, several police units were deployed to the front, including the Calama Carabineros Regiment in the Chuquisaca Lagoon sector, as well as other detachments such as the 15th and 16th Infantry Regiments made up of gendarmes, commissioners and police officers which participated in the battles of Boquerón and Kilometre 7, in addition to the Murguía Regiment made up of the most seasoned carabineros known as the *Cuchilleros de la Muerte* (Knives of Death).

On 26 February 1937, President David Toro Ruilova signed the Supreme Decree creating the National School of Police and Carabineros of Bolivia, and that same year an Italian Carabinieri Mission was hired to professionalise the country's police forces. The institution was commanded by a General Director of Police and Carabineros.

Due to the determined support they gave to the MNR during the 1952 Revolution, the police received numerous weapons that were confiscated from the military. In 1962, the name *Carabineros* was changed to *Policía Boliviana* (Bolivian Police) and the figure of general director changed to that of general commander of the Bolivian Police.

On 4 November 1964, the military coup led by the Air Force General René Barrientos and the Army General Alfredo Ovando instructed the confiscation and surrender of weapons of the police force, which were returned to the army. Even though the army uniform was olive green, the police uniform continued to be the same colour.

By the mid-1960s, the Bolivian Police had a Higher Command and the country was divided into regional, district, border commands and police zones, each with its commanders and chiefs. The Superior Command had three Police Directorates: Scientific, Technical and Administrative. There was also a *Departamento de Investigación Criminal* (Criminal Investigation Department/DIC), a sort of Bolivian FBI. The country was divided into three Police Regions (RP) and the following Police Districts (DP):

- Región Policial No. 1 (RP1): Its headquarters was in the city of Oruro and included the Police Districts of La Paz, Oruro and Potosí.
- Región Policial No. 2 (RP2): Its headquarters was in the city of Sucre and included the Police Districts of Cochabamba, Chuquisaca and Tarija.
- Región Policial No. 3 (RP3): Its headquarters was in the city of Trinidad and included the Police Districts of Santa Cruz, Beni and Pando.

During 1967, due to the fight against the guerrillas, police units were deployed to the Ñancahuazú area and a police officer and his dog were killed by the subversives.

6
US MILITARY TRAINING IN BOLIVIA

At the time of the guerrilla insurgency in Bolivia, the US ambassador in that country was Douglas Henderson, a career diplomat. Meanwhile, John Tilton was the head of the CIA in La Paz.

The poor military preparation of officers, NCOs and troops in the Bolivian Army led the government to seek a a mission of US Army instructors in 1962. This was made up of a captain, a lieutenant and 12 specialist sergeants, and they arrived in Bolivia to provide COIN training. Courses were held first with the cadets of the Military School and then with officers and NCOs in the army detachment in Cochabamba and finally in Challapata, where the *Teniente Méndez Arcos* Infantry Regiment 24 was created as an assault unit, which was known by the name of Rangers. However, all this training was only theoretical, and as a result, all the army's tactical exercises were still for a conventional conflict. At that time, there was still no thought of a foreign guerrilla force on Bolivian soil, but rather of mining groups, the focus of conflicts being led by communist-leaning trade unionists.

After the seizure of power by the military, the armed forces openly declared themselves anti-communist and tight control began to be exercised over the left-wing political parties and movements in the country.

After his popular election in 1966, President General René Barrientos had requested additional military training for the Bolivian Army during an official visit to Washington. One of the first measures taken by the American government was to help organise and train the Airborne Battalion of the Bolivian Army in Cochabamba. It was to be the first of several elite units oriented for mountain, river, and jungle warfare. Bolivian officers had been attending COIN courses at the School of the Americas in Panama as well. Early in 1967, the US Military Group (MILGP) under the command of Lt Col Joseph P. Rice based in Cochabamba, Bolivia, assigned two of its members, Major John D. Waghelstein and Master Sergeant Gustavo Fabian to give COIN classes to Bolivian Army officers and NCOs. Major Waghelstein became an instructor at the *Escuela de Armas* (Weapons' School) for captains and lieutenants, and Master Sergeant Fabian did the same at the Bolivian NCO Academy. Major Waghelstein and Sergeant Fabian even

The Bolivian Naval Force received four 12-ton PBR Mk. I patrol boats (Patrol Boat Riverine Mk I) similar to the ones in the photos donated by the American government in 1963. On the left, Rear Admiral Horacio Ugarteche, Commander of the FNB in the mid-1960s. (Open source).

Chiefs and instructing officers of the National Police Academy in the mid-1960s (left). Bolivian Police NCOs, sergeants and corporals (right). (Policía Boliviana).

managed to be driven to the Red Zone, the area where it was thought a guerrilla base had been created. The MILGP also sent Sergeant First Class Del Toro to La Esperanza training centre to teach vehicle driving and maintenance (jeeps and trucks) to the Bolivian Army Rangers.

In April 1967, in the middle of the fight against Che's guerrillas and perhaps at the most appropriate moment, given the first setbacks of the Bolivian Army in that conflict, the 8th Special Forces Group MTT (designated BL 404-67X), which were popularly known as the Green Berets, commanded by Major Ralph W. 'Pappy' Shelton arrived in Bolivia in order to train the local Ranger troops. This US Army group was made up of 16 members, officers and non-commissioned officers specialised in anti-guerrilla warfare, with different specialties as instructors, light and heavy weapons, radio operators, medical specialists, intelligence specialists, engineering and logistics. All of them could speak Spanish. This special mission had been assigned by the Commander of the 8th Special Forces Group, Colonel Magnus Smith, stationed in the Panama Canal Zone.

Major Ralph W. Shelton had first become a NCO in the US Army and participated in the Korean War (1950–1953) where he was wounded twice. After returning home, he got into the Officer School Program and became a Green Beret and as such he saw action in Laos and the Dominican Republic. He studied Spanish and was very fluent. It was probably because of that he skipped the Vietnam War since the Army High Command gave him posts in Latin America, firstly in the Panama Canal Zone. At the time when he was assigned to lead the MTT to Bolivia, he was 37 years old. Major Shelton chose all the members of his MTT personally.

Once all the MTT effectives had been briefed about their mission, they and all their equipment, including weapons, ammunition and food, boarded two USAF Lockheed C-130 Hercules and departed from Howard Air Base in the Panama Canal Zone towards Santa Cruz de la Sierra, Bolivia. The MTT effectives and all their equipment were transported in Bolivian Army trucks to La Esperanza, a small town with few inhabitants. Once there, they established their base in the abandoned facilities of a sugar mill.

The task was difficult since at that time the Bolivian Army had 15,000 troops, the vast majority conscripts (mostly peasants and aborigines) with very poor training and moderately armed, although their morale was very high. The idea was to select the best army effectives for rapid training so that they could immediately go to the front to fight the subversives. It was then decided that the second Ranger battalion, known as Ranger-2, was to receive such training at La Esperanza Army Base in the Department of Santa Cruz. The Ranger Battalion was to be organised in nine infantry rifle companies, all to be trained in COIN operations. The training was also extended to the Army Airborne Battalion, especially to junior officers at the Combat Arms School in Cochabamba.

This military cooperation between the two countries was framed in the national security policy during the Cold War, which consisted of containing the advance of communism across the world and especially in the American continent, given the successful revolution that had taken place in Cuba in 1959. Cuban plans to 'export' the Marxist revolution to all Latin American countries were well known, creating different 'National Liberation Armies'. According to Che Guevara himself, the idea was to create as many 'Vietnams' as possible.

Central and South America were the responsibility of the United States Southern Command (SOUTHCOM). They were in charge of administering the Military Assistance Program for Latin American countries, directing US participation in hemispheric defence exercises, mapping and charting activities, and directing disaster relief and search and rescue operations. The army component command of SOUTHCOM was US Army Forces Southern Command (USARSO), based at Fort Amador, in the Panama Canal Zone. The army was represented in US MILGP throughout Latin America. When the 8th Special Forces Group went to Bolivia, they learned how the MILGP provided support, mostly by liaison.

The MILGP was the 'doer' for military support on US Ambassador Douglas Henderson's country team. Lieutenant Colonel Joseph Rice headed the MILGP detachment in Cochabamba advising the Bolivian Army NCO Academy, the *Escuela de Armas*, and the Bolivian Airborne Troops School. He assumed the role of Ranger Battalion Project Officer. Visiting units outside La Paz was difficult because of the terrain and the primitive Bolivian road network. The mission of the MILGP was to assist the Bolivian military with its internal security. This was critical because Bolivia's military was ill-prepared to combat the growing internal insurgency.

The severely constrained budget of the Bolivian Army prevented effective training of the new soldiers. Military spending was around 28 million dollars which accounted for only 2.2 percent of Bolivia's gross domestic product, which in 1967 was estimated at 1,287 million dollars. While Shelton's team struggled to obtain basic soldier items such as canteens and load-bearing equipment from the US MILGP, the Bolivian Army had no field rations for its soldiers. The state of the Bolivian Army, considered one of the weakest in Latin America, made it a prime target for revolutionaries. However, Che's dream of mounting a successful insurgency was destroyed when the US trained a counterinsurgency force, the Rangers, to eliminate the guerrilla threat.

With the influx of the 12 million dollars of American military aid in the 1960s, the Bolivian Army was able to motorise some infantry battalions and create a special high-altitude assault battalion with soldiers from the Altiplano. They made significant advances in the schooling of the officers and non-commissioned officers. With the assistance of the United States, they established an Airborne Troops School and Battalion and a Non-commissioned Officer's School in Cochabamba. For all the services, the training of officers began with a five-year basic course at the Gualberto Villarroel Military School in La Paz. Each December the school commissioned about 95 cadets as sub lieutenants to fill the ranks in the armed forces. Officers and non-commissioned officers attended courses at the US Army-run School of the Americas in the Canal Zone. After the Academy, army officers attended career branch schools, a two-year staff course for promotion to major, and ultimately the National War College. This education strengthened the officer and NCO corps, but it did not adequately address how to combat an insurgency.

When the main body of the 8th Special Forces Group MTT BL 404-67X arrived in La Esperanza, on 29 April 1967 to begin a 179-day deployment, the men were struck by the primitive conditions of the tiny village. According to one of the members of the MTT, Sergeant First Class Harold T. Carpenter, the conditions there were pretty Spartan. La Esperanza was a tiny village with no more than 200 inhabitants, no electricity or running tap water, and not even indoor plumbing. However, the place was chosen to train the new Bolivian Army Ranger Battalion by their team leader, Major Ralph W. Shelton for its access to suitable training areas and the necessary operational security due to the town's remote location.

Major Shelton and his team developed a comprehensive 19-week training programme with four phases:

- **Phase One**: Six weeks of basic individual training, a necessity for the untrained conscripts, from May to mid-June 1967. World War II vintage training manuals from the School of the Americas at Fort Gulick (the Canal Zone, Panama) that had been translated into Spanish were used. This phase included physical training (PT), weapons training, land navigation, camouflage techniques, and basic patrolling.
- **Phase Two**: Three weeks of advanced individual training, carried out in June and the first week of July 1967. It was devoted to the different military occupation specialties (MOS) requirements such as medical, communications, advanced marksmanship for snipers, and crew-served weapons gunners, and leadership and staff training for the officers and NCOs. Ranger training was introduced. It consisted of rappelling, ranger operations (ambushes, raids, and patrols), and combat conditioning exercises with makeshift confidence tests and obstacle courses. This phase was designed to bring the troops to a high level of individual soldier proficiency before the collective training in small unit operations began. An abandoned sugar mill structure provided the training platform. There was also advanced sniper and counter-sniper training using the much heavier M-1D Garand rifles and also some old Mauser rifles. In this phase, the Bolivians received training in the use of M20A1 3.5-inch antitank rocket launchers, U.S. 81 and 60mm mortars and the older French 82mm systems.
- **Phase Three**: Three weeks of basic unit training starting with the rifle squad, progressing to the platoon (Bolivian Army Section), and company tactics, during the month of July 1967. The basic collective training concentrated on squad and platoon-level movement techniques, fire and manoeuvre, and patrolling, with hand and arm signals.
- **Phase Four**: It lasted seven weeks and concentrated on advanced unit and counterinsurgency training, which culminated in a two-week field training exercise at the end. This phase lasted from 30 July to 17 September. The Field Training Exercise was conducted 15 miles southwest of the town of Santa Cruz (75 miles from La Esperanza) because it closely replicated the Red Zone terrain where the Rangers would soon be operating. The Special Forces team worked to inject as much realism into the instruction as possible. As part of the immediate action training, they set up a little mock village to teach the soldiers how to properly clear buildings without harassing the local people. This was their final evaluation before being committed to combat against Che Guevara and his guerrillas.

Table 8: US Army 8th Special Forces MTT Members[1]

Rank	Name	Role
Major	Ralph W. 'Pappy' Shelton	Commander/ Executive Officer S-3
Captain	Edmond L. Fricke	Deputy Commander/S-3
Captain	Leroy Mitchell	Executive Officer S-3
Captain	Margarito Cruz	S-2 Officer
Captain	James Trimble	S-1/S-4 Officer
First Lieutenant	Harvey Wallender	S-2 Officer
Master Sergeant	Oliverio Gómez	Team Sergeant
Master Sergeant	Roland Milliard	Intelligence Sergeant
Sergeant First Class	Daniel V. Chapa	Light Weapons Instructor
Sergeant First Class	Héctor Rivera-Colon	Heavy Weapons Instructor
Sergeant First Class	Harold T. Carpenter	Heavy Weapons Instructor
Sergeant First Class	Johnnie E. Reynolds	S-1/S-4 Sergeant
Staff Sergeant	Jerald Peterson	Medical Specialist
Staff Sergeant	James Hapka	Medical Specialist
Staff Sergeant	Wendell Thompson Jr.	Radio Operator
Staff Sergeant	William W. Burkett	Communications Supervisor
Sergeant	Alvin Graham III	Radio Operator
Sergeant	Byron R. Sigg	Assistant Instructor
S-1: Personnel Administration, S-2: Intelligence, S-3: Plans, Operations and Training, S-4: Logistics.		

The team's mission was to turn brand-new draftees into Rangers. The Bolivian troops arrived in groups beginning in early May 1967, and the training program started on the 8th of that month.

The Bolivian soldiers just had one uniform on their backs and a variety of weapons. They had no load-bearing equipment (LBE), canteens, or ponchos. The Bolivian Army did not have packaged field rations. Food and water determined how far from La Esperanza they could train. Despite the best efforts of the SF team, the soldiers would not get these critical items until the training was nearly complete. The team worked through Lieutenant Colonel Joseph

US Army Major John D. Waghelstein, COIN operations instructor at *Escuela de Armas* (Weapons' School) for captains and lieutenants of the Bolivian Army. He also trained paratroopers. (US Army).

The 8th Special Forces Group Mobile Training Team (MTT designated BL 404-67X) officers and NCOs sent to Bolivia (left) and its Commander Major Ralph W. 'Pappy' Shelton. (US Army).

The two USAF Lockheed C-130 Hercules that brought the MTT to Bolivia together with all their equipment from Howard AFB in Panama to Santa Cruz Airport. (US Army).

Rice of the MILGP to obtain the equipment from war stocks in storage in the Canal Zone. Another hindrance was the quality of food provided by the Bolivian Army. The normal diet, which did not provide enough calories to sustain troops undergoing rigorous training, consisted of rice, pork, potatoes, all boiled, and bread.

It was immediately noticed that the conscripts barely spoke Spanish and had no military training and a very poor education, if any. In contrast, the officers were of European origin and were well trained and educated, a situation that had persisted since long before the Chaco War. The MTT had to make a great effort to unite officers, non-commissioned officers and troops in the same training to create an esprit de corps and to build a bond among them as the training progressed.

Besides COIN tactics and weapons handling, the Green Berets MTT also trained a group of intelligence officers. They learned techniques such as how to blend in among civilians to get vital information.

The President General René Barrientos Ortuño visited La Esperanza on 29 July to talk with the Rangers. His address was a great morale booster to the battalion. He came at an opportune time and carried them through some of the more arduous training in Phase IV. As part of the celebration of the Bolivian Army's anniversary on 7 August, the troops donned green berets, the distinctive unit headgear chosen for the Ranger Battalion, which was a sign that the training was nearing completion.

Another important visitor was that of General Robert W. Porter Jr, Commander of SOUTHCOM. He brough some gifts for Bolivian Rangers, gold wristwatches for officers and silver ones for the best soldiers of each company.

A formal graduation ceremony and parade was held at the headquarters of the VIII Army Division, which was the Rangers' parent headquarters, on 17 September in Santa Cruz. The Vice President of Bolivia, Adolfo Siles and the VIII Army Division Commander Colonel Joaquín Zenteno Anaya presided over the ceremony. Both them and Major Shelton addressed the troops in turn, and it was broadcast on Bolivian National Radio. Each member of the Special Forces team was given a special certificate. During the graduation, the Rangers were awarded a gold pin, the Condor Badge, with the word 'Ranger' on it, their distinctive qualification badge. MTT BL 404-67X returned to La Esperanza when the Rangers boarded trucks for the Red Zone.

After the graduation of the 2nd Ranger Battalion of the Bolivian Army effectives, some members of the MTT returned to the United States, being replaced by others.

Once the first training of Bolivian troops was finished, the MTT provided refresher tactical and COIN training to nine Bolivian infantry companies starting on 4 October 1967. Three rotations of three infantry companies each trained at La Esperanza. Each rotation was four weeks long. The first programme was for Company A of the IV Army Division, Company B of the V Army Division, and Company C of the III Army Division, for a total of 337 officers and troops. The second cycle was Company B of the IV Army Division, Company C of the V Army Division, and the Squadron Braun of the VIII Army Division; 338 men in all. The final rotation included Companies A and C of the VII Army Division and Company E of the III Army Division, totalling 316 soldiers.

The MTT left Bolivia on 19 December for Fort Gulick and the main body returned to the Canal Zone on 22 December. Altogether, the team trained 1,600 Bolivian Army Rangers and infantrymen.

7
THE ÑANCAHUAZÚ GUERRILLA IN 1967

The Ñancahuazú (a Guarani language word meaning *big ravine*) campaign against the guerrillas took place in an area of approximately 40,000 square kilometres (15,444 square miles) in southeast Bolivia. The area was located in the Departments of Chuquisaca and Santa Cruz. It was a rugged, little explored zone, located between the Incahuasi, Iñao and Ilochupa mountains. The terrain was uneven, covered with vegetation typical of the area: scrubland with some tall trees, sparse and widely dispersed population, scarce animal life, and poor livestock limited to the area of Lagunillas and Monteagudo. These were the most important towns in the area with no more than a thousand inhabitants. This area was divided into two sectors: North, which corresponded to the jurisdiction of the VIII Army Division, whose headquarters were in Santa Cruz de la Sierra; and South, under the jurisdiction of the IV Army Division, based in Camiri, with both sectors separated by the Rio Grande.

Guevara chose this location purportedly for the agrarian nature of its economy and the proximity to some oil fields. The area itself forms a rectangle with its north boundaries delimited by the Cochabamba-Santa Cruz road, to the west by the Mizque River, to the east by the Boyuibé-Abapó-Santa Cruz railways and to the south by the Parapetí River. The area in question has several small towns, the largest being Vallegrande, which at that time had a population of 7,800. Most towns are located in mesothermic valleys, and the area is generally mountainous and warm, vegetation is low and irrigated by mighty rivers which are difficult to cross in rainy seasons.

The means available to sustain the guerrilla included two major rivers and their small tributaries crisscrossing the area, the only sources of clean water. The peasants maintained small plots of corn, rice, sugar cane, yucca and some fruits, although some farmers had small quantities of cattle. Nine main roads connected the towns with each other and the larger cities of Cochabamba and Santa Cruz. The only permanent airfield in the area was located near Camiri in Choretí, although some stretches of land or dry riverbed were usable for emergency landings. A landing strip was built on the town of Vallegrande during the campaign, and used extensively.

Che Guevara and his guerrillas had already settled in the Ñancahuazú area since November 1966 and they dedicated themselves to reconnoitring the terrain for future actions and training. The presence of the guerrillas did not go unnoticed by the government, which began to prepare plans for their repression and sent military and police patrols to the area.

Before the discovery of the guerrillas in the Ñancahuazú zone, the IV Army Division in Camiri had the following units:

- Infantry Regiment No. 6 (RI.6) Campos in Carandayty;
- Infantry Regiment No. 11 (RI.11) Boquerón in Charagua;
- Artillery Group No. 4 (GA.4) in Choreti;
- Cavalry Group No. 1 (GC.1) in Yapiroa;
- Divisional Company in the Achaval Barracks in Camiri.
- Total troops: Ten senior officers, 21 junior officers, 54 non-commissioned officers and sergeants, and 244 soldiers.

Another large neighbouring unit of the previous one was the VIII Army Division in Santa Cruz, whose component units were:

- Infantry Regiment No.12 (RI.12) Manchego in Montero;
- Infantry Regiment No.10 (RI.10) Warnes in San Ignacio;
- Cavalry Group No. 8 (GC.8) Braun in Santa Cruz;
- Engineering Battalion No.3 (BATING 3) in Vallegrande.
- Total troops: Fourteen senior officers, 21 junior officers, 55 non-commissioned officers and sergeants and 308 soldiers.

When General Ovando returned from his tour of Europe and the United States, his first act was to organise an Anti-Guerrilla Operations Command in Camiri, in the Department of Santa Cruz, urging the government to declare that territory a military zone. At the beginning, IV and VIII Army Division troops were deployed to the area but they were not really prepared to face the guerrillas. The commander of the IV Army Division, Colonel Humberto Rocha Urquieta, organised four companies of infantrymen to support operations in the area.

However, both the President General Barrientos and the Army Commander General Ovando wanted to confine the guerrillas to one area, to make it easier for the army to track them down. The IV Army Division area was located south of the Grande River and the VIII Army Division north of the river, whose headquarters was in Santa Cruz de la Sierra.

In addition to military preparations, the Bolivian government also contacted intelligence services in the United States, Brazil and Argentina, specially to determine if Che was behind the guerrilla in Bolivia. General Ovando requested military cooperation from all the neighbouring countries so Argentina provided arms (FAL assault rifles), ammunition and napalm bombs, and Brazil sent combat rations for the troops, besides all the military aid from

As of 1967, armour of the Bolivian Army included 18 M3A1 Stuart light tanks, 24 M3 Half Track and some 60 M113 armoured personnel carriers. However, none of these were deployed in the fast-paced action against the Ñancahuazú guerrilla. In addition to venerable M38A1 Willys Jeeps, the primary utility vehicle was the Dodge M37 ¾-ton 4x4 truck. Based on the WC 51-series built during the Second World War, but significantly improved, more than 63,000 examples had been manufactured by 1958, when the further improved M37B1 entered series production. As can be seen from its insignia (including the military registration EB-21-3351), this vehicle was one of several dozen donated by the USA to Bolivia in the 1950s and 1960s, and assigned to the Ranger Battalion of the Infantry Regiment 12 Manchego. (Artwork by David Bocquelet)

Another crucial vehicle of the Bolivian Army in 1967 was the REO M35 2 ½-ton 6x6 cargo truck. Inheriting the nickname 'Deuce and a Half' from an older 2½-ton truck (the GMC CCKW from the Second World War), the M35A1 was in production from 1950: the improved M35A2, with a canvas 'soft top' and a winch, followed by 1958. Although considered an 'interim solution' until better variants became available, the M35 proved simple, dependable and highly popular in service: they were manufactured by additional companies in the USA, and by KIA Motors in South Korea, and remained in widespread service well into the 2000s. The exact number of M35A2s delivered to Bolivia by 1967 remains unknown, but they were the primary cargo vehicles during the campaign against the Ñancahuazú guerrilla. (Artwork by David Bocquelet)

To bolster the riverine capabilities of the Bolivian Naval Force (BNF), in 1962 the USA donated four Patrol Boat Riverine (PBR) Mk I patrol boats. These 12-ton vessels, powered by two Detroit Diesel 6V53N engines with 216 horse powers each, could carry four crewmembers at a maximum speed of up to 27 knots. Usual armament consisted of two Browning .50cal/12.7mm M2 heavy machine guns, a 60mm mortar and a 40mm grenade launcher. This example was christened Commandante Arandia. Like all ground vehicles of US origin too, it was left in the I Forrest Green overall livery, as delivered. (Artwork by David Bocquelet)

The standard uniform of the Bolivian Army in 1967 was of a traditional design. Made from cotton in olive drab colour, it consisted of a shirt and long jacket with four pockets, reinforced trousers with two large side pockets, and leather boots. While US-made M1 steel helmets were available, they were rarely worn: this soldier is shown wearing a black baret instead. His other gear is limited to a leather belt with a large metal buckle, and two pouches for magazines for his firearm: the M1 semi-automatic .30cal (7.62mm) carbine. (Artwork by Renato Dalmaso)

Although present in Bolivia since November 1966, Che officially established the 'National Liberation Army' (abbreviated to ELN in Spanish) only on 25 March 1967. As so often in the case of movements of this kind, ELN combatants wore no standardised uniform: Che and the operatives that arrived with him from abroad wore a miscellany of fatigues of Western and Eastern origin, frequently including shirts in either olive drab or khaki, and different models of trousers, including some with cargo pockets, as shown here. Their armament varied as well, and included captured M1 Garand rifles, M1 carabines (shown here), M3 submachine guns, Mauser rifles, BARs, and Walther PPK pistols. (Artwork by Renato Dalmaso)

Tailored to military specification, the CWU-27 Nomex IIIA orange flight suit was highly popular in the 1950s – and worn with pride by Bolivian fighter pilots well into the 1970s. Made of flame-resistant fabric, it had double safety stitched seams with flame-resistant sewing threads, pleated action back, an adjustable waist belt with Velcro fastener, wrist closures with Velcro tapes, and six pockets on chest, legs, and sleeves (as well as a knife pocket on the left thigh). This was usually worn in combination with contemporary flight helmets, like the General Textile Mills Type P-1A or Type P-3, the Type A-13A oxygen mask (on P-51 Mustangs), protective glasses, leather gloves, and black leather boots. (Artwork by Renato Dalmaso)

By the mid-1960s, biplanes such as the Boeing-Stearman PT-17 Kaydet, as well as the ancient (and Brazilian-built) Fairchild PT-19A/Galeão PT-3FG (top), and Vultee BT-13A Valiant (bottom) still formed the backbone of the FAB's training fleet. Most important were 11 PT-19As (which originally carried their Brazilian serials 0340, 0376, 0385, 0389, 0402, 0452, 0469, 0484, 0489 and 0529) and 37 BT-13As delivered within the Lend-Lease Program in two batches, in 1942 and 1945. Kaydets wore a red overall livery, and PT-19As had their wings painted in orange, but otherwise all were left in bare metal overall. (Artworks by Luca Canossa)

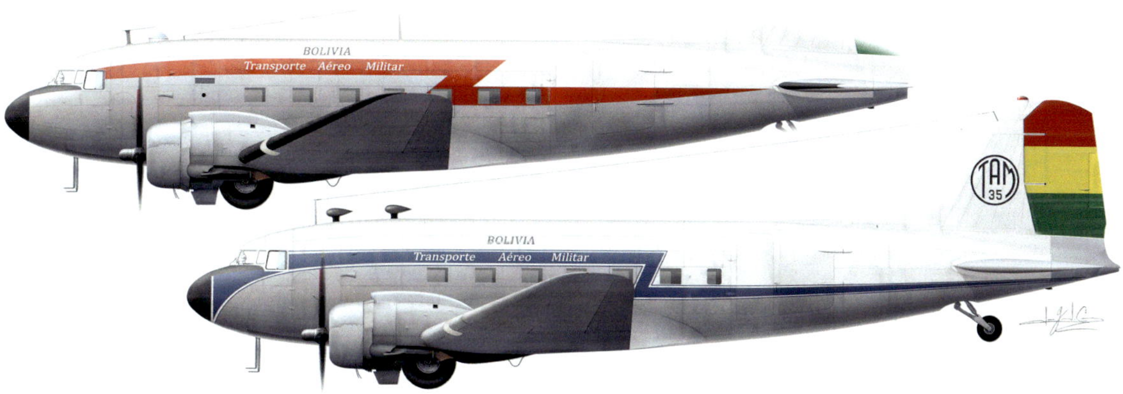

Between 1945 and 1997, Bolivia acquired and operated nearly 50 Douglas C-47 and DC-3 transports. Starting in 1955, they were all operated by the Transportes Aéros Militares (re-organised as the Transporte Aéreo Militar in the 1970s). The example shown, TAM 16, was one of the C-47s donated by the USA through the MAP in the 1960s; TAM 01 was equipped with a 'VIP'-interior and used as the presidential aircraft. As of 1967, the majority of the C-47s and DC-3s appeared as shown in the artwork, with the top of their fuselage in white, bottom and wings in bare metal or light grey, and the blue cheat line. Heavily tasked during the campaign against the Ñancahuazú guerrilla, they hauled troops, ammunition, and supplies to forward airstrips and also parachuted supplies to units underway in isolated areas. (Artworks by Luca Canossa)

Between 1963 and 1992, Bolivia operated a total of seven Cessna U-17A (military version of the Cessna 180, provided through the MAP), followed by 15 Cessna 185E and 185F, making a total of 22 aircraft. Despite their 'civilian-like' livery of white overall, with thick blue cheat lines down the full length of the fuselage, during the campaign against the Ñancahuazú guerrilla, they primarily served in liaison roles, but also flew aerial reconnaissance missions. At least two – including the aircraft with serial number FAB 205, illustrated here – were operated as forward air controllers guiding air strikes by P-51s and T-6s. An additional Cessna 180 (serial FAB 001) was acquired in 1960 and served for VIP-transport purposes until 1973. (Artwork by Tom Cooper)

In 1954-1955, Bolivia acquired its first batch of 12 North American F-51D piston-engined fighters and three TF-51D conversion trainers (with full combat capability). They were left in bare metal overall, with a large black anti-glare panel on the forward fuselage, as shown on the example illustrated here. By 1967, nearly all carried large 'shark-mouth' insignia on the lower part of the forward fuselage, and had their spinners painted in red. All were assigned to the *Grupo Aéreo de Combate* (Air Combat Group, redesignated to *Grupo Aéreo de Caza* in 1968), based at El Alto AB, outside La Paz. Standard armament consisted of six .30cal/7.62mm Browning machine guns installed in the wing. Up to 907kg (2,000lbs) of bombs or unguided rockets could be carried on underwing hardpoints. (Artwork by Tom Cooper)

At least six of the original 15 F-51D/TF-51D are known to have been written off in various accidents between 1955 and 1966 (including serials FAB 19, FAB 20, FAB 21, FAB 501, FAB 502, and FAB 505). Correspondingly, in 1960, La Paz acquired another batch of second-hand aircraft from the Uruguay Air Force (FAU), and in 1966, the third batch was purchased from the Nicaraguan Air Force. Most of the Mustangs in question were overhauled in the USA before being delivered to Bolivia. Two such examples were FAB 510 and FAB 511: the latter is shown here, and is confirmed to have had its serial number repeated on the bottom of the left wing. Whether this remained in place following delivery, or was accompanied by a roundel, or entirely removed, remains unclear. (Artwork by Tom Cooper)

In 1957, Trans Florida launched a project envisaging a complete overhaul and upgrade of surplus military P-51s into high-speed, private aircraft. Ten years later, after – amongst others – overhauling and delivering 30 F-51Ds to the Dominican Air Force, Trans Florida was renamed the Cavalier Aircraft Corporation and contracted by the Department of Defense to create military specification F-51Ds for export. In the same year, seven of the resulting Cavalier F-51D and two TF-51D Mustangs (one of which is shown here) were given to Bolivia within the framework of Project Peace Condor. Their known serials were from FAB 515 to FAB 523. The first few Cavalier Mustangs were delivered wearing light grey overall, with spinners in red and the traditional, and large 'shark-mouth' insignia on the lower part of the forward fuselage. (Artwork by Tom Cooper)

Bolivia received its first three Hiller UH-12B/OH-23 Ravens in 1966. Twelve additional UH-12B/OH-23s followed starting in April 1967 and they saw heavy utilisation during the campaign against the Ñancahuazú guerrilla. FAB 604 is known to have crashed in a remote area on 30 July, stranding its crew for more than three weeks: the two airmen, and the helicopter, were eventually found, evacuated and the Raven was subsequently repaired and returned to service. FAB 601 is known to have been regularly used by President Barrientos: two years later, on 27 April 1969, an unidentified example struck telephone cables in the canyon of Rio Arque, killing the president, the pilot Teniente Carlos Estivariz, and Capitan Leovegildo Orellana. (Artwork by Tom Cooper)

Between 1943 and 1965, Bolivia received a mix of 96 North American AT-6, T-6G Texans, SNJ3s and SNJ6Bs. Most were kept in bare metal overall, but all retained their anti-glare panel in black or olive drab along the upper forward fuselage, and many received a blue strip around the engine cowling, and blue wing-tips. On mobilisation in March 1967, five aircraft – FAB 316, FAB 321, FAB 324, FAB 340, and FAB 351 – were redeployed to an airstrip outside Choreti (near Camiri). While FAB 324 was left in bare metal overall, the other four were camouflaged with whatever colours were available, in a great rush, without an application of varnish. This is a reconstruction of FAB 316, based on several photographs of different aircraft: this Texan is known to have retained its blue band around the engine cowling, and seems to have received a pattern in tan and two shades of green. The insets show 50lb/25kg bombs known to have been deployed for attacks on he guerillas led by Che Guevara. (Artwork by Tom Cooper)

Another of the first five AT/T-6Gs deployed to combat the guerrillas was FAB 321. This example seems to have received a camouflage pattern applied in a similar fashion to that used on several OH-23s, consisting of three or four shades of green and earth brown. It is unclear if the undersides were overpainted, but none of the five Texans in question carried any markings there. The serial was 'applied' by leaving parts of the central fuselage unpainted. The FAB 321 lacked the three machine guns installed on the FAB 316 (one in front of the cockpit and one in each wing), and instead was armed with unguided rockets (some used for marking targets for other aircraft, and others for ground attacks). Of other Bolivian AT/T-6s of the time, FAB 333 is known to have been written off on 29 March 1967, while FAB 302 crashed at El Alto on 18 July 1967. (Artwork by Tom Cooper)

US experience from the Vietnam War, dominated by 'COIN doctrine', exercised their influence upon the development of camouflage and markings on FAB Mustangs once they were sent into combat against the Ñancahuazú guerrilla in 1967. The aircraft received disruptive camouflage patterns applied in three colours from the famous 'South East Asia' (SEA) scheme, also applied on US Air Force aircraft around the same time, including tan (FS30219), and two shades of green (FS34079 and 34102) on top surfaces and sides. It remains unclear if undersides were painted in light grey (FS36622) or left in bare metal. Nevertheless, the Bolivians applied their shark-mouth insignia, too. This is a reconstruction of the F-51D with serial number FAB 506. (Artwork by Tom Cooper)

In the case of at least two Cavalier Mustangs delivered to the FAB in 1967, the use of camouflage colours appears to have gone so far that the F-51Ds serial numbers FAB 517 and FAB 518 were not only repainted in SEA colours, but appear to have received a 'toned down' version of their shark-mouth insignia. While their primary weaponry consisted of six Browning .30cal/7.62mm machine guns, general purpose bombs such as the AN/M57 (250lb/125kg) and AN/M64 (500lb/250kg), and unguided rockets, during the campaign of 1967 they reportedly deployed quantities of 'napalm bombs'. The exact types of the latter remain obscure: they were either reconditioned drop tanks, as shown on FAB 506 at the top of this page, or some may have been containers developed during the Korean War, shown here. (Artwork by Tom Cooper)

During the campaign against the Ñancahuazú guerrilla, the USA donated a number of additional aircraft and helicopters to Bolivia. Amongst these were 12 North American T-28D Trojans, which arrived on 14 July 1967, but saw no action, and two Sikorsky H-19 Chickasaw transport helicopters. Initially left in silver grey overall, they received only the Bolivian national markings and – reportedly – serials FAB 604 and FAB 605. Deployed for MEDEVAC purposes, one was quickly lost in a non-fatal accident: the other is known to have received a camouflage pattern (probably consisting of tan and two shades of green), but details of this as applied on the left side remain unknown. (Artwork by Tom Cooper)

Territorial losses claimed by Bolivia since its independence in 1825. (Map by author)

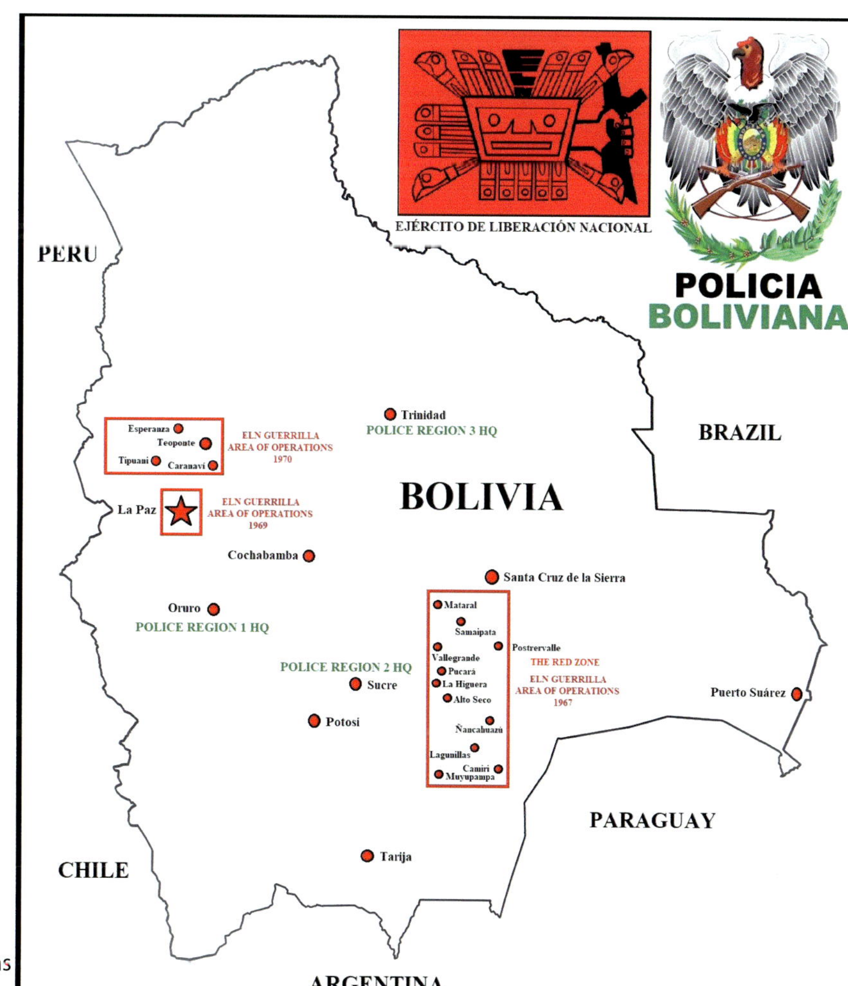

Police Regions and Guerrilla Operations Areas in 1967, 1969 and 1970. (Map by author)

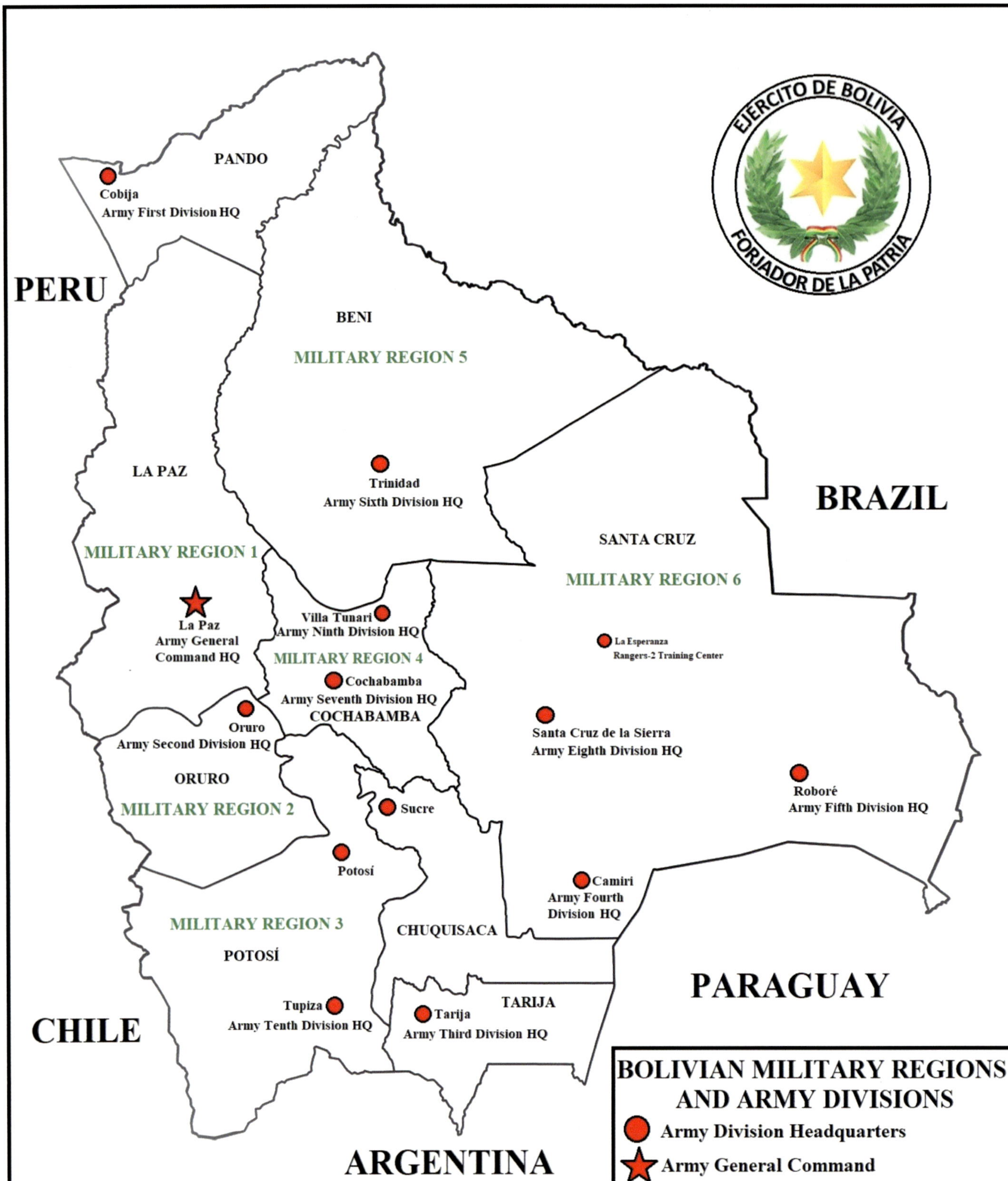

Bolivia's Military Regions and Army Divisions

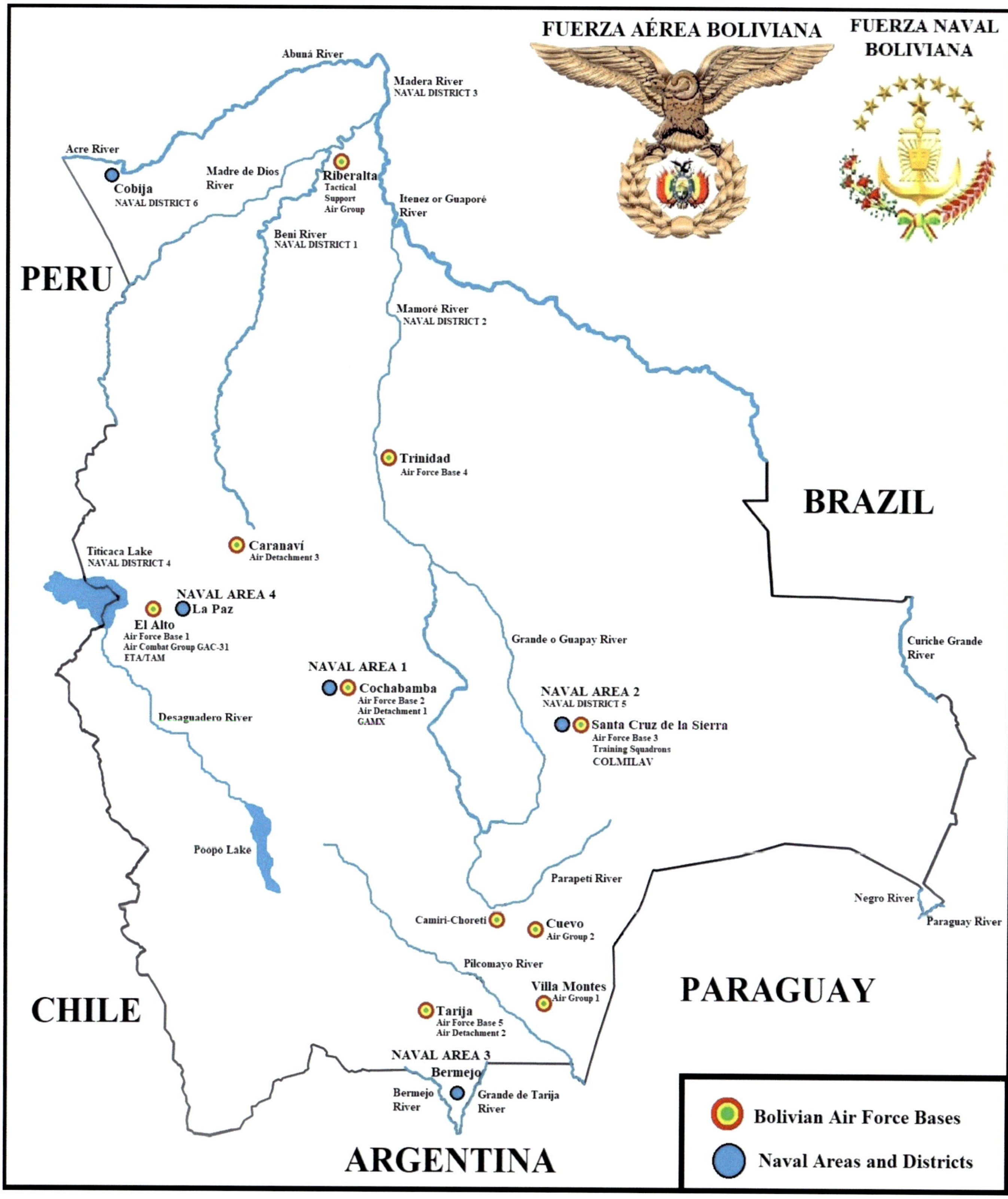

Bolivia's Air Force and Naval Force bases

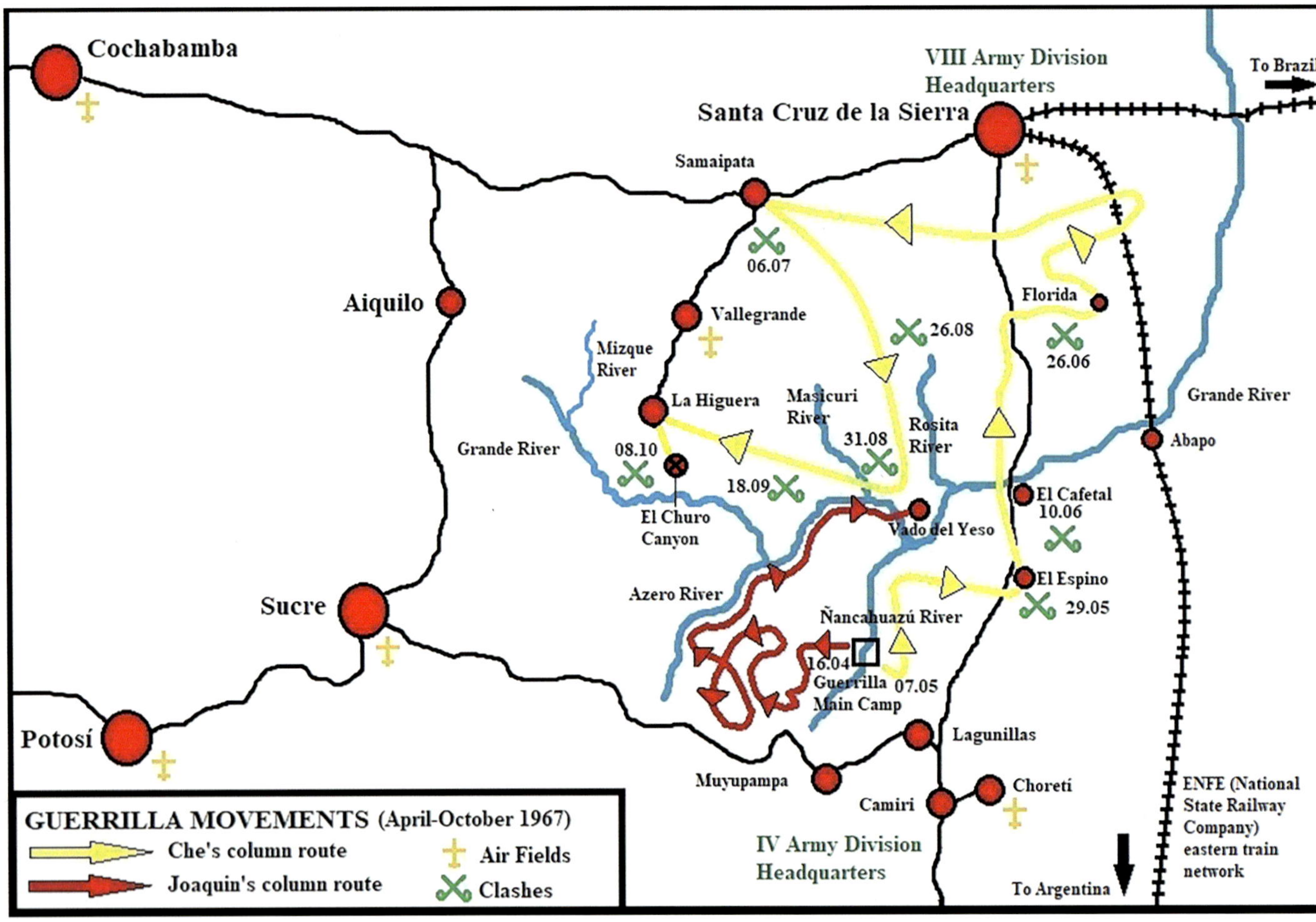

(Map by author)

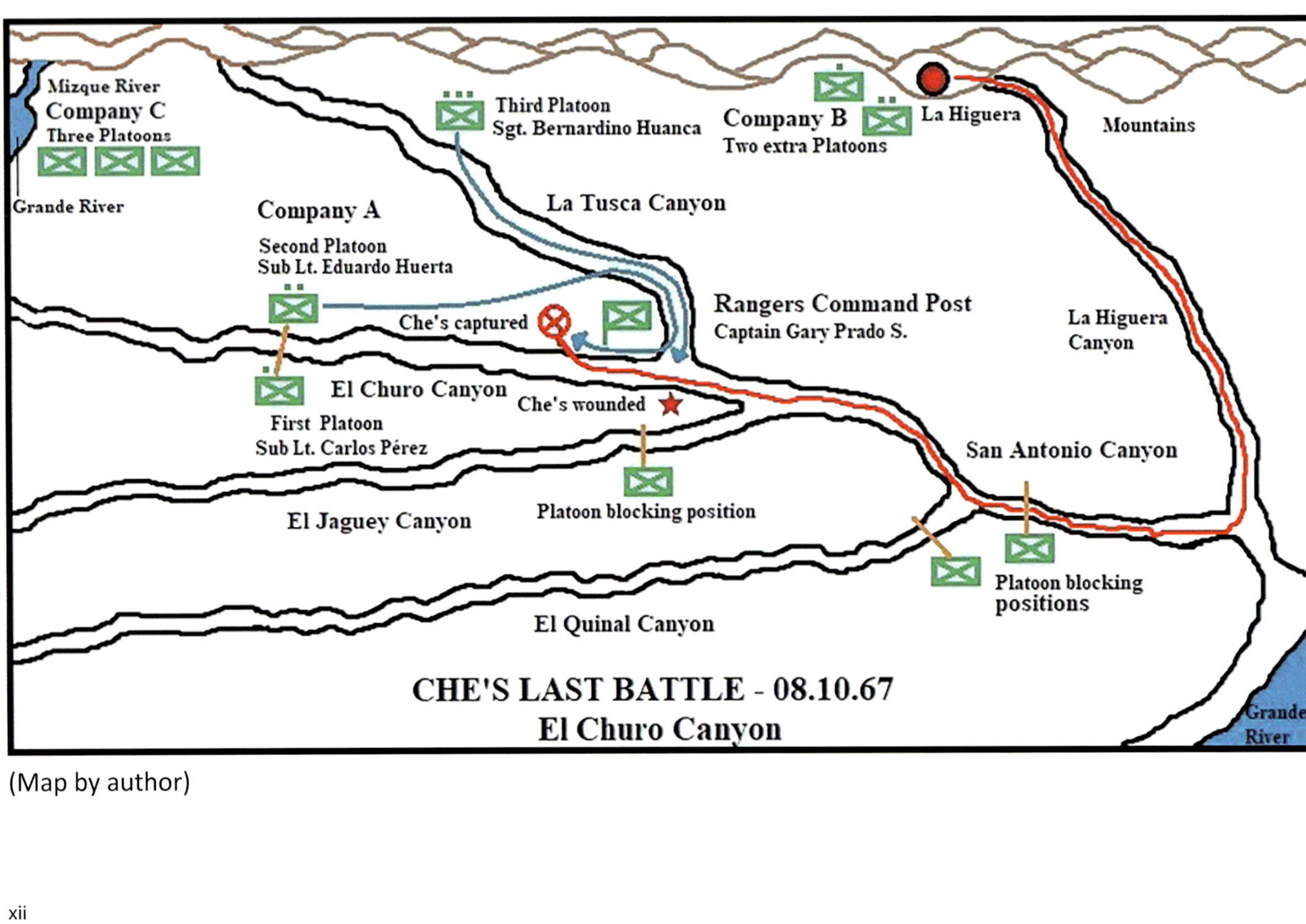

(Map by author)

the United States. Intelligence agencies agreed to increase surveillance on the common borders to detect and track the guerrilla movements.

President Barrientos established military law in the whole country. He outlawed the PCB and the Revolutionary Workers' Party, arresting 41 of their leaders, in order to prevent them from helping the guerrillas both in combat and logistics. He also cracked down on labour unions.

It is noteworthy that the ELN issued various communiqués, at least six, to the public, some of which were published during the conflict and others after the capture of the guerrilla documentation. It was also revealed that there was fluid communication with Fidel Castro in Havana via radio communication, using, of course, coded messages, at least at the beginning of the campaign. The daily details of the guerrilla operations became known when the various war diaries of Che, Pombo, Rolando, Braulio, Pacho and Morogoro were published in subsequent years and in several languages.

Some members of the US Army MTT Team. In the top row, from left to right: Staff Sergeants Jerald Peterson, Wendell Thompson Jr, James Hapka and Captain Margarito Cruz. In the bottom row, from left to right: Staff Sergeant William W. Burkett with a bazooka, Sergeant First Class Daniel V. Chapa, and Sergeant Alvin Graham III. (US Army).

The abandoned facilities of a sugar mill in the town of La Esperanza, Department of Santa Cruz, was used as a training base for the Bolivian Army Rangers. (US Army)

March

Despite previous brief encounters with the police, coincidence brought the first news about the presence of the armed band to the military command of the IV Army Division. On 7 March 1967, YPFB technicians denounced the presence of certain bearded characters in military fatigues before the President of the Fiscal Entity, Major Engineer José Patiño Ayoroa, who informed the Commander of the IV Army Division Colonel Humberto Rocha Urquieta. The news reached La Paz immediately.

On 9 March, the Bolivian Army High Command presented the so-called *Plan de Operaciones Sararendá*, with the premises that the guerrilla group would soon initiate the following actions:

- Trigger violent actions in different areas of the country.
- Carry out acts of terrorism and destruction of pipelines, pumping stations and YPFB camps.
- Incite peasants to join the revolutionary cause.
- Create a climate of unrest in the country.

For this purpose, military commissions were formed that, in coordination with YPFB personnel, provided security and surveillance in Monteagudo, Tatarendá, Lagunillas, Chorétí and Camiri, carrying out reconnaissance with the objective of capturing guerrillas and suspicious persons.

On that very same day, Army Captain Augusto Silva Bogado, who was coming back from a civic action mission, hitched a ride with a YPFB vehicle on the road to Camiri. During the trip, the driver informed Captain Silva that some days earlier they had encountered six suspicious 'bearded and foreign-looking' men at the Tatarendá pumping station. The men described were armed, wore olive drab fatigues, had purchased food and had plenty of money. As soon

Major Pappy Shelton (centre) in a meeting with some officers and NCOs prior to a training session in La Esperanza (left). The emblems of the Green Berets of the US Army. (US Army).

as he arrived in Camiri, Captain Silva informed his commanding officer of the news. On the following day both met with the local YPFB superintendent, Engineer Humberto Suárez Roca, in order to coordinate a search. The first aerial sortie of the campaign, a reconnaissance flight, was flown on the YPFB Cessna 185A utility plane, registration CP-711, with Colonel Juan Fernández, IV Army Division Chief of Staff and Captain Silva. On the morning of the 11th, as the plane returned from Santa Cruz to Camiri, both army officers were able to see a group of four men on the shores of the Rio Grande who, upon sighting the plane, ran for cover in the bush. This became sufficient reason to organise a search on foot. The Silva patrol, composed of six soldiers and the officer plus an YPFB guide named Epifanio Vargas, reached Tatarenda by road on the 12th and continued in a westbound direction towards the Ñancahuazú River;

Much of the training of the Bolivian Rangers was in the use of light and heavy weapons, assault rifles, mortars, heavy machine guns and rocket launchers. (US Army).

poorly supplied and armed only with five submachine guns and a pistol, the patrol reached *Casa de Calamina* on 17 March.

The guerrilla had 50 troops at the time and Che decided to split them into three groups:

The first group had not returned from its reconnaissance trip to the northeast.

The second group, encamped some two kilometres north from *Casa de Calamina*, did not notice the military presence.

The third and smallest group, based at the property, withdrew from the area as soon as the patrol arrived, although they managed to wound one of the soldiers.

Captain Silva occupied the house and set up to guard the place. Unbeknownst to him, two guerrilla deserters, Vicente Rocabado Terrazas *aka* Orlando and Pastor Barreno Quintana *aka* Daniel, had been captured and interrogated, probably under torture, on the 14th, providing valuable information about their guerrilla comrades, and after hearing their confession, the military command of the IV Army Division began to organise its response in coordination with the air force.

When the Ñancahuazú Campaign began, the following units and troops were mobilised. On 17 March, a third guerrilla, Salustino Choque *aka* Salustio, was captured. On that day, to complement the data provided by Captain Silva's patrol, it was decided to send Colonel Alberto Libera Cortéz and six troops to explore the Lagunillas-Itimiri-Ñancahuazú-Pincal area. During the mission, Colonel Libera and Captain Silva met at the *Casa de Calamina*. On that same date, the guerrilla Jorge Vázquez Viaña *aka* Loro wounded the soldier Sebastián Rojas.

Now the presence of guerrillas was confirmed on Bolivian soil, the government of General Barrientos obtained the support of his Argentine counterpart Lieutenant General Juan Carlos Onganía and Paraguayan Army General Alfredo Stroessner. Both countries promised strict control of their borders with Bolivia, to prevent guerrillas from fleeing abroad. On the other hand, both Brazil and

The shooting practices were carried out with all the weapons available to the Bolivian Army. In the top photo, Sergeant Thompson assists a Bolivian Ranger with a Mauser rifle. In the photo below, American sergeants instruct their Bolivian counterparts in the use of light machine guns. (US Army).

Training was carried out regularly and the Bolivian Rangers wore their camouflaged combat uniforms for the first time. (US Army)

Captain James Trimble, MTT Team S-1/S-4 officer in Bolivia (left). Bolivian Rangers training in rappelling (right). (US Army).

Major 'Pappy' Shelton and Captain Margarito Cruz speaking with a Bolivian Army officer in La Esperanza (left). The officers and NCOs of the MTT integrated very well with the local population, sharing food, music, dances, and parties in La Esperanza. (US Army).

Some Bolivian paratroopers also received training from US Army instructors. (US Army).

Chile showed indifference to the matter. The Bolivian Military High Command issued Order No. 1/67 on 21 March to locate and destroy them, especially in the area between the Ñancahuazú River, Pampa de Tigre and the Incahuasi mountains. In general terms, the order determined to 'annihilate the enemy' which had to be done with two groups of forces, one under the command of Colonel Libera, with four officers, three NCOs and 59 troops who had to move along the Lagunillas-ltimiri-lti-Monte Dorado-Yuqui-Quebrada Overa axis, the margin of the Ñancahuazú River and comply with the Central Camp in coordination with the second group. The second group was commanded by Major Hernán Plata, with three officers, three NCOs and 55 troops and had to move from the Pical-Río Nancahuazu-Quebrada de Iripiti axis, continuing along it until reaching the height of the Central Camp; then, occupy the area, and capture or annihilate the guerrillas who escaped from the attack of Colonel Libera. To mobilise such a force, troops from the Campos Infantry Regiment RI.6 and the Military Police had to be used, many of whom had not yet received adequate military training for combat. The other regiments' effectives were not in the area.

The group led by Major Hermán Plata reached *Casa de Calamina* on the 22nd, joined the Silva patrol and continued the operation. On 23 March, the group was divided into three segments. The vanguard, commanded by artillery Lieutenant Rubén Amézaga Faure and led by the civilian Epifanio Vargas as a guide, fell when struck down by

Two MTT sergeants supervising a Bolivian Ranger cleaning a mortar (left). An American sergeant training a pair of Bolivian Rangers with a heavy machine gun (right). (US Army)

A Bolivian Ranger poses proudly in his combat gear (left). President Barrientos visited La Esperanza on 29 July 1967, meeting with Captain Gary Prado Salmón (right). (Ejército Boliviano).

the fire of the Cuban guerrilla ambush as they were about to cross the Ñancahuazú River. Lieutenant Amezaga, despite being wounded, attacked the machine gun nest that was located on the right bank of the river, until he fired the last cartridge of his machine gun and then fell dead. The ambush yielded a terrible result, as one officer, six troops and the civilian guide were killed, five were wounded and 18 captured, including Major Plata and Captain Silva. Furthermore, the guerrillas obtained a copy of the army's plan to combat them. The rest of the troops withdrew to Pincal and waited for orders. The guerrilla booty consisted of 16 Mauser rifles with 2,000 bullets, three 60mm mortars and 64 rounds, three Uzi submachine guns with 24 magazines, two bazookas and a .30 calibre machinegun with two belts of ammunition. The prisoners were interrogated and endured a political speech and the wounded soldiers were treated. Stripped of their clothes, they were freed a day later. The guerrillas' baptism by fire was a success.

The FAB immediately dispatched a Hiller OH-23 helicopter for a reconnaissance flight over the area where the fighting had taken place. That same day it was decided to deploy five North American T-6 Texan attack aircraft, serials FAB-316, FAB-321, FAB-324, FAB-340 and FAB-351, and the Hiller OH-23 helicopter serial FAB-601, establishing their bases in the town of Chorettí near Camiri. In addition, TAM Douglas C-47s brought supplies, food and ammunition to the Lagunillas airstrip for the army troops. In addition to all that, five North American P-51D Mustang fighters were also deployed to Santa Cruz El Trompillo Airport. On 24 March, given the urgency in the deployment of troops and due to the existing bad roads, two TAM Douglas C-47s were used to airlift troops and supplies, including a paratrooper company with 81 men from the *Centro de Instrucción de Tropas Especiales* (Special Troops Training Centre/CITE) from Cochabamba to Camiri, and on the following day, a couple of TAM Douglas C-54s transported a mixed company of soldiers from the Braun and Manchego Regiments from

Another important visit to La Esperanza was that of General Robert Porter, Commander of the United States Southern Force, who brought gifts for officers, non-commissioned officers and the best soldiers of each company of the Bolivian Army Rangers. (Open source).

Sergeant First Class Harold T. Carpenter of the MTT receiving a Diploma of Recognition from Vice President Adolfo Siles at the graduation ceremony of the Bolivian Rangers in Santa Cruz on 17 September 1967. (US Army).

Ranger troops of the Bolivian Army parading during the graduation ceremony at the VIII Army Division Base in Santa Cruz on 17 September 1967. (Ejército Boliviano).

Major Pappy Shelton pinning the Rangers' metal insignia on graduates of the training course (above). The metallic Condor Badge of the Rangers of the Bolivian Army (below). (US Army).

Santa Cruz to the area of operations. These aircraft also carried out medevac missions for wounded and sick military personnel.

Also on the 24th, two AT-6s flying from Camiri bombed the suspected guerrilla positions up river in the first attack mission of the campaign.

Although the ELN guerrillas had been on Bolivian soil since November 1966, it was not until 25 March 1967 that Che Guevara officially founded the *Ejército de Liberación Nacional* (National Liberation Army) according to his own notes in his war diary.

Major Shelton flanked by Major Miguel Ayoroa and Lieutenant Romero together with Ranger troops (left). Bolivian Army Rangers parading in the town of Vallegrande upon being deployed to the Red Zone at the end of September 1967 (right). (Luis Ernesto Padilla).

On 26 March, two Mustang fighters loaded with napalm bombs attacked the area of the guerrilla main camp in Ñancahuazú. They dropped not only the bombs but also machine-gunned the entire area. Although they did not cause any casualties among the guerrillas, the attack served to demonstrate that the legal security forces were using their full potential against the subversives. That very same day, President General Barrientos arrived in the Red Zone on board an Air Force Hiller OH-23 helicopter that landed very close to the *Casa de Calamina*. Air Force Major Niño de Guzmán was the personal pilot of General Barrientos and he was the first certified helicopter pilot in Bolivia. After a brief stay just a few miles from Guevara himself, Barrientos returned to Camiri and gave a press conference. During that event, two senior army officers, Generals Jorge Belmonte Ardiles and Juan José Torrez González, showed some of the guerrilla belongings that had been found by the army in the area of operations. The news of the presence of a guerrilla group in southeast Bolivia was made public not only in the country but internationally.

Aerial reconnaissance missions continued on the following days, with one aerial supply sortie recorded on the 27th carried out by a TAM C-47 dropping supplies using parachutes at the troops stationed at the Argañaraz farm, as landing in the area was impossible. Also, five armed T-6s were involved in another bombing mission on the 29th. On the other side, army troops occupied all the towns in the area to try to cut off the logistics and supply chain for the guerrillas, as well as to control all the routes to block the possible escape of the subversives. The orders of the High Command of the Military Forces were to annihilate the guerrillas.

At the end of March, President General Barrientos returned to visit the area of operations on the C-47 serial TAM-01, landing in Camiri where he harangued the troops on the importance of annihilating the subversive group. General Barrientos himself piloted the NA T-6 serial FAB-351 together with another pilot officer flying over the Ñancahuazú area. Also at the same time, four guerrillas, Pepe, Paco, Chingolo and Eusebio, were removed from the category of combatants by Che for their poor performance and motivation, but they were forced to remain in the group for menial jobs. They received the nickname of *resacas* (hangovers or drags).

On 30 March, some AT-6 and P-51 Mustang aircraft machine-gunned the area around *Casa de Calamina*.

A very important factor that decided the final victory of the security forces was that the population in general strongly supported the fight against the guerrillas, helping with valuable information, denouncing the presence of subversives to both the police and the military and even providing food to the troops. In fact, several civilians who acted as guides for the Bolivian Army were killed by the guerrillas. The ELN failed to win the support of the Bolivian 'proletariat' and despite initial successes in combat, it ultimately failed miserably.

April

On 1 April, the Army High Command issued the General Order of Operations No. 2/67 which reorganised the guerrilla repression forces into four companies:

- Company A: This company was led by Major Rubén Sánchez Valdivia and was to occupied the town of Yuqui.
- Company B: Led by Captain Alfredo Calvi, to be deployed to Pincal.
- Company C: Under the command of Captain Raúl López, sent to Pirirendá Lagoon.
- Company D: This was a reserve company led by Captain Celso Torrelio, which was to be kept in Lagunillas.

Each company began its patrol operations on 3 April, but they did not encounter the guerrillas until days later. As a consequence, General Order of Operations No. 3/67 was issued with new instructions for the companies: Company A should remain in the Ñancahuazú River area; Company B should explore all the ravines that lead to the guerrilla camp; Company C was to be deployed for reconnaissance of the Gutierrez-Pirirendá-Tiraboy area and Company D was to

A typical road and village in the Red Zone of operations in southeastern Bolivia. (Open source).

A *Lloyd Aéreo Boliviano* Douglas DC-3 on the Choretí airstrip, near Camiri in 1967. (LAB).

The main camp of the guerrillas in Ñancahuazú. From left to right: Urbano, Miguel, Che, Marcos, Chino, Pachungo, Pombo, Inti and Loro. (Centro de Estudios Che Guevara).

From left to right: Vice President Siles, President Barrientos, Commander of the Armed Forces General Ovando and General Torres in 1967. They were four Bolivian political actors: Siles was overthrown months after the tragic accident of Barrientos; Barrientos had overthrown Paz Estenssoro; Ovando was overthrown by Torres and he in turn was overthrown by Bánzer. (Ejército Boliviano).

occupied Gutiérrez and patrol the areas of Ipitá and La Herradura. All four companies got to their new destinations on 9 April.
With information gathered from the guerrilla deserters, the army located and occupied the Central Camp in Ñancahuazú on 4 April.

On 10 April, Company A under the command of Major Sánchez was divided into three platoons led by Lieutenants Hugo Gutierrez Heredia, Luis Saavedra Arambel and Remberto La Fuente. Their commander assigned different patrol areas to the three platoons: Lieutenant Gutierrez was sent to the Yuqui River, Lieutenant Saavedra to Iripiti and Lieutenant La Fuente to Piraboy.

When the patrol of Lieutenant Luis Saavedra reached the Iripiti ravine, they were attacked by the guerrillas with heavy machine gun fire. As a result, Lieutenant Saavedra and eight soldiers were killed and the rest of the patrol surrendered. Three soldiers could escape and went to the *Casa de Calamina*, the command post of Major Sánchez. After being informed of the situation, a rescue mission led by Major Sánchez himself was prepared. Once in the area, the rescue patrol was ambushed by the guerrillas who killed several soldiers and Sub Lieutenant Jorge Ayala, and finally captured Major Sánchez and the rest of the team. A small fraction of this force led by Sub Lieutenant Carlos Martins was able to escape. In the clash, the Cuban guerrilla Jesús Suárez Gayol *aka* Rubio was killed and several guerrillas were wounded. A total of 11 army effectives had been killed, 14 were wounded and 23 were made prisoner. The military prisoners were released the following day. The booty this time consisted of 21 M-1 Garand rifles, 12 M-1 carbines, nine Mauser rifles, four M-3 submachine guns, another mortar, and a Browning Automatic Rifle (BAR). They then had more weapons than they needed. Another resounding victory for the guerrillas.

All these casualties caused great discouragement among the army troops and as a consequence of these clashes, it was clear for the army that their troops were not trained for this kind of combat. Even close air support was not enough to beat the guerrillas since it was almost impossible to locate them due to the thick forest. That same day, the government issued Supreme Decree No. 07961 which outlawed the activities of the Communist Party and the Partido Obrero Revolucionario (Revolutionary Workers Party). The provinces of Luis Calvo and Hernando Siles of the Department of Chuquisaca, and the provinces of Cordillera and Vallegrande of the Department of Santa Cruz, were declared military zones.

The military command began to reformulate its strategy, and slowly reinforce its troops: 375 more soldiers arrived from other parts of the country including the Bolivar Artillery Regiment RA.2 from Viacha, effectives from the NCO school in Cochabamba and also from the *Centro de Operaciones de Selva* (Jungle Operations Centre/CIOS) from Riberalta, plus the Sucre Infantry Regiment RI.2, a welcome addition to the 200-troop force already deployed in the area. In addition, the Bolivian government received the help of its American counterpart to strengthen the anti-subversive fight. That help consisted of sending a specialised commando unit from the US Army Green Berets as instructors for the Bolivian Army. In addition, weapons and military advice were received and the Bolivian Air Force got two Sikorsky H-19 Chickasaw and three Hiller OH-23 Raven helicopters, which arrived in the country between 19 and 28 April of that year.

On 17 April, Guevara divided his forces, appointed Juan Vitalio Acuña Nuñez *aka* Joaquín as commander of the second column with 13 effectives, some of them sick and wounded, including Tania, the only woman among them and at least four guerrillas considered not fit for combat. According to Che himself, these members were delaying the march and endangering the operations, so he decided to send them to the rear as a kind of 'reserve'. The other column led by Che had 33 troops. Both columns separated, took different roads and would never meet again.

On 20 April, the guerrillas arrived at a place called Ayanago, eight kilometres from the town of Muyupampa. They requested food and medicine for the wounded, and the population led by the sub-prefect, a priest and a doctor, agreed to their request. Once the guerrillas withdrew from the place, they informed the army. Three Air Force T-6 Texans bombed the area shortly after, wounding one of the guerrillas of Cuban origin. Army effectives immediately got to Muyupampa and arrested Jules Régis Debray and Ciro Roberto Bustos who had left the guerrilla column and tried to leave the area. They also captured a British-Chilean freelance journalist, George Andrew Roth, who had wandered into the guerrilla bivouac on 19 April. This was a severe blow for the guerrillas since they provided information about the subversives. It was then that Regis Debray definitively confirmed the presence of Che Guevara. Debray and Bustos were taken separately to Camiri in a private Hughes 269B helicopter, registration CP-780, which belonged to the Oil Industry Supply Company. This company worked under contract with YPFB. Roth was never charged with a crime and was released in July.

As the army reorganised and regrouped, the air force continued its reconnaissance missions using the half-dozen utility and light attack planes deployed to the area, mainly armed T-6 Texans and

Effectives of the IV and VIII Divisions of the Bolivian Army being deployed throughout the Red Zone in rivers, jungle and mountains. (Ejército Boliviano).

The first aerial reconnaissance of the Red Zone was carried out with Cessna 185A registration CP-711 of the state oil company YPFB on 9 March 1967. The aircraft was flown by a civilian pilot of the company with Colonel Juan Fernández, IV Army Division Chief of Staff and Captain Augusto Silva managing to spot several guerrillas in the Ñancahuazú area. (YPFB).

Cessna U-17s. The Texans also performed some strafing sorties. Guevara registered in his diary that on 20 April a flight of three AT-6s attacked his position and wounded one of his men, Ricardo. Che also wrote that on the following days his movements were hindered by the constant air patrols, which continued with more strafing close to the guerrilla positions on the 24th.

The guerrillas also used the time for reorganisation, hiding some captured equipment and gathering supplies. On some occasions, the guerrillas paid the peasants for food, but their economic resources dwindled rapidly, so they resorted to confiscating animals and food 'in the name of the revolution'. But they had more pressing problems since Guevara noted that their presence had been detected too soon. The guerrillas had been careless in their movements, since they left very visible and easy-to-follow tracks, which greatly facilitated the pursuit of the army.

One of the measures taken by the military during this time of re-alignment was the re-activation of the Manchego Infantry Regiment in Santa Cruz. With 650 new recruits, the regiment began training in mid-April. Among the instructors were 16 US Army Special Forces officers and NCOs. The staff of the new unit was completed with officers from other regiments, among them Captain Gary Prado Salmón. Lieutenant Colonel José R. Gallardo was appointed as Regiment Commander and Major Miguel Ayoroa Montaño as Battalion Commander.

With that reserve force in training, the army decided to use the troops already deployed in the zone to surround the Ñancahuazú area, thus encircling the guerrilla forces there. The army forces was reorganised one more time, this time with six companies:

- A in Lagunillas and El Pincal;
- B in Yumau;
- C in Tiraboy;
- D in Tatarendá;
- E in Ñancahuazú;
- F in Pirirendá.

The manoeuvre was accomplished on 17 April. However, having left on the 16th, the guerrillas were able to escape the encirclement. When they noticed that, the military ordered two companies to march south to Muyupampa where some guerrillas were captured on 20 April. On the same day, one Air Force T-6 aircraft strafed and attacked the guerrilla positions with rockets.

The guerrilla group moved towards Taperilla and on 21 April they occupied the Coripote ranch, imprisoning its occupants. That day they also captured a van and a YPFB food truck. Realising that they were very close to one of the guerrilla groups, the army tracked them towards Coripote Ranch where a brief skirmish took place. The following day, army troops occupied the ranch without resistance, since the guerrillas had abandoned the place. They found some 15 handcuffed civilians, who reported that the guerrillas had taken supplies, a pick-up truck and some mules, heading north. Immediately the CIOS Special Troops Company led by Sub Lieutenant Carlos Monje Landívar was sent after the guerrillas. The guerrillas were then in full retreat towards El Mesón canyon, located between Ticucha and the Iquira River where they prepared an ambush and fought against the military on 25 April. Casualties of this encounter with the CIOS Company included a civilian guide and one policeman with his German Shepherd dog named Tempestad (Tempest).

The guerrilla troops then began to circulate through the area in order to escape from the encirclement that the Bolivian Army was carrying out. The ELN began to suffer casualties in isolated combats. On 27 April, Jorge Vázquez Viaña *aka* Loro disappeared during an exploration mission but in reality, he had been wounded and was later captured by the army and taken to a hospital. According to one version, he later was kidnapped from the hospital by the army and thrown alive from a helicopter. The official version though stated that he actually escaped from the hospital but was found by the army and immediately executed. Later, Eliseo Reyes *aka* Rolando, who had accompanied Guevara since the Sierra Maestra campaign in Cuba, was also killed. This loss greatly affected Che, as Rolando was with Guevara in Sierra Maestra, Cuba, when he was barely 14 years old. Guevara considered him his best man. He was personally buried by the Guerrilla Chief one kilometre from the improvised camp.

Table 9: Mobilised army units for the guerrilla campaign[1]

Units	Regiment	Army Division	Effectives
Division Company	-	IV	62
Campos Company	Infantry Reg. RI.6	IV	64
Boquerón Company	Infantry Reg. RI.11	IV	46
Abaroa Squadron	Cavalry Reg. RC.1	IV	81
Bullain Battery	Artillery Reg. RA.1	IV	17
Company A	-	IV	87
Company B	-	IV	86
Company C	-	IV	87
Engineering Platoon 8	-	VIII	50
Manchego Company	Infantry Reg. RI.12	VIII	63
Braun Squadron	Cavalry Reg. RC.8	VIII	37
Ranger-2 Battalion	Infantry Reg. RI.12	VIII	650
Escuclases 1 Company	NCO School	VII	85
Escuclases 2 Company	NCO School	VII	85
Ustarez Company	Infantry Reg. RI.13	VII	72
Sucre Platoon	Infantry Reg. RI.2	VII	24
CITE 1 Company	Special Troops Training Centre	VII	67
CITE 2 Company	Special Troops Training Centre	VII	81
Florida Company VI			145
Trinidad Company	Cavalry Reg. RC.2	VI	158
CIOS Company	Infantry Reg. RI.9	VI	71
Ranger-1 Company	Infantry Reg. RI.24	II	82
Colorados Company	Infantry Reg. RI.1	I	81
Toledo Company	Infantry Reg. R.I.23	I	81
Ingavi Squadron	Cavalry Reg. RC.4	I	81
Bolivar Battery	Artillery Reg. RA.2	I	174
Marine Infantry Company	Abapó Battalion	Naval Force	56
Total effectives: 2,673			

The air force bombed that area with two T-6s so the guerrillas fled towards Iripití. An air force Hiller OH-23 helicopter surveyed the area and then called for close air support, so some armed AT-6s strafed the suspected guerrilla positions.

By the end of April, the Army had blocked the guerrillas' exit to Rio Grande, forcing them to cross the mountains. In the summary for the month of April, Che Guevara wrote the following in his diary:

[…] the isolation remains total; illnesses have undermined the health of some comrades, forcing us to divide forces, which has made us less effective; we have not yet been able to make contact with Joaquín; the peasant base remains undeveloped; although it seems that, through planned terror, we will achieve the neutrality of the majority, the support will come later. There has not been a single addition […][10]

May

During May the guerrillas escaped again and again from the encirclement. Che then decided to return to their main base camp on the banks of the Ñancahuazú River. They did not encounter resistance on the way, as the bulk of the military force was deployed elsewhere and the CIOS Company had temporarily lost track of the subversives. Che sent a vanguard to check the *Casa de Calamina* camp and they found out that the place was occupied by the army, so the guerrillas headed for the second camp, *Cueva del Oso*.

The guerrillas arrived in their second camp on 7 May, and settled there. On the following day, they were met by a patrol led by First Lieutenant Henry Laredo Arze, who was killed with two soldiers, and 12 other army effectives were captured, two of them wounded. The armament booty this time consisted of seven M-1 and five Mauser rifles. One soldier managed to escape and informed his commanding officers. Immediately the High Command decided to send two companies towards the encampment and the air force proceeded to bomb the place only a few hours after the prisoners were released. The T-6s continued bombing the area over the next two days.

General Barrientos, in the photo together with General Ovando (left), obtained the support of the Argentine government of General Onganía (centre) and the Paraguayan General Stroessner (right) in the fight against the guerrillas in 1967. (Open source).

On 14 May, 120 army effectives gathered in Piraboy under the command of Lieutenant Colonel Augusto Calderón. These were troops from the CITE, the Sergeants' School, the Braun Squad and the IV Army Division. That same night the chase began, detecting the subversives one kilometre from La Manga. A section of three AT-6s also strafed the Platanal and

Army artillery Lieutenant Rubén Amézaga Faure attacked a guerrilla machine gun nest, where he was killed. (Ejército Boliviano).

Army troops disembark from a TAM C-47 in Vallegrande (above). Major Jaime Niño de Guzmán, arriving in Vallegrande aboard a Hiller OH-23 (below). (FAB via Jorge Cornejo).

Manga areas on 14, 15, 16 and 24 May, albeit ineffectively; the army patrols marched parallel to the guerrilla line of movement without encountering them.

On 21 May, one of the newly Sikorsky H-19B helicopter, serial FAB-604, piloted by Captain Estivariz, crashed near Lagunillas. The pilot survived uninjured but the loss of the helicopter was total. Meanwhile, the Army High Command allowed Bolivian and foreign war correspondents to accompany members of the army and air force in their anti-guerrilla missions to document and inform the general public.

On 24 May, the guerrilla Julio Velasco *aka* Pepe deserted but was captured and executed by the army. The guerrillas then moved eastward, while the military prepared a ground counterattack that arrived days after the enemy had left the location. After many days of searching, an Air Force Cessna U-17A utility plane spotted the guerrillas on the premises of the Pirirenda Ranch. The guerrillas entered the brush again and were not found until 28 May, when they reached the town of Carahuatarenda and captured two vehicles, which were used to move east towards the Yacuiba-Santa Cruz railways. The army then deployed two mobile

One of the P-51D Mustang fighters, serial FAB-504, deployed to Cochabamba in March 1967. Noteworthy in the photo are several instructors of the US Army conducting an airborne proficiency jump with the Bolivian Airborne School. (US Army).

Part of the FAB-armed North American T-6D Texans deployed on the Choretí airstrip in March 1967 (left). The arrival of the Hiller OH-23 serial FAB-601 in Choretí (right). (FAB via Jorge Cornejo).

The first operational sortie of the FAB camouflage Cavalier TF-51D Mustang fighters took place on 26 March, with a napalm raid over the guerrilla positions in Ñancahuazú. In the photo, four FAB fighter pilots are posing in front of their Mustangs. (FAB).

President Barrientos carrying a Uzi submachine gun (left) poses with the pilot Major Jaime Niño de Guzmán, who is also armed (right), on his first visit to the Red Zone in Ñancahuazú aboard a Hiller OH-23 helicopter. (FAB).

companies from the Infantry Regiments RI.24 Mendez Arcos and RI.1 Colorados, which reached El Espino on 30 May. RI.1 continued its search eastward while RI.24 went northward, parallel to the railway line. One patrol from the latter regiment was ambushed while detached from the main group, which led to Sub Lieutenant Eduardo Velarde and soldier Wilfredo Banegas being killed and four other soldiers wounded. The next day, one of the trucks of the Infantry Regiment RI.11 Boquerón, which had joined the persecution along the Muchiri road, was struck by a grenade killing the civilian guide Alejandro Saldías and wounding five army effectives, Sub Lieutenant Max Siles and four soldiers.

Cavalry Lieutenant Luis Saavedra Arambel was killed in a guerrilla ambush on 10 April in the Iripití ravine (left) The funeral of honour of Lieutenant Saavedra, whose coffin was carried by the Commander of the Armed Forces himself, General Ovando, and by the Commander of the Naval Force Rear Admiral Ugarteche, among other high-ranking officers. (Ejército Boliviano).

June

After three months of operations, the balance clearly stood in favour of the guerrilla force; the military casualties had reached 24 killed and 21 wounded, in addition to four civilians and one policeman. The handful of guerrilla deaths was unknown at the time, thus compounding the military's frustration. As the situation worsened, radical actions were taken. Colonel Joaquín Zenteno Anaya was assigned commander of the VIII Army Division based in Santa Cruz de la Sierra, replacing Colonel Roberto Vargas Claros, and Colonel Luis Reque Terán was to lead the IV Army Division based in Camiri, replacing Colonel Humberto Rocha Urquieta. They both assumed their commands on 5 June.

Che with two babies and a farmer (left). Che studying a map surrounded by peasants, who looked at him with fear and curiosity though none of them joined the guerrilla. (Centro de Estudios Che Guevara).

Soldiers from the platoon of Sub-Lieutenant of the Cavalry Jorge Ayala lift the corpse of the officer heroically killed in combat on 10 April 1967. (Ejército Boliviano).

An extremely unusual and unprecedented event in Latin American guerrilla history was that Che released all the prisoners of the Bolivian Army and the captured civilians as well. The photos show some of the liberated officers and soldiers, without their weapons and sometimes even without their uniforms and boots. (Ejército Boliviano).

The jurisdictional limit between both Army Divisions was the Rio Grande.

Colonel Luis Antonio Reque Terán immediately proceeded to visit all the units engaged in the fight against the guerrilla. It was then arranged that Colonel Fernández Calzaga remained in Camiri as Logistics Chief and Colonel E. Sanchez Gironda as Operational Chief of Staff.

Thanks to a reconnaissance mission carried out by Colonel Fernando Sattori in a T-6, two guerrillas, Antonio Sánchez Dias *aka* Antonio and Casildo Condori Vargas *aka* Víctor, fell into an army ambush in the Peñón Colorado area, near Bella Vista on 2 June.

As mentioned before, President Barrientos had favoured the peasants over the miners and workers because the latter had been the source of numerous conflicts since the 1952 Revolution. On 6 June, there was an assembly of the Huanuni miners to protest against the precarious working conditions, unfair practices and miserable pay. In an open demonstration and supported by leftist political and union leaders, they declared their solidarity with the guerrillas. Due to the social unrest, especially in the mining sector, the government declared a state of siege throughout the national territory on 7 June. Barrientos did not lose time and sent army troops who quickly occupied the Catavi and Siglo XX districts, key tin-mining centres. The miners were armed and resisted so the soldiers opened fire, with tragic consequences. According to official sources, there were 16 dead and 71 wounded but the miners later declared that there were at least 90 dead and hundreds of wounded, including women and children. This tragic episode took place on 24 June, during the Catholic festivity of *San Juan Bautista* (Saint John the Baptist) and it was known as the Saint John's Day Massacre.

On the other hand, the new army structure made it possible to decentralise the sections with their own responsible commands, with an efficient communications network and sufficient logistical support. This began to be carried out on 15 June under the code-name *Operación Cynthia* (Operation Cynthia, named after Colonel Reque Terán's favourite daughter). Besides this, police and military forces increased repression in mines and cities, searching for guerrilla supporters and sympathisers.

As part of Operación Cynthia, the order of battle was reformulated according to the General Order of Operations No. 8/67 to add 564 combatants to then existing forces, which had gradually built up to 693 men, as some units were shifted and equipment re-assigned. The VIII Army Division also entered the campaign as the guerrilla forces had crossed to its jurisdiction. The area of operations was then divided in three sectors and new responsibilities were given to troops on the ground. The additional 564 men came from the CITE Company, the First Ranger Battalion of the Infantry Regiment RI.24 Méndez Arcos (Ranger-2 was being trained by the MTT in La Esperanza at that time), the Colorados Company of the Infantry Regiment RI.1 Colorados, the Toledo Company of the Infantry Regiment RI.23 Max Toledo, the Ingavi Squadron of the Cavalry Regiment RC.4 Ingavi and the Trinidad Company of the Cavalry Regiment RC.2 Ballivián.

These reserve units were organised into three infantry battalions:

- BI.1 under the command of Lieutenant Colonel Augusto Calderón.
- BI.2 led by Major Rubén Sánchez.
- BI.3 commanded by Major Ives de Alarcón, with the troops that had already been deployed to the Red Zone previously.

At the air force level, AT-6 attack aircraft and F-51D fighters began employing napalm on their bombing raids. K-17 aerial reconnaissance cameras as well as ammunitions were requested from the US government. Furthermore, coordination with ground commanders was implemented in order to improve air strike results.

With the arrival of the two Sikorsky H-19 helicopters, medevac missions could be carried out more efficiently. A tan and dark green camouflage was painted on these helicopters, as can be seen in the photo. (FAB via Jorge Cornejo).

A trio of FAB North American T-6 Texans flying over the jungle during a training sortie. (FAB via Jorge Cornejo).

Company leaders operating in areas considered to be 'hot' were provided with PRC-9 and PRC-10 radios which were used to relay communication to each other or to Cessna U-17A liaison planes flying overhead. These planes acted as Forward Air Controllers (FAC) to guide the T-6s and P-51s to the guerrilla targets. Two of the Cavalier Mustangs involved in those attacks were serials FAB-518 and FAB-519, which received a South East Asia-style camouflage. The Mustang fighters had been painted with large shark mouths when they had the bare metal colour scheme, and these were retained when receiving the two-tone green and brown camouflage.

Regarding combat situations, the first armed clash of this phase took place in the Cafetal area on 10 June, when the army's Trinidad Company led by Captain Faustino Rico Toro encountered a group of guerrillas on a margin of the Río Grande. As a result, soldier Antonio Melgar was killed and soldier Eladio Arias was wounded. The company used its mortars to attack the guerrilla position and called for support; one company from the Mendéz Arcos Regiment was quickly deployed to the area. The guerrilla force diverted its route and started marching towards Rosita River in order to reach the town of La Florida, while the air force continued its patrol missions using both P-51 Mustangs and Cessna U-17s. Though they were unable to spot the guerrillas, the patrols forced them to walk at night and slowed their progress.

On 22 June, the guerrillas were sighted in the Moracos region, led by a civilian named Paulo. On their march to Rosita River, they left very visible traces, presumably with the intention of ambushing the closest army unit. On the following day, the army's Trinidad Company received the order to stop its march in order to coordinate operations with the Escuclases Company (*Escuela de Clases,* NCO Training School) and the Ingavi Squad. The army's High Command sent an AT-6 Texan piloted by air force Colonel Fernando Sattori on a recce flight over Santa Cruz-Camiri route and at the height of Filo, the presence of a group of mounted guerrillas was sighted.

At 1530 hours on 24 June, a general order was issued to deploy two army companies to Quebrada Pilaí and organise an ambush, with the Trinidad Company to attack from the north in a 'hammer and anvil' operation to destroy the enemy.[11]

On 25 June the guerrillas reached the outskirts of La Florida and sent some men to purchase goods. A mixed company from the VIII Army Division, which included a platoon from the Alianza Marine Infantry Battalion, arrived that same night there. On the following day a patrol from the mixed company was ambushed in the Piray zone and three soldiers were killed, and one of Guevara's men, the Cuban guerrilla Carlos Coello *aka* Tuma, was also killed. The guerrillas then withdrew northward towards the Cochabamba-Santa Cruz road, having been unable to recruit new combatants and gather supplies. The guerrilla force was reduced then to 24 men.

By the end of this month, Che was so ill and weak that he could no longer keep up with his men on foot. During the long marches, he would normally ride on a mule or horse. Sometimes he had to be helped to mount and dismount his horse.

Air Force Cessna A185F serial FAB 233. The U-17/185s were used during the Ñancahuazú campaign as reconnaissance aircraft and also as Forward Air Controllers (FAC) for the T-6 and P-51 in their attack missions. (Dick Lohuis).

President Barrientos emerges from the Hughes 269B helicopter registration CP-780 of the Oil Industry Supply Company in Camiri. Several FAB T-6s can be seen in the background. (Via Jorge Cornejo).

RI.13 Ustariz, occupied the town of Samaipata. On 6 July, using its vanguard group, the guerrillas managed to surprise the officer in charge, Lieutenant Juan Vacaflor Alfaro, and captured him; they then tried to subdue the soldiers. One of them, soldier José Verazaín Llanos, valiantly attempted to free his fellow men and was killed in the act. The guerrillas seized five assault rifles and one machine gun from the army troops and withdrew after gathering some food and medicines from a grocery store and a pharmacy, which they paid for. It is important to clarify that Che had received a large sum of money in US dollars and Bolivian pesos from the Cuban government. That money was used to 'earn the appreciation' of the peasants, paying for the goods they took, whether food or medicine. Although the peasants always accepted the money offered, it never meant a commitment to the guerrilla.

The following day, the subversives confronted the military forces in Peñón Colorado, and since they were outnumbered and outgunned, they escaped towards Mataral. Three days later, the guerrilla Serafín Quispe *aka* Serapio was killed by the army.

On 9 July troops from the IV and VIII Army Divisions found an abandoned guerrilla camp around 100 kilometres south of Santa Cruz, in a place called El Dorado, near Rio Grande.

On 14 July, the FAB officially received 12 North American T-28D Trojan advanced trainers from the US. That same day, TAM Douglas C-47 aircraft dropped supplies to the army troops using parachutes, since there were no adequate conditions to land near the area where those troops were deployed.

Joaquín's guerrilla column evaded pursuit until 19 July, when the army's Campos Company located them in the village of Tapera; the subversives immediately withdrew to the south. The army troops began the pursuit and a section of the Colorados Regiment occupied Tarepillas in order to block the subversives' escape through that area.

On 21 July, the Campos Company located the subversives and attacked them, forcing them into retreat. The Battalion Commander, Major Rubén Sánchez, in the vicinity of Monteagudo, captured two guerrilla deserters: Hugo Choque Silva, *aka* Chingolo and Eusebio Tapia Aruni *aka* Eusebio. Both were subjected to intense interrogations carried out by the chief of staff.

Expecting a strong military response, the guerrillas diverted their march south, and despite their need for medicines they continued marching without occupying any other towns, hiding from the locals.

July

In the month of July, the Fourth Peasant National Congress took place, which represented the vast majority of Bolivian peasants. During the congress, it was decided to give unrestricted support to General Barrientos and the army in the fight against the guerrillas and, if necessary, to take up arms to support the initiative. In fact, the great majority of the conscripts that complied with the obligatory military service were peasants. This gave rise to the so-called *Pacto Campesino-Militar* (Peasant-Military Pact), a strong alliance of the peasantry with the armed forces. That is why when a farmer talked to an army officer, non-commissioned officer, or soldier, he was talking to someone from his own social stratum and sometimes even to a neighbour or friend. In addition, the army always took into account the information brought by peasants and, in fact, this allowed the annihilation of the guerrillas in Bolivia. On the other hand, in the mining and student sectors there was great admiration for the guerrillas, but ultimately, no miner or student ever actually went to Ñancahuazú to join Che's guerrilla. It was just a 'moral' sympathy.

Meanwhile, the VIII Army Division organised its positions in the various towns on the sides of the Cochabamba-Santa Cruz road; the zone to cover was around 250 kilometres, so the companies available were divided in small platoons in order to cover the whole area. One of these platoons, in this case just 20 men from Infantry Regiment

Liaison and reconnaissance flights continued over the area and the Trinidad Company was sent to track the guerrillas on their march south. They lagged behind them by a few days.

On 27 July both forces reached the area of Corralones. One of the Bolivian Army groups spotted the guerrilla from one side of the canyon and attacked their positions with mortar fire. They also called for close air support from the Air Force T-6s but it did not arrive from Camiri on time. Another group of the military was ambushed by the rearguard of the guerrillas and as a result one civilian guide was killed.

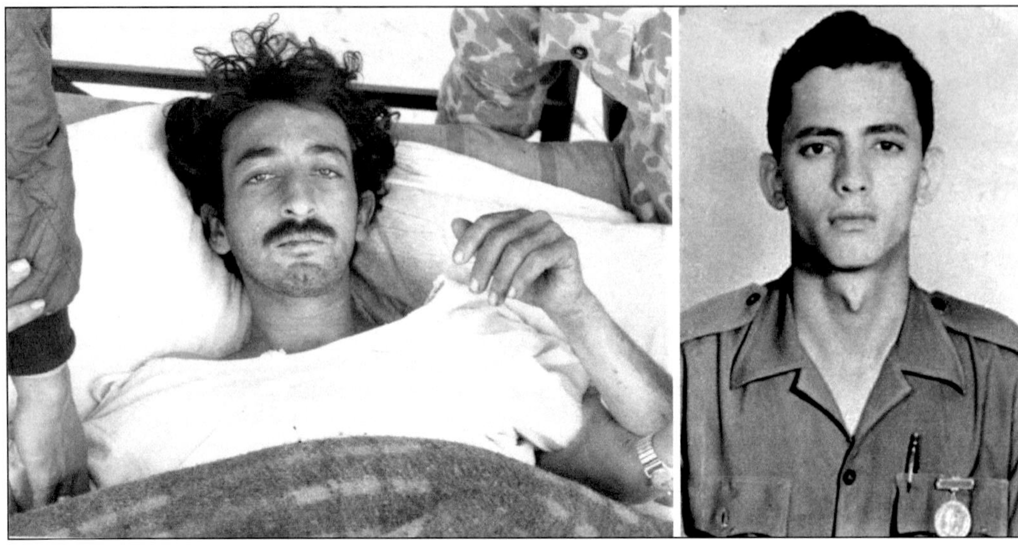

The guerrilla Jorge Vázquez Viaña *aka* Loro was wounded in combat and captured. He was taken to the Camiri Hospital from where he escaped, but he was killed by the army as he fled (left). Another guerrilla killed was Eliseo Reyes *aka* Rolando (right). (Ejército Boliviano).

On July 28, the Army High Command issued Operations Directive 13/67 for the forces of the IV and VIII Army Divisions. Three phases of operations were established, namely:

Heavily-armed army troops occupied the mining districts of Cataví and Siglo XX in June 1967 to repel the miners, causing armed confrontations and unfortunate fatalities. (Ejército Boliviano).

- First Phase: Both army divisions would simultaneously eliminate the guerrilla nuclei in Yerba Buena and Monteagudo.
- Second Phase: IV Division to undertake occupation and plugging of the probable escape routes to the east and west of the Ñancahuazú River, with a search from north to south. VIII Division to undertake raking and cleaning of guerrilla pockets from north to south in its area of influence.
- Third Phase: Once the enemy was isolated, the Ranger Unit would be sent to destroy them in the area.

On 30 July, on the area known as Morocos, the vanguard group of the Trinidad Company accidentally collided with the enemy and a fierce combat followed through the night. Two of Guevara's men were killed, Ricardo and Raúl, and others were wounded. In the case of the army, they had four fatalities and another four wounded. Close air support had been limited in this instance as no helicopters were available to rescue the casualties. One Hiller OH-23, commanded by Lieutenant Rolando Arévalo with the mechanic Captain Rolando Sandoval, had crash-landed on the hills north of Postrervalle about a month earlier. Its two-man crew remained stranded for three and a half weeks and was rescued on the verge of starvation. The helicopter was recovered and repaired, and served again in the campaign. The second OH-23 was deployed to the Paraguayan border, in the Choroveca region at the time of the combat described above.

In the months of June and July the ELN lost seven men in a series of small clashes: Casildo Condori Vargas *aka* Víctor, Antonio Sánchez Díaz *aka* Marcos, Carlos Coello *aka* Tuma, Julio Velazco Montaño *aka* Pepe, actually a deserter who surrendered to the army and was later executed, Serapio Aquino Tudela *aka* Serapio, Raúl Quispaya Choque *aka* Raúl and José María Martínez Tamayo. At the end of July, the guerrilla group had 22 fit members but three sick, including Che, with asthma attacks that made it impossible for him to walk much. Che himself recorded in his diary that his illness delayed operations. Also at the same time, FAB Commander General Jorge Belmonte Ardiles stated that T-6 aircraft machine-gunned the guerrillas in the Florida area and that napalm had begun to be used against them.

August

On 1 August, a USAF Lockheed C-141A Starlifter from the Military Air Command (MAC) brought 30,000 kilos of military aid for the Bolivian Army.

On the very same day, two CIA agents arrived in La Paz to join the hunt for Che Guevara: the Cuban-Americans Gustavo Villoldo and Félix Rodríguez. They arrived in La Paz El Alto International Airport aboard a regular flight of Braniff International Airways DC-8-62 from Miami, with stops in Panama City and Lima. Both agents came with passports with false names to cover their true identity: Félix Ramos Medina (Rodriguez) and Eduardo González (Villoldo). They were received by John Tilton, the head of the CIA mission in Bolivia. Both agents had been veterans of the 2506 Brigade force at the Bay of Pigs in 1961 and other Cuban missions. They had very good reasons to hate communism and especially Castro and Che.

Both had belonged to wealthy families in Cuba and had to leave the country after 1959.

As soon as they reached La Paz, they were taken to a meeting with President Barrientos and then with General Ovando, who gave them army identification cards. Both CIA agents were 'officially' captains in the Bolivian Army and wore the corresponding uniforms. Félix Rodríguez stayed in the city of Santa Cruz as an adviser to Colonel Joaquín Zenteno Anaya, of the VIII Army Division, and Major Arnaldo Saucedo, head of intelligence. Meanwhile, Gustavo Villoldo went directly to La Esperanza and dedicated himself to the intelligence training of a group of young aborigine soldiers who only spoke Quechua, Aymara and Guaraní so that they would be 'the eyes and ears' of the troops, going ahead dressed as civilians to obtain information from the peasants.

Soon, both agents got together in La Esperanza and met Major Shelton. There, they talked about their plans. Shelton confessed to them that they were working hard to train the Bolivian Rangers. If it was up to him, the Green Berets would go into the forest and in a few days they would locate the guerrillas to eliminate them, but they had precise instructions from the American government not to get involved in the fight and to limit their participation only to the training of Bolivian troops.

The month of August was spent by the guerrillas marching south towards Río Grande. On 4 August, thanks to the information given by deserters, some guerrilla supply depots were discovered by the army.

At the beginning of August, a new offensive was launched by the VIII Army Division led by Colonel Zenteno under the name of Operación Parabanó in the area of operations of that particular Army Division, north of the Rio Grande.

Between 4 and 8 August, the search intensified in the Major Sánchez sector, especially in the Serranía del Iñao. On 7 August, the army seized the *Cueva del Oso* guerrilla camp where they found food and medical supplies, weapons including submachine guns, grenades and even a mortar, documents including passports, maps, dozens of pictures of guerrilla members, a list of contacts in Bolivia, deciphered radio messages from Havana and codebooks. Many subversives, either combatants or logistics supporters were identified; among the latter, Loyola Guzmán, a 25-year-old member of the Communist Youth. She was arrested and taken to the Ministry of the Interior building in La Paz for interrogation. She provided vital information for the security forces and having realised that in some way she betrayed her comrades, when her guards were not looking, she threw herself out through a window. Her fall was not fatal and she was taken to the hospital. She survived and would later go into exile in Sweden.

The army's incursions on the guerrilla territory bore fruit on 10 August when Joaquín's column was located when they were trying to cross the Iñao mountain range. A fierce combat took place that lasted three hours and as a result of it, the subversives were expelled from the IV Army Division's jurisdiction. They had one fatal casualty, Antonio Jiménez Tardío *aka* Pedro or Pan Divino.

On 14 August, the army took over the Ñancahuazú camp where, among other things, they found a number of photos of the guerrillas taken by Tania. In the following days, *the* army found other temporary guerrilla camps: *Arroyo Podrido* (Rotten Creek), *Piscina* (Swimming Pool), *Clínica* (Clinic) and *El Elevador* (The Elevator), where guns and ammunition, identity documents, photographs, personal diaries, books and magazines, surgical material and medical drugs, a radio and batteries, and even Che's camera were seized.

The high command of the armed forces appointed two new Army Division Commanders in June 1967: Colonel Luis Reque Terán, Commander of the IV Army Division (left) and Colonel Joaquín Zenteno Anaya, Commander of the VIII Army Division (right). (Ejército Boliviano).

Three officers of the Bolivian Army killed in combat: Engineering Sub Lieutenant Eduardo Velarde Rodríguez, Cavalry First Lieutenant Henry Laredo Arze and Infantry Lieutenant Jorge Ayala Chávez. (Ejército Boliviano).

Demoralised and suffering from the lack of contact with the outside, lack of supplies and carrying their wounded, the guerrillas avoided contact with the military until 26 August when they failed to ambush a seven-man army detachment patrolling the area. One soldier, Vicente Choque Mamani, was wounded as a result, while the guerrillas hurriedly left the area. Meanwhile, the guerrilla column under the command of Joaquín, who, following orders from Guevara had remained in the southern part of the area of operations while marching in a seemingly haphazard manner for three months, was finally detected by the military on early July. A company of the Manchego Regiment led by Captain Mario Vargas Salinas tracked the group for the next two months. Towards the end of August, the aforementioned company was ordered by Colonel Constantino Valencia Oblitas to establish its base in the military post in Masicurí. The other military post in Lajas was commanded by Sub Lieutenant Pedro Barbery Arzabe. The subversives were located near that area and Captain Vargas set up an ambush with a peasant named Honorato Rojas Vaca, who had contact with the guerrillas and had acted as their guide on several occasions. Besides this, Captain Vargas had infiltrated two soldiers, Faustino Garcia and Fidel Rea, in the civilian population of that area and thus they were able to find out the exact place where the subversives were going to cross the Masicurí River near the its juncture with Rio Grande.

On 31 August, in the area known as Vado del Yeso (the site was also known as Puerto Mauricio) 150 kilometres south of Vallegrande, Captain Vargas and his troops, 44 effectives from Infantry Regiment RI.12 and the Cavalry Regiment RC.8, prepared for the ambush, taking positions on both sides of the Grande River bank in a U formation, ordering absolute silence and immobility. At around 1730 hours, a sentry soldier alerted them to the approach of the subversive group. Captain Vargas held the fire until most of the guerrillas showed up to cross the river. At the appropriate moment, while the guerrillas were crossing the river holding their weapons and supplies above their heads, heavy fire was opened on them and eight of the 10 subversives were killed. One army soldier,

A North American P-51D Mustang fighter with a South East Asia type camouflage (left). North American T-6D/G Texan light attack aircraft. (FAB).

Che recorded in his diary that the month of August was the worst of all, since his guerrillas lost all the camps, supplies, weapons, and ammunition hidden in those places plus Joaquín's column was exterminated. They had been left with only what they could carry. And Che's illness kept getting worse, plus his troops suffered from malnutrition, thirst and other symptoms such as diarrhoea, cramps, dizziness and fainting. All these contributed to constant quarrels among them.

Che riding a mule. His chronic asthma prevented him from taking long walks and he had to be mounted most of the time. Sometimes he was so ill that he had to be helped to dismount or mount. (Centro de Estudios Che Guevara).

Antonio Vaca Céspedes, was killed in the battle. Two surviving guerrillas, Ernesto and Paco, tried to escape but they were cornered by the effectives led by Sergeant Barba. Ernesto tried to fight back and was immediately killed, and Paco surrendered. The guerrillas' fatal casualties were Juan Vitalio Acuña Nuñez *aka* Joaquín, Haydee Tamara Bunke Bider *aka* Tania, Apolinar Aquino Quispe *aka* Polo, Walter Arencibia Ayala *aka* Walter, Moisés Guevara Rodríguez *aka* Moisés, Gustavo Machín Hoed de Beche *aka* Alejandro, Restituto José Cabrera Flores *aka* Negro, Freddy Maymura Hurtado *aka* Ernesto and Israel Reyes Zayas *aka* Braulio. The only survivor was José Castillo Chávez *aka* Paco. Their bodies were first exposed publicly and then clandestinely buried. This resounding victory for the army raised the morale of the troops, who finally avenged their comrades killed by the guerrillas. President Barrientos himself promoted Vargas to major and Barbery to lieutenant in the area of operations. Just two days later, the other guerrilla column led by the Che got to that place, completely ignoring the fact that Joaquin's column had been exterminated.

The Battle of Vado de Yeso marked a milestone in the fight against the guerrillas, since the Bolivian Army, after several combats with many casualties, was able to prevail over the subversives, who had already definitively lost the initiative, thus beginning its decline and subsequent disappearance. Right after Vado del Yeso, the IV Army Division sector was definitively free of insurgents. All that remained was to liquidate Che's group that operated in the VIII Army Division's sector.

Meanwhile, the peasant Honorato Rojas was rewarded by the army and he was incorporated into the ranks as a sergeant in the Manchego Regiment, in addition to receiving a five-hectare farm in the Department of Santa Cruz as a gift where he moved. He would be killed by a communist named Luis Pérez Aponte in the early hours of Monday, 14 July 1969 to avenge Honorato's betrayal of Joaquín's guerrilla column two years earlier.

September

A reinforced platoon under the command of Sub Lieutenant Guillermo Román Carranza arrived in Yajopampa on 3 September. They camped near the house of Honorato Rojas. Some sentinels from the platoon spotted a group of guerrillas under Inti's command approaching Rojas's house, with the intention of buying food supplies. Sergeant José Ortíz reacted quickly by starting a confrontation, where the soldier Benito Velazco was killed and the soldier Fanor Lino wounded, with no casualties for the guerrillas, who then left the place.

The army Company Tigre from the Manchego Regiment, commanded by Sub Lieutenant Eduardo Galindo Grandchant, was sent to the area. A few days later, on 7 September, they found the body of Tania, who had been killed in Vado de Yeso and dragged down river. A Hiller helicopter was requested to transport the corpse. She was given a funeral and her remains were buried in the Vallegrande Cemetery. Even President Barrientos was at the funeral, since he had travelled to that area to visit the troops. Incredibly, as part of her infiltration activity in La Paz, Tania had become a German teacher for General Barrientos's children.

The president stayed with the troops for two days, north of Rio Grande. From there, he sent a message to the guerrillas urging them to surrender in exchange for respecting their lives. The president even participated in some patrol incursions into the woods armed with a SMG. This action strengthened the morale of the troops. In fact, and as part of the psychological operations campaign, several FAB T-6 aircraft dropped flyers offering rewards: 50,000 Bolivian pesos (around 4,200 US dollars) to those who provided information about the subversives. As has been mentioned on several occasions, the peasants openly collaborated with the army and were very reluctant to do so with the guerrillas. They even fled from them when they appeared in a town or village.

On 8 September, Che and his group decided to rest for a few days – primarily because he was very exhausted and sick. Then, they headed towards Rio de la Pesca in order to proceed to Monteagudo following the Azero River. On the 14th, they captured some peasants and seized their food.

By then the guerrilla group was completely isolated and its commander Ernesto Che Guevara was severely affected by asthma and without medication. The group then left the Ñancahuazú River area to climb the high mountain ranges located to the west, and headed towards La Higuera area.

By mid-September, the Bolivian military already knew the route that the guerrilla column was following, through the information they received from the inhabitants. Meanwhile, the guerrillas spent

President General Barrientos arriving at a town in the interior of Bolivia, being warmly received by the peasants, some of whom are presenting their weapons as a sign of respect. (Open source).

Bolivian Air Force Douglas C-47 serial TAM 16. C-47s were vital for transporting troops, weapons, ammunition and supplies for operations against the guerrillas. (FAB).

Major Rubén Sánchez (centre) with some of his soldiers. (Ejército Boliviano).

weeks escaping from the military and avoiding contact with the locals and as a result they suffered from hunger and internal strife.

On 14 September, the guerrillas captured some peasants in the Rio la Pesca. After liberating them, they walked for days and days until they reached San Rafael, where they rested and then continued to Alto Seco. They finally reached that town on the 24th. They remained all day there, obtaining food, clothing, shoes and medicines. Meanwhile, on 17 September, the trial against Debray and Bustos was held in Camiri, in which they were sentenced to 30 years in prison. This attracted worldwide attention and was heard on the radio by the guerrillas. In those days the police captured numerous members of the guerrilla logistics in several cities, most of them members of the PCB.

Meanwhile, the VIII Army Division led by Colonel Zenteno implemented a strategy to trap Che and his men, which included three phases:

- The first stage was to isolate the guerrillas in a well-defined area. A good number of Colonel Zenteno's men were deployed to the north of the Cochabamba-Santa Cruz road so as to block a possible escape route. Other effectives were sent along the Rio Grande in the south to block that area. However, if the guerrillas managed to cross that river, the IV Army Division would be waiting for them.
- The second stage was the VIII Army Division's penetration into the Red Zone itself by deploying effectives along the Yacuiba-Santa Cruz railroad on the west. These first two stages were completed by the first week of October.
- Finally, the third stage was to tighten the siege around the guerrillas as much as possible in order to finally destroy them.

On 22 September, Che and his guerrillas arrived at the village of Alto Seco, where they seized food supplies and clothes from a grocery store. Although they invited the men in the town to join the guerrillas, none volunteered. Just by seeing what the guerrillas looked like, the peasants knew that it was a lost cause and furthermore, they would never betray President Barrientos. They stayed in that area for a day and then left, heading towards the Santa Elena River and the village of Loma Larga. Army troops arrived in Alto Seco three days later.

On 25 September, with the authorisation of the Army Command, the Rangers Infantry Regiment No. 12 consisting of companies A, B and C, was transferred to Vallegrande on army trucks, arriving there in the morning of 26 September. The commander of that regiment was Colonel José Gallardo, the deputy commander was Major Miguel Ayoroa, and the company commanders were Captains Celso Torrelio Villa (A), Gary Prado Salmón (B) and Ángel Mariscal Gómez (C), in all totalling 600 troops. Among the officers were Sub Lieutenants Germán Venegas, Hugo Loza, Tomás Aguilera, Carlos Pérez, Eduardo Huerta, César Peredo and Mario Romero. Among the outstanding sergeants were Bernardino Huanca and Mario Terán. The following day, Company B was transferred to La Higuera, Company A to patrol the northern area of the Rio Grande, and Company C remained as reserve.

On the 25th, the guerrillas left Loma Larga and headed to the villages of Trancamayo and Abra del Picacho, finally ending up in La Higuera on the 26th. The guerrilla survivors were dirty and smelled very bad, with torn clothes and many without shoes. Even Che was wearing pieces of leather tied to his feet as makeshift shoes. They looked demoralised and pitiful, but the peasants remained alert, since they were armed. Che then sent a vanguard of six guerrillas, Coco, Benigno, Miguel, Julio, Aniceto and Pablito, toward Jaguey, where they engaged in combat with Company A effectives of the army that were patrolling the area. In the clash, Coco Peredo was first wounded and then killed. Benigno was also wounded. The guerrillas had to retreat and the troops under the command of Sub Lieutenant Galindo were ordered to pursue them to La Higuera, but upon reaching there, they did not find any guerrillas. They had left, heading towards San Antonio Canyon. Prado's men rode to the village of Pucará and marched through the night to take up positions at the southern entrance of San Antonio Canyon, led by a civilian guide.

Troops from the IV and VIII Divisions of the army mobilised to the Red Zone with full combat gear. While some troops wore American M-1 helmets, most wore only caps or berets. (Ejército Boliviano).

The primitive conditions in which the guerrillas lived in the jungle. From left to right: Alejandro, Inti, Urbano, Rolando, Che, Tuma, Arturo and Moro. (Centro de Estudios Che Guevara).

Bombs being loaded onto the underwing pylons of a FAB T-6D for an operational sortie against the guerrillas. (FAB via Jorge Cornejo).

As an irony of fate, the army troops were using the classic manoeuvres detailed in the manual written by Che himself called *Guerra de Guerrillas* (*Guerrilla Warfare*), surrounding the guerrillas inside a deadly trap. Incredibly, perhaps because he was physically and mentally very weak, Che did not follow his own manual to avoid being caught.

On 26 September, 190 army effectives ambushed seven guerrillas at a place called Quebrada de Batán, killing three of them: Roberto Peredo Leigue *aka* Coco, Mario Gutiérrez Ardaya *aka* Julio and Manuel Hernández Osorio *aka* Miguel, leaving Benigno and Pablo wounded. Orlando Jiménez Bazán *aka* Camba and Antonio Rodríguez Flores *aka* León could escape but were captured days later by effectives of Company B. The military did not sustain any casualties. This was the baptism of fire for the Bolivian Army Rangers, who had been trained by instructors from the US Army.

By 30 September the insurgents were bottled up. Che and his forces were given a brief respite as army troops conducted thorough sweeps along the Rio Grande, but did not venture into the narrow canyons. Ernesto Guevara and the 16 surviving ELN guerrillas sought to escape by climbing even higher, managing to hide for three days, though in miserable conditions since they could not set a fire to cook their food and their water supply was almost gone. At that time, only two military units were present in the area: Ranger-2's Company B under the command of Captain Prado with 145 men and the Braun Squad under the command of Sub Lieutenant Lara with 37 men, patrolling all the canyons and ravines on the 28, 29 and 30 September. The Braun Squad was replaced by Ranger-2's Company A.

On 30 September, President General Barrientos arrived in Vallegrande to visit the army troops in operations once again and motivate them for the definitive defeat of the guerrillas.

During the month of September, the only Cuban contact in La Paz, Renán Montero *aka* Iván, returned to Cuba and no one else was sent in his place, a clear example that Fidel left Che without communication with Cuba – even the radio transmitter had broken. Che's poor guerrilla force was totally isolated.

October

Ranger-2's Company B searched along the north and south banks of Rio Grande until 4 October when they set up a patrol base near Abra del Pichaco at the mouth of the San Antonio Canyon. Two platoons from Company A led by Captain Celso Torrelio were attached to Prado's company and positioned near La Higuera. Prado then had 200 rangers under his command. The remainder of Torrelio's company was given the mission of combing the ravines to the east of the San Antonio Canyon. The ranger companies continued searching the area without success for some days.

Both companies of Rangers, who were joined by the Florida Company of the VI Army Division assigned to the VIII Division, carried out searches on 5, 6 and 7 October from their bases in La Higuera, Abra del Picacho and Loma Larga, without meeting the guerrillas.

Under these conditions, Che Guevara tried to find a descending route that would take them to Rio Grande and allow them to flee through it. On 7 October they began to go down a steep gorge towards the river. That night he made the last entry in his diary:

A USAF Lockheed C-141A Starlifter brought 30,000 kilograms of military aid to Bolivia in early August 1967. (USAF).

The two Cuban American CIA agents sent to Bolivia, Félix Rodriguez (left) and Gustavo Villoldo (right). (Open source).

On 7 August, Bolivian Army troops captured Che's secondary camp called *Cueva del Oso*, seizing weapons, medicines, and canned food. Some days later, the guerrilla main camp in Ñancah*uazú* was also taken. (Ejército Boliviano).

The 11 months of our guerrilla inauguration were completed without complications, until 1230 when an old woman, herding her goats, entered the canyon where we had camped and we had to arrest her. The woman has not given any reliable news about the soldiers, answering everything that she doesn't know, that she hasn't been there for a long time. She only gave information about the roads; from the results of the old woman's report, it can be deduced that we are approximately one league from Higueras and another from Jagüey and about two from Pucará. At 5:30 p.m., Inti, Aniceto, and Pablito went to the house of the old woman who has a bedridden daughter and a half-dwarf; they gave her 50 pesos with the order that she would not speak a word, but with little hope that she would comply despite her promises. The 17 of us left with a very small moon and the march was very tiring and leaving a lot of traces through the canyon where we were, which has no houses nearby, but potato fields irrigated by ditches from the same stream. At 2 we stopped to rest, since it was useless to continue advancing. El Chino becomes a real burden when you have to walk at night.[12]

Che's capture

It was only around 0200 hours on Sunday 8 October that Che and his guerrillas stopped the march to rest. Some hours later, a farmer named Pedro Peña saw 17 guerrillas sleeping at a place called Quebrada del Churo (sometimes also called del Yuro) near his potato field and quickly reported their position to army Sub Lieutenant Carlos Pérez, commander of the First Platoon, Company A (attached to Company B) at La Higuera. The Second Platoon was led by Sub Lieutenant Eduardo Huerta, and both platoons got ready for a search mission in the area mentioned by the farmer.

Right before departing, Sub Lieutenant Pérez immediately contacted Captain Prado on his AN/PRC-6 radio and was ordered to move both Company A platoons to the north end of El Churo Canyon. That canyon was 300 metres long, running downhill northeast to southwest, and at its southern end, it merged with La Tusca Canyon making a big letter Y, and fed into the San Antonio Canyon. Captain Prado and the Third Platoon, led by Sergeant Huanca, went directly to the zone to support Company A.

Captain Prado would position himself with one rifle company with two 60mm mortars and one Browning M1919A4 MG on the high ground overlooking the south end of the small ravine, so as to close off both ends of the canyon. It was there that he established his command post so as to block any guerrilla attempt to cross the area. The steep ravine was as much as 200 metres deep with thick vegetation, particularly along the canyon floor, becoming sparser near the top. Captain Prado sent his third platoon, led by Sergeant Bernardino Huanca up to the north end of La Tusca Canyon.

Che had split his force into three groups, sending four men, Pombo, Inti, Darío, and Ñato, forward into the upper part of El Churo Canyon and four others to the southerly confluence of the two canyons. The rearguard, Chapaco, Moro, Pablo, and Eustaquio, slipped out before the rangers got into position. Che stayed hidden in the centre of El Churo with the remaining guerrillas. His intent was to block the troops from entering the canyon and escape with his main body by climbing to the high ground. The ranger forces

Colonel Constantino Valencia Oblitas, Commander of the Tactical Group No. 3. (Ejército Boliviano).

Captain Mario Vargas Salinas (left), commander of a company of the Infantry Regiment RI.12 Manchego which annihilated Joaquín's guerrilla column in an ambush in Vado del Yeso on 31 August 1967. (Ejército Boliviano).

began searching the canyons, closing in on Che. Immediately there was contact at the north end of El Churo.

At 1100 hours, the shooting began at the north end of El Churo. The 17 surviving guerrillas were surprised by the newly arrived rangers while trying to descend the Quebrada del Churo. Two rangers were killed in the initial exchange. Captain Prado had positioned his crew-served weapons to watch over the area where El Churo and La Tusca canyons converged. When the guerrillas emerged to begin their breakout, he engaged them with mortar and machine gun fire. The guerrillas retreated back into El Churo with casualties but they were trapped. There was no way out for them. Che was wounded in the right calf, and his M-1 carbine was damaged. A second breakout attempt resulted in another wounded guerrilla. The tide of battle began to run against the guerrillas.

Bolivian Army soldiers in the Vado del Yeso area, where they killed eight of the 10 guerrillas from Joaquín's column. (Ejército Boliviano).

When the first casualties occurred in the army, Captain Prado, using his PRC-10 radio, requested from Sub Lieutenant Tomás Totti a Hiller OH-23 helicopter to evacuate the wounded and he also briefed him about the situation of the fight. Immediately, Sub Lieutenant Totti radioed the command of the VIII Army Division in Vallegrande to send the Hiller. The command also dispatched two AT-6 Texan aircraft armed with bombs and machine guns to provide close air support. Once both T-6s were overflying the area,

Bolivian Army Sub Lieutenant Eduardo Galindo Grandchant (left) commanded the Tigre Company of the Manchego Infantry Regiment (right). (Ejército Boliviano).

the pilots requested instructions to drop their bombs. Captain Prado called off the bomb raid, as it was impossible to attack the enemy without affecting the army troops, so they had to return to Vallegrande. Then the Hiller OH-23 helicopter piloted by Major Jaime Niño de Guzmán appeared to evacuate the wounded. He was about to land near Captain Prado's command post when he received shots from the guerrillas, causing the pilot to abort the landing; he then received instructions to go to La Higuera. Instead, Company A effectives were to rescue the wounded and dead to be transported to La Higuera on foot first.

Sergeant Huanca and his platoon, having completed their sweep of La Tusca Canyon, were directed into El Churo to drive the guerrillas against the two platoons of Company A atop the ravine in a hammer and anvil manoeuvre. Sergeant Huanca courageously attacked Che's main body with hand grenades, killing two guerrillas, Antonio and Arturo. This forced the insurgents to fall back and enabled the rangers to get into the canyon. Then Che had no choice but to try to escape, and the only way out was up. Separated from the rest of his men, the wounded Che with Simeón Cuba *aka* Willy helping him, began climbing out of the canyon. Three rangers manning an observation post near Prado's command post caught sight of the two fleeing guerrillas. They held their fire and stayed hidden, allowing the insurgents to climb up the ravine. When they were 10 feet away, the three rangers, Balboa, Choque and Encinas, told the guerrillas to surrender and they were taken prisoner. According to those rangers, these words were said by Che when he was captured: 'Don't kill me, I am Che. I am worth more alive than dead…'[13] They immediately shouted to Captain Prado since the command post was just 20 metres away. It was 1330 hours and the main combat had lasted three hours, but the rangers continued to sweep the canyons for insurgents.

Besides being wounded, Guevara was dirty, smelly, sick, with long hair and a beard, and above all, demoralised. His appearance was pitiful because more than a guerrilla, he looked like a homeless beggar. Still, he was arrogant and defiant. Captain Gary Prado got closer and identified Che and proceed to tie his hands behind his back, and did the same to Willy. They both sat down under a tree. Right after asking a few questions to them, Captain Prado returned to his command post because he was concerned about his own men who were still fighting in the canyon. Meanwhile, Prado called Lieutenant Colonel Andrés Selich Chop, commander of the Ranger-2 Regiment, who was in Vallegrande. The communication was in code: 'I have Papá Cansado and Willy. Combat goes on.'[14] (*Papá Cansado,* meaning Tired Dad, was the code for Che Guevara. This code's real meaning was 'in custody and wounded'.)

Alberto Fernández Monte de Oca *aka* Pacho, who was severely injured, was captured and also Juan Pablo Chang Navarro *aka* El Chino, who had lost his glasses and was practically blind. During the combat, three other men lost their lives: René Martínez Tamayo *aka* Arturo, Orlando Olo Pantoja Tamayo *aka* Antonio, and Aniceto Reinaga Cordillo *aka* Aniceto. Alberto Fernández Montes de Oca *aka* Pacho was seriously injured and died the following day. On the other side, the army casualties were soldiers Mario Characayo, Mario La Fuente and Manuel Morales from Company A (killed in action) and soldier Beno Jiménez (wounded). In Company B, soldier Sabino Cossío was killed and soldiers Valetín Choque, Miguel Tabada and Julio Paco were wounded. In several flights, all casualties were flown on the Hiller helicopter to the hospital in Vallegrande that day and the following day.

First, Che and Willy were detained at Captain Prado's command post until dusk. Lieutenant Colonel Selich immediately went to La Higuera on board an air force Hiller OH-23 helicopter piloted by Major Jaime Niño de Guzmán. Once there, Selich ordered the transfer of the prisoners to La Higuera, just three kilometres away, so Captain Prado and his men took the prisoners to that village on foot. Che was helped to walk by two soldiers. Some troops in the canyon were left blocking all the exits. Once there, Che, Pacho and Willy were confined in the two classrooms of the school, a precarious adobe hut with a dirt floor. Major Miguel Ángel Ayoroa, Commander of the Rangers Battalion, also appeared.

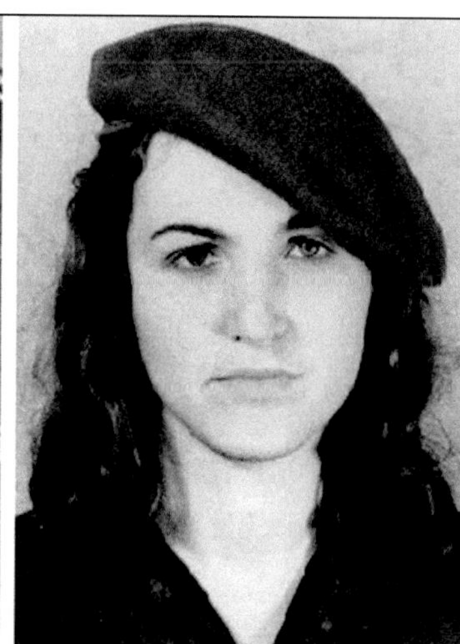

Senior Bolivian military commanders and President Barrientos next to Tania's corpse, brought to Vallegrande on a FAB Hiller OH-23 (left). Haydée Tamara Bunke Bider *aka* Tania (right). (Open source).

President Barrientos accompanied by an army officer receiving explanations in the middle of the jungle on one of his many visits to the front (left). Major Ayoroa (centre) informing General Ovando (left) about the latest operations against the guerrillas. In the background, the Hiller OH-23 in which Ovando had arrived (right). (Open source).

Various scenes of the military trial of the Frenchman Régis Debray and the Argentine Ciro Bustos in Camiri in September 1967. This trial produced tremendous negative propaganda against Bolivia as various world leaders demanded the release of the accused. Note that the effectives of the Military Police were wearing German helmets. (Open source).

Captain Gary Prado Salmón (centre), commander of the Rangers Company B. In the photo below, Captain Prado (second from the right) with some of his troops in La Higuera at the end of September 1967. (Ejército Boliviano).

The Bolivian military found several documents in Guevara's backpack, including:

- His diary in two notebooks (one corresponding to November–December 1966 and the other to January–October 1967).
- A notebook with addresses and instructions.
- Two notebooks with copies of the messages received and sent.
- Two small codebooks.
- Twenty different maps.
- Two books on socialism.
- Two smoking pipes.
- A damaged M-1 carbine.
- An altimeter.
- A 9mm Walther PPK pistol.
- A Solinger dagger.
- Twelve undeveloped rolls of 35mm film.
- Four Rolex watches.
- A small bag containing 20,000 Bolivian pesos and 2,500 US dollars.

That day, Lieutenant Colonel Selich held several conversations, not very extensive, with Guevara. He was tied hand and foot and bleeding from an unattended wound, lying on the ground, where the bodies of the dead guerrillas were also placed. Another version of this event, however, states that his wound was taken care of. However, Pacho's wounds were not treated and the guerrilla finally bled to death around midnight that day.

During the long hours that passed between his arrival at the school premises and his subsequent execution, Che was visited by some high-ranking officers, junior officers, NCOs and soldiers, and even some civilians. Those who insulted him or even hit him were treated with contempt by Che, while those who were respectful were able to converse with him without problems. These included the CIA agent Félix Rodriguez, as well as the village teacher who brought him food and even Major Jaime Niño de Guzmán, the pilot of the Hiller, who got some tobacco for Che. Even the conversation with Captain Gary Prado was friendly. Also, some soldiers came up to ask a few things and Che answered them sincerely. Some even wanted a picture with him.

Meanwhile, in La Paz a meeting was held led by the President General René Barrientos with the Armed Forces Commander General Alfredo Ovando, the Armed Forces Chief of Staff General Juan José Torres, the Commander of the Army General David Lafuente Soto, the Air Force Commander General Jorge Belmonte Ardiles, the Naval Force Commander Rear Admiral Horacio Ugarteche, the Army Chief of Staff General Marcos Vasquez Sempertegui, the CIA Chief in Bolivia John S. Tilton and the Chief of the American Military Mission in Bolivia. It is essential to clarify that the decision to execute Che was not rushed at the last moment by the Bolivian military authorities. This had already been discussed weeks before Che's capture. After the huge worldwide campaign against Bolivia that took place as a result of the trial of Debray and Bustos, the government and the entire military leadership, including of course General Barrientos, could not afford to tolerate the

President Barrientos with his ubiquitous submachine gun having coffee in a military kitchen (left). Army troops being transported in REO trucks to the Red Zone from La Esperanza to Vallegrande. Some of the instructors from the US Army can be seen in the picture. (US Army).

Captain Celso Torrelio Villa (centre), commander of Rangers Company A, along with several of his soldiers disguised as peasants for intelligence tasks (left). Ranger troops carrying heavy machine guns, mortars and rocket launchers (right). (Ejército Boliviano).

Ranger troops in the middle of the jungle chasing the guerrillas (left). Major Ayoroa (left) and Captain Gary Prado (right) leading the Rangers. (Ejército Boliviano).

repercussions that putting Che on trial would have had, so they had to opt for his summary execution. In fact, if Che's guerrilla adventure had been successful, he would surely have shot Barrientos, Ovando, Zenteno, Reque Terán, Selich, Prado and many others, just as he did in Cuba with the authorities of the Batista government. So, from having been a shooter, Che went on to be shot.

On the other hand, Che's followers and also the Cuban government have stated that on 8 October at 2300 hours, General Barrientos received a message from the US government through Ambassador Henderson specifying that Che should be eliminated in order to avoid all the international scandals that followed the Debray trial. Keeping him alive was not an option since it would cause numerous problems for the Bolivian Armed Forces and the government itself, and besides, 'the dead enemy was the best enemy.' His extrajudicial execution and the burial of his body in a secret place was finally decided.

Back to the military operations against the subversives, four other guerrillas were persecuted and killed four days later, being buried in clandestine graves: Octavio de la Concepción de la Pedraja *aka* Moro, Francisco Huanca Flores *aka* Pablo, Lucio Edilverto Garvan Hidalgo *aka* Eustaquio and Jaime Arana Campero *aka* Chapaco. Notably six guerrillas known as Pombo, Benigno, Urbano, Inti, Darío and Ñato, managed to break the encirclement and escape. The army pursued them, killing Ñato, but the remaining five managed to remain hidden in Bolivian territory for months until they finally escaped to Chile, thanks to the help of some members of the Bolivian Communist Party and a series of Chilean organisations, headed by the then-socialist senator Salvador Allende.

Che's execution

In the early hours of 9 October, Colonel Joaquín Zenteno Anaya and CIA agent Félix Rodríguez arrived at La Higuera in the Air Force Hiller OH-23 helicopter serial FAB-601 from Vallegrande, the latter in Bolivian military uniform and under the name of Capitán Ramos. Rodríguez sent a coded message to his superiors, had brief conversations with Guevara and photographed each page of the diary. Colonel Zenteno tried to interrogate Che but he did not answer any questions, so the officer left the room angrily. Rodriguez was luckier, probably because he was Cuban and also treated him with respect. Rodriguez told Che the following: 'Commander, I didn't come to question you. Our ideals are different, but I admire you. You were a minister of state, you are here because you believe in your ideals, even though I know they are wrong. I've come to talk to you...'[15] So, after checking that he was serious and not joking, Che answered, 'May I sit down? Would you untie me?'[16] Rodriguez requested a soldier to untie him and they began to chat. When Che was asked why he chose Bolivia, he answered that it was a very poor country and that 'Yankee imperialism' was not going to defend it; also, he knew that

The guerrilla Orlando Jiménez Bazán *aka* Camba when he was captured by army troops. Bloodstains can be seen on his fatigues. (Ejército Boliviano).

Captain Gary Prado Salmón, commander of Company B of Ranger-2, carrying an M-2 carbine. (General Gary Prado Archives).

the typical Bolivian Army soldier was very poorly trained but above all, if he were successful in Bolivia, it was going to be easier to export the revolution to Brazil, Paraguay, Argentina, Chile and Peru later. They also talked about the disastrous Cuban economy because of the American embargo and their guerrilla adventure in Africa.

Also, and although it was not explicit (perhaps he still had the hope of getting out of there alive) Che gave Rodriguez to understand that there were 'ideological confrontations' with Fidel Castro and that if he remained alive, he would not return to Cuba. In fact, in his last years of life, Che moved closer to Mao's orthodox Chinese line, distancing himself from the Soviet Union, which caused severe diplomatic problems for Fidel Castro, who needed to continue counting on Soviet economic support.

Years later, Rodriguez stated that Castro, in order to maintain his hegemony in Cuba, gradually got rid of other revolutionaries who could 'shadow' him, including Che, and that was why he sent him to Bolivia and practically took all support away from him in his guerrilla adventure. Castro knew perfectly well that Che would not leave Bolivia alive.[17]

The conversation was interrupted by a call from the Bolivian Army High Command at 1000 hours that passed a message in a secret code: 500-600 (500 meaning *Che* and 600 meaning *dead*). Then Colonel Zenteno returned and communicated the government's orders to eliminate the prisoner. Rodriguez warned him that the US government's instructions were to try to keep him alive at all costs and take him to Panama for questioning. The Colonel's answer was, 'Félix, we thank you very much for your help, but they are orders from the President and the head of the Armed Forces, which I cannot break. If I don't carry it out, I will get dishonourably discharged from the military…'[18]

On the other hand, it is interesting to clarify that retired General Gary Prado has denied this version of events involving Félix Rodriguez, arguing that the few meetings that agent had with Che were violent and that the guerrilla fighter refused to speak with him. Besides this, some authors, especially Cuban and Latin American, but also American, have also questioned Rodriguez's version.[19] Based on alleged declassified CIA documents, they have affirmed that the US government in general, and the CIA in particular, pressured the Bolivian government of General Barrientos to execute Che. They even mention that everything performed and published by Rodriguez and Villoldo was to cover up the CIA's order to kill Che.

However, after receiving the order, Félix Rodríguez spoke again with Ernesto Guevara and took several photographs of him, the last in which he appeared alive. Then Rodriguez simply told him, 'Commander, I'm sorry…'[20]

Che turned pale and said, 'It's better this way, I should never have been taken prisoner alive.'[21]

Rodriguez then asked Che if there was anything he wanted to say to his family, to which Che first responded in an ironic way: 'Tell Fidel that the Revolution will triumph sooner or later, and if you happen to talk to Aleida, tell her to get married again and try to be happy.'[22]

They shook hands and Rodriguez left the room, but not before giving him his pipe.

Meanwhile, Colonel Zenteno asked for two volunteers for the execution of Che and the other prisoners. Sergeants Mario Terán and Bernardino Huanca volunteered and Colonel Zenteno ordered Huanca to execute Willy and El Chino and Terán to execute Che. Both had M-2 carbines and they carried out the order immediately.

At about 1310 hours, Sergeant Terán shot Che with a M-2 automatic carbine bursts under his head to simulate his death in combat and Sergeant Huanca did the same with Willy. Years later, Sergeant Terán told the press that upon receiving the order, he went to see his commander, Colonel Pérez, to confirm the execution. He was furious and ordered him to carry out the order. So Terán went to Che and killed him.

There are two versions of what Che's last words were before his execution. According to his followers, Che stared at his executioner and told him to calm down and aim well, because he was going to kill a real man. The other version, however, tells that Che, realising that he was going to be executed, trembled with fear and said nothing.

On 9 October in the morning, a FAB Douglas C-47, serial TAM 14, transported the Commander of the Armed Forces General Ovando, the Commander of the Army General Lafuente Soto, Rear Admiral Ugarteche, Colonel Fernando Sattori, Lieutenant Colonel Heberto Olmos and Captains Oscar Pammo, Ángel Vargas and René Ocampo to Vallegrande. On the afternoon of that day, the body of Ernesto Guevara was taken by the Air Force Hiller OH-23 helicopter serial FAB-601 to Vallegrande and placed in the laundry room of

Quebrada del Churo (or Yuro), a typical landscape of southeastern Bolivia (left). Che with his backpack and his M-1 carbine in 1967 (right). (Open source).

The exact place where Che and Willy were captured in Quebrada del Churo (left). La Higuera school, where Che and two guerrillas also captured were imprisoned and later executed (right). (Open source).

The deplorable physical condition of Che when he was captured. On the left, posing with the CIA agent Félix Rodriguez and several Bolivian soldiers. Che was wounded, weak, filthy and smelly. (Félix Rodriguez Archives). Che's damaged M-1 carbine (right). (Ejército Boliviano).

Lieutenant Colonel Andrés Selich Chop (fourth from the left), commander of the Ranger Regiment together with the VIII Army Division commander Colonel Joaquín Zenteno Anaya (centre), Captain Gary Prado and other officers, after the capture of Che (top). Colonel Zenteno Anaya with Sub Lieutenant Eduardo Galindo Grandchant (left) and the Tigre Company effectives of the Manchego Infantry Regiment. The troops have FAL, M-1 and Mauser rifles (bottom). (Ejército Boliviano).

The last pictures of Che still alive on the morning of 9 October 1967. (Félix Rodriguez Archives).

Sergeant Bernardino Huanca, who executed Willy and El Chino (left). Sergeant Mario Terán, who executed Che (right). (Ejército Boliviano).

Colonel Joaquín Zenteno Anaya, commander of the VIII Army Division (second left) and other army officers, during a press conference in Vallegrande. One of the officers is holding Che's diary. The table was full of tape recorders from the press. (Freddy Alborta).

President Barrientos together with several military officers reviewing the documents seized from Che after his capture. (Ejército Boliviano).

the Nuestro Señor de Malta Hospital, where it remained on public display that day and the entire following day, being injected with a large amount of formaldehyde to avoid decomposition. The famous and widely distributed and published photos of Che's corpse were taken precisely in that place. Then it was officially announced that Che had 'died in combat', news that quickly spread throughout the world. Of course, few believed the official version, especially after the autopsy carried out by doctors in Vallegrande. It was impossible to stay alive for so many hours with the number of injuries that Che's body had. The vast majority sensed that Che had been taken prisoner alive and that he was later executed.

Because it had already been decided that the body of the guerrilla Guevara would be made to disappear, like that of the rest of the guerrillas, on the night of 10 October, the hands of the corpse were cut off to keep them as proof of death. The members of the ELN believed Bolivian Army Colonel Roberto Quintanilla Pérez was responsible for cutting off Guevara's hands to guarantee his identification, although in reality the hands were cut off by order of the head of the Bolivian Army, General Alfredo Ovando Candia. At that time, Colonel Quintanilla was the Head of Intelligence for the Minister of the Interior, Antonio Arguedas, and was in the area of operations. The next day, early in the morning, the bodies were secretly buried in a common grave in an area near the Vallegrande airstrip.

Two days later, some of Guevara's relatives appeared at the scene accompanied by international journalists, but they were mistakenly informed that his remains had been cremated. The authorities at the time wanted to prevent the place from becoming a kind of 'sanctuary' for communists and sympathisers.

In the area of operations, the remaining army troops begin their demobilisation on 21 November 1967, with the last unit, the Rangers Regiment, stood down on 30 December. The Bolivian Air Force carried out many flights transporting troops back to their units with Douglas C-47 and C-54 aircraft. Furthermore, all the P-51, T-6, Cessna U-17 aircraft deployed for this campaign returned to their bases in La Paz and Cochabamba on 31 December.

A short time later, the Minister of the Interior of the Barrientos government, Antonio Arguedas, sent a copy of Che's diary to Cuba. He also sent the hands amputated from Che's corpse, preserved in formaldehyde, supposedly without financial compensation, and when he was discovered by the security forces, he fled Bolivia and was considered a traitor. He later declared himself to be a CIA agent and a member of the Communist Party.

The escape of the guerrilla survivors to Chile

As not all the subversives had yet been captured, the military forces maintained Company A of the Rangers in La Higuera, Company B in Abra de Picacho, and Company C in Alto Seco and Cajones. In addition, Florida Company was in San Lorenzo and the NCO School Company in Chasamonte. All these forces dedicated themselves to patrolling those areas on 10 and 11 October, but without results. The surviving guerrillas had escaped from El Churo led by Urbano. Early on the morning of 12 October, a peasant reported to Captain Prado's B Company Command Post that he had seen a group of six guerrillas in the area of the Santa Elena River. The pursuit began immediately, sending a platoon under the command of Second Lieutenant Germán Venegas to that area through the lower part of the canyon and another platoon with Major Ayoroa, Captain Prado and Sergeant Huanca to the same area but in the upper part of the canyon.

When the troops reached the Quebrada de El Potrero, Second Lieutenant Raúl Espinoza, who was leading his platoon, found himself face to face with Urbano and his guerrillas, beginning a confrontation that resulted in no casualties. A blockade was established in the area surrounding the ravine to prevent the guerrillas from leaving the zone, but they managed to escape through a fissure called El Socavón, near El Naranjal hill. The commander sent Corporal Daniel Calani and a platoon to follow the guerrillas through the fissure. While the platoon was carrying out this task, Corporal Calani was wounded and when the medic Franz Muriel approached him to help, he was killed with a shot to the head. The guerrillas then killed Corporal Calani. During the night, the subversives killed two other soldiers, Facundo Cruz and Abel Callapa and a civilian guide, and then they managed to escape.

The other group of surviving subversives made up of Chapaco, Moro, Eustaquio and Pablito moved towards the Cajones area on 13 October. While making a fire to cook food, they were spotted by the sentry of Ranger Company C who alerted the commander, Sub Lieutenant Guillermo Aguirre Palma. The company waited until dawn and established an encirclement that ended in a confrontation, with the four guerrillas being killed. After this clash, there were only six guerrillas left.

After learning of Che's death, the Cuban government remained silent for a few days. On 15 October, the Prime Minister of Cuba, Fidel Castro, gave a press conference where he confirmed the death of Che and mentioned that he had been entrusted with a mission, thus admitting Cuban interference in Bolivia. He also denounced that Che had been captured alive and later executed.

The six guerrilla survivors, then led by Pombo, escaped north avoiding any contact with the military or the population. They reached the town of Mataral on 13 November and attempted to purchase civilian clothing and supplies. They were once again denounced by peasants and the army sent the Ranger-2 Battalion to establish checkpoints along the Santa Cruz-Cochabamba route, and the Florida Company and a NCO School Company to conduct raids in the area between Alto Seco and Los Sitanos. The NCO School Company, under the command of Captain José Meruvia Lazarte, captured the civilian guide of the guerrillas, Honorato Linares, who revealed that the guerrillas had been in a ravine near his house. Immediately a platoon from the NCO School under the command of Sub Lieutenant Jorge Castellón began a chase that culminated in the heights of the Mataral area, where they engaged in combat on 15 November with the subversives, Ñato being killed and the five remaining guerrillas managing to escape.

Mataral is considered the last combat of the army campaign against the guerrillas. After that, the persecution of the guerrilla survivors became a police affair. They all reached San Isidro area. Days later, Inti and Urbano went out onto the road that connected Cochabamba with Santa Cruz and were able to take a bus to Santa Cruz. From there, they flew to Cochabamba on a LAB plane and began preparations so that the other three survivors could leave the San Isidro area, 200 kilometres from Cochabamba. Once there, they made contact with members of the PCB who offered to help them.

Members of the Communist Youth volunteered to contact the three guerrillas who were waiting in the San Isidro area. The meeting took place in December 1967. To get them out of the place, they used a truck loaded with wood where the guerrillas hid. The operation was carried out successfully and they were able to reach Cochabamba without problems, where they secretly stayed at the house of a sympathiser. Similarly, members of the PCB contacted their Chilean counterparts to organise the reception of the surviving guerrillas in that country. At the beginning, all these actions were carried out without the knowledge of the PCB leadership, since the operation was going to be made public. Meanwhile, all the guerrillas stayed in different sympathisers' houses in Cochabamba. However, Inti travelled incognito to La Paz to take steps to transfer the others to the capital. The plan to take them to Oruro was also considered, but finally La Paz was the choice. Besides, the government had distributed flyers with photos of the guerrillas in La Paz, Oruro and Cochabamba, offering large sums of money as rewards.

In Chile, the members of the PCB contacted the Senator Salvador Allende to plan the reception of the survivors there. In the end, the general secretary of the PCB Jorge Kolle got involved in organising the escape of the five surviving guerrillas to Chile. The guerrillas were then taken to Oruro by car on 2 February 1968. In fact, it had been planned that only the three Cubans – Benigno, Pombo and Urbano – would cross into Chile, while the two Bolivians, Inti and Darío, would remain in the country to reorganise the ELN and thus continue the fight. From there, the escape to the border with Chile was planned. The guerrillas would make the last leg to Chile carrying small arms, pistols and revolvers, as a precaution. They all arrived in cars at the Desaguadero River, which they crossed on a boat. The three Cubans and a pair of Bolivian guides, Estanislao Villca *aka* Tani and Efraín Quicañez Aguilar, both communist sympathisers, reached the town of Sabaya either by walking or on a bus.

The authorities learned of the presence of these Cubans in the area through a telegram sent by the mayor of Sabaya and began to mobilise the police and the army to capture them, so that the guerrillas had to flee hastily. On 14 February, they left the village on foot and hid in a mountainous area. Soon after, they already heard that aircraft were flying over the area, a TAM C-47 with troops, a

Mustang fighter and a Cessna U-17. Then they walked for about seven hours and at midnight they arrived at a village called Todos los Santos, around 40 to 50 kilometres from the border with Chile. However, the Bolivian authorities also contacted their counterparts in Chile, so that if the Cubans crossed the border, they could be detained by the army or the carabineros. Paratroopers were preparing to descend in the area of border markers No. 24 to 30 with Chile and once on the ground they would be supported by troops from the Cavalry Regiment R.C.4 Ingavi, but the rainy weather prevented such actions.

In the early morning of 18 February, the two Bolivian guides and the three Cubans crossed the border on foot without knowing it. It was only in the morning that they asked some peasants of the area and they were told that they were in Chilean territory. They also learned that the Chilean carabineros were looking for them.

After a long walk, they arrived at the town of Camiña where they met Luis Berenguela, a journalist from the newspaper *El Mercurio*. They told him that they were the Cuban guerrillas who had escaped from Chile and that they wanted to turn themselves into the authorities to seek political asylum. Almost immediately, on 22 February, members of the Chilean Communist Party contacted the Cuban refugees in that town when they were already in custody of the carabineros. With all the corresponding guarantees, the three Cubans and two Bolivians were transferred in Jeeps to Iquique. Once there, they were taken to a Chilean Air Force base where they remained in custody.

On 23 February, the Cubans and Bolivians were transferred to Santiago on a Chilean Air Force aircraft under strict security measures. Once there, they were taken to a police station. Several Chilean socialist senators appeared there, including Salvador Allende. In a typical communist communiqué, these senators issued a statement to the press and the population stating that: '...the guerrillas were already in Chilean territory, after having circumvented a military-police siege of the Bolivian gorillas, the CIA and the Green Berets mercenaries of the Imperialist Army...'[23] It also praised Che Guevara and his fight with innumerable adjectives and attacked the oligarchies of Chile and Bolivia.

The following day, and after a general medical examination, they were airlifted to Easter Island on a Lan Chile aircraft. They stayed there for a few days before being transferred to Papeete, Tahiti on another flight from the same airline, this time with the company of the Senator Salvador Allende. Once there, Allende delivered them to the Cuban Ambassador in France, Baudilio Castellanos. From Tahiti, the five went to Paris on an Air France flight and from there to Prague where they arrived on 3 March. Then they went to Moscow, from where they took a direct flight to Cuba.

The end of the journey happened on 7 March, when they finally arrived in Havana, Cuba, on board an Aeroflot Tupolev Tu-114 from Moscow. They were welcomed by Fidel Castro himself and high authorities of that country.

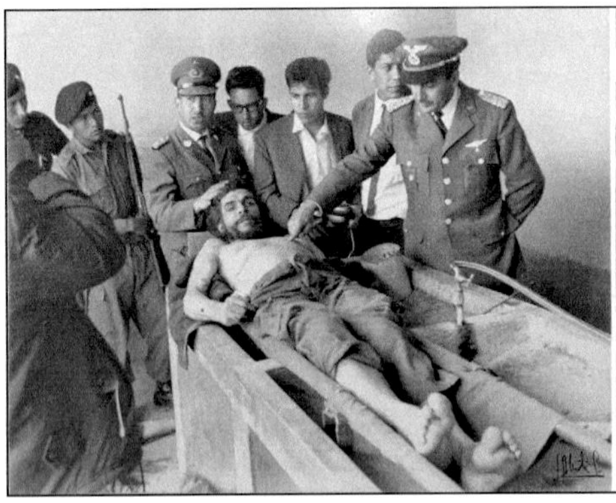

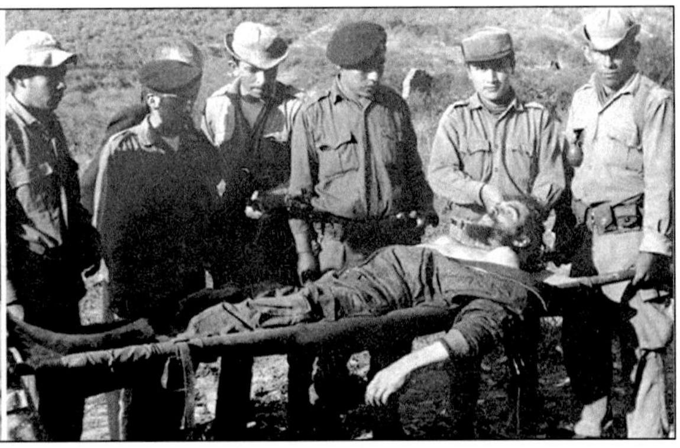

Military officers, including army Colonel Roberto Quintanilla Pérez (touching the head of Che's corpse) and several journalists in the laundry room of Nuestro Señor de Malta Hospital in Vallegrande (left). (Freddy Alborta). Army soldiers carrying Che's corpse on a stretcher (right). (Ejército Boliviano).

The Air Force Hiller OH-23 that carried the mortal remains of Che from La Higuera to Vallegrande. The pilot was Major Jaime Niño de Guzmán and CIA agent Félix Rodriguez was on board as a passenger. (FAB via Jorge Cornejo).

Vallegrande airstrip was crowded with TAM C-47s and other aircraft due to the arrival of journalists all over the world for Che's capture and death in October 1967. (Freddy Alborta).

Che's remains

There are various versions about the final destination of Che's corpse. General Juan José Torres stated that the body had been cremated, while General Alfredo Ovando stated otherwise. There was a consensus among the Bolivian military present at the scene that the cremation order was real, but that it could not be carried out due to lack of adequate means; there was also the risk of a negative reaction from the population as in Bolivia, cremation was illegal. There was also a certain consensus that the body of Guevara was buried in the early morning of 11 October by Lieutenant Colonel Selich, in a separate grave from the other six guerrillas.

The laundry room where Che's body was exhibited to the population of Vallegrande. (Freddy Alborta).

Thirty years later, on 28 June 1997, teams of Cuban scientists found five bodies clandestinely buried in a single common grave in Vallegrande, and identified among them, with the support of an Argentine forensic anthropology team, the body of Ernesto Guevara and four of his men. The corpse lacked hands, registered a high formaldehyde content, and wore clothing and items compatible with those that Guevara was supposed to be wearing at the time of being buried. On 12 July of that year, Che's remains were taken to Cuba, where they were received by a crowd to be buried at the Santa Clara Memorial, which also holds the remains of most of the leftist guerrillas who accompanied him on his failed expedition.

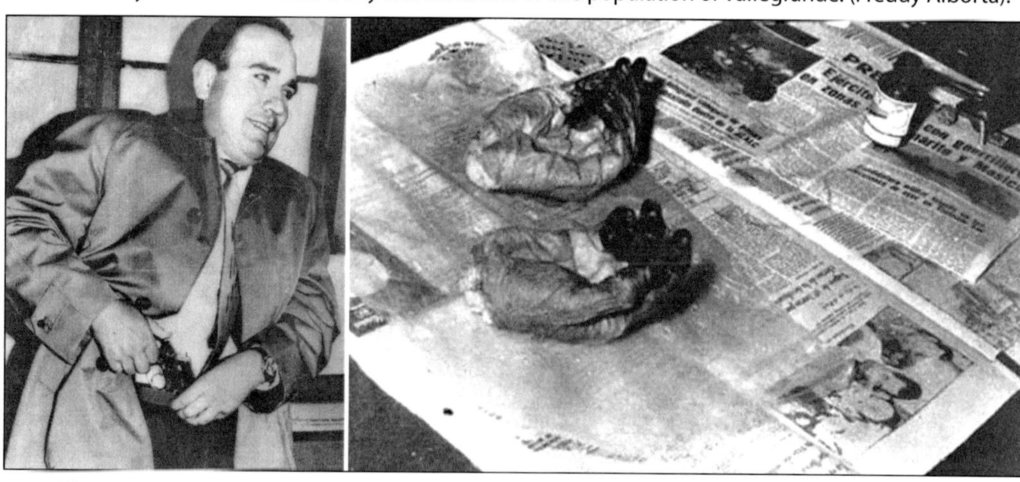

The controversial Minister of the Interior of the Barrientos government, Antonio Arguedas, was responsible for sending not only a copy of Che's diary to Cuba but also the hands amputated from the corpse of Ernesto Guevara, preserved in a glass jar in formaldehyde. (AP/Ejército Boliviano).

8 THE AFTERMATH

ELN's failed relaunch in 1969

The imprisoned guerrillas were tried in a military criminal summary trial. These included Antonio Rodriguez, Régis Debray, Ciro Bustos, José Carillo, Vicente Rocabado, Pastor Barrera, Salustino Choque and Eusebio Tapia, and they were tried for crimes against state security. All were sentenced to military prison for 30 years.

During the de facto government of General Juan José Torres and through Supreme Decrees No. 9527 and 9528, the Bolivian former guerrillas and foreigners Régis Debray and Ciro Bustos were granted amnesty. In the cases of Debray and Bustos, they were expelled from Bolivia aboard the Air Force Douglas C-47 serial TAM-18 piloted by Captain Marcelo Campos Castillo and flown to Iquique, Chile, on 23 December 1970. The Bolivian former guerrillas were allowed to return to their homes in the country. Many army officers did not agree with this amnesty since they had lost many comrades during the operations against the guerrillas in 1967.

Some of the few survivors of the Ñancahuazú guerrillas, such as Guido Álvaro Peredo Leigue *aka* Inti and David Adriazola Veizaga *aka* Dario, both Bolivians, decided to reorganise the ELN in July 1968, just nine months after its defeat by the Bolivian Army. They had, in theory, the help of the Cuban government for this task. They remained in hiding in Bolivia and planning the revival of the ELN. Inti Peredo then travelled to Cuba where, together with Manuel Piñero *aka* Barbarroja, the Cuban officer responsible for Cuban military operations abroad, they planned the return of the guerrillas to Bolivia, with the approval of Fidel Castro. Between 60 and 70 Bolivians who would form the new ELN gathered in Cuba, where they received guerrilla training in Baracoa, along with some Chileans, Argentines and Peruvians. All were militants of the communist, Maoist, Trotskyist, or socialist organisations of their countries.

The slogan was to return to the mountains, organise themselves better in order to defeat the government forces and impose a socialist-communist regime in Bolivia, in the 'best' Cuban style.

On 9 May 1969, Inti returned to Bolivia clandestinely. Around 40 of the trained guerrillas were already on Bolivian soil, waiting for the opportune moment to relaunch the revolution. On 5 September of that year, he published a message to the Bolivian people that shocked national public opinion by announcing that the battle started in Ñancahuazú was but briefly interrupted; it would start again. He did this in such a way that it publicly announced the return of the ELN to the armed struggle. The promised Cuban support did not come, so that the ELN was already in serious trouble at the beginning; furthermore, the rest of the guerrilla group that had been trained in Cuba was not allowed to leave that country until December 1969, by which time the Bolivian government had already captured and executed the guerrilla leaders.

Soon the intelligence services of the Bolivian government, as well as the CIA, discovered this new attempt and the mission was to defeat it as soon as possible. Key data on this new guerrilla attempt had been obtained through infiltrators from the army intelligence services. Added to this was the total disinterest of the Bolivian population in general towards that 'revolution', the lack of economic resources, weapons and training. The government responded with an extensive tracking campaign. On 4 September, the ELN made another announcement. Meanwhile, Inti had moved to La Paz where he remained in hiding but not for long. Once his hiding place was located, 150 policemen surrounded the house where he was taking refuge on 9 September. There was a serious clash that lasted around an hour until the police force threw a grenade through a window that severely injured Inti in his legs and arms. The police took the opportunity to break into the house and capture him. He was transferred to a jail in Achocalla where, in spite of his wounds, he was tortured. Versions about the last moments of his life indicated that Colonel Roberto Quintanilla hit him on the head with the butt of a shotgun for two hours. Finally, Dr Hebert Miranda Pereira killed him with an injection. At 2200 hours that day, the government revealed the guerrilla's body to the press with obvious signs of torture.

Months later, David Adriazola Veizaga *aka* Dario would suffer the same fate when he was captured by the police in La Paz and executed on 31 December of that year. With its leaders dead, the ELN disbanded although they would return briefly in 1970 for another revolutionary attempt. In 1969, however, the ELN could not even start its operations.

Che's avenger

But this story had other facets. A German immigrant, Monika Ertl *aka* Imilla, who had fled Germany after WWII with her family, would be in charge of avenging the death of Che and Inti. Her father, Hans Ertl, had been one of Hitler's photographers. The whole family travelled to Chile first and then to Bolivia. In 1951 they settled in the lands of Chiquitania, on a 3,000-hectare property called La Dolorida, where Hans would start a new life accompanied by his wife and daughters.

Monika became a communist and sympathised with Che Guevara's cause, although she had not been involved in the Ñancahuazú fighting. In fact, Monika later lived in Cuba where she received guerrilla training. There she became involved with Régis Debray and they planned the kidnapping of the Nazi war criminal Klaus Barbie in Bolivia to take him to France to be tried for the crimes committed during the Second World War.

On 15 October 1967, the Cuban Prime Minister Fidel Castro informed the Cuban people and the press about the death of Che Guevara in Bolivia. Castro is showing a picture of high-ranking Bolivian officers with General Ovando celebrating Che's death. (Open source).

FUERZAS ARMADAS DE BOLIVIA
4a. DIVISIÓN DE EJÉRCITO
CAMIRI

DIPLOMA
CAMPAÑA CONTRA - GUERRILLERA

Grado Nombre y Apellidos: Dgto Augusto Obendo Carrion
Unidad o Repartición: Compañia Divisionaria
Cargo que Desempeñó: Fusilero
Tiempo de Servicios: Seis Meses
Acciones en las que tomó parte: Tiraboy, Yumao, la Pesca, Rio Rositas y Operación "CINTHYA"

COMTE. 4a. DIV. DEL EJÉRCITO
Cnel. Luis Reque Terán
Camiri 30 de NOV. de 1967

Each soldier who participated in the fight against the guerrillas received a certificate of recognition with his name and the places where he fought. The specimen above belonged to a rifleman of the IV Army Division. (Ejército Boliviano).

As Monika grew closer to the ELN, she distanced herself from her family. Although her father Hans maintained a good relationship with Monika, when she proposed to turn the family farm into a guerrilla training camp, he expelled her without further consideration. Monika had had a love affair with Inti Peredo and swore to avenge his death; she was also motivated because Colonel Quintanilla had cut Che's hands off. Monika considered Che as a god.

For his part, Colonel Quintanilla, fearing an attack on his person, managed to get the government to name him Bolivian Consul in Hamburg, Germany. Monika travelled to Germany in March 1971 determined to kill Colonel Quintanilla. On 1 April of that year, she requested an interview at the Bolivian Consulate in Hamburg, posing as an Australian tourist who wanted to visit Bolivia. Colonel Quintanilla himself attended her in his office. At one point during the conversation, Monika pulled out a Colt Cobra .38 calibre revolver and fired three shots at the consul, killing him instantly.

After carrying out the murder, Monika fled, leaving behind her blonde wig, her glasses, the revolver and a handbag which contained a piece of paper saying: 'Victory or death. ELN.' From then on, the persecution of the Bolivian intelligence services and the CIA began. She was seen in France and Cuba and used an Argentine passport, although she eventually returned to Bolivia.

The poster widely distributed to the press and the population in search of the five survivors of the guerrilla, whose text in Spanish reads: '*REWARD. 10 Million Bolivian Pesos for each one. These are the mercenary bandits at the service of Castrocommunism. These are the causes of mourning and pain in Bolivian homes. Information that turns out to be true will entitle you to the reward. Bolivian citizen, help us capture them alive if possible.*' (Open source).

The Chilean Socialist Senator Salvador Allende in 1967. (Open source).

If there was someone in La Paz who knew her well, it was 'Onkle' Klaus (Uncle Klaus) and he was behind her steps. Due to his relationship with his father Hans Ertl, Onkle Klaus, as Monika called him, was none other than former *SS Hauptsturmführer* Klaus Barbie Altmann, who had settled in Bolivia. with the help of the American Counter-Intelligence Corps under the name of Klaus Altmann Hansen. He became a Bolivian Army lieutenant colonel *Honoris Causa* since he was a military advisor for the government.

Monika moved often, living clandestinely and it was not easy to locate her. On one occasion, in the heart of La Paz, she was recognised by Barbie even though she was very well disguised. She looked like a gypsy or a hippie but Barbie singled her out for her striking legs and elongated earlobes. Barbie immediately put the 'system' on alert and three days later she was located in the El Alto neighbourhood when she arrived at a clandestine safe house accompanied by an Argentine. It was 12 May 1973, and when the police arrived and surrounded the place, Monika and her partner put up a tenacious resistance with their guns until they ran out of ammunition. They were captured and taken to a police station. After torturing her, she was executed and buried. It was later declared that she had died in combat but her father denounced that, saying before she died she had been tortured.

During the first democratic government after the era of de facto military regimes in Bolivia, Barbie was deported to France in 1983. He was tried and finally, on 4 July 1987, was sentenced to life imprisonment for crimes against humanity. Four years later, while in prison on 25 September 1991, he died of leukaemia.

The final attempt: the 1970 Teoponte Guerrilla

Another attempt to form a guerilla movement occurred in 1970 and was known as the Teoponte Guerrilla, because it took place in the area with that name (*Teoponte* is a compound word in the Lecos language; *teo* is a thorny bush with red flowers and *ponte* means bridge or pampa), north of La Paz. Many of its members had belonged to Inti Peredo's ELN and they decided to make another revolutionary attempt. The far-left guerrilla group was led by the Chilean journalist Elmo Catalán Avilés *aka* Ricardo and the Bolivian Osvaldo Peredo *aka* Chato, who was Inti Peredo's brother. Chato was a militant member of the PCB and received medical training but left that profession when he joined Che Guevara's Ñancahuazú guerrilla logistic chain in 1967. However, due to the need for medical services,

After Ñancahuazú and fleeing, from left to right: Harry Villegas *aka* Pombo, Dariel Alarcón *aka* Benigno, Leonardo Tamayo *aka* Urbano, Guido Peredo *aka* Inti and David Adriazola *aka* Darío. The Cubans crossed to Chile with their guides, and the two Bolivians guerrillas remained in their country in hiding. (Open source).

he was sent to the Soviet Union where he received advanced medical and ideological training at Patrice Lumumba University in Moscow. When he returned, he became one of the leaders of the ELN.

Elmo Catalán *aka* Ricardo and his partner Genny Köhler *aka* Victoria would be murdered by an ELN member, Anibal Crespo Ross, in Cochabamba on 8 June 1970 in obscure circumstances, with all the trappings of a crime of passion.

On 18 July 1970, in order not to arouse suspicion, the 67 ELN members travelled in two buses and a van to Teoponte with credentials as literacy teachers, with their weapons hidden in their suitcases and handbags.

On the following day, Chato Peredo officially relaunched the ELN for another guerrilla attempt. This organisation was made up of young people linked to the leadership of the Bolivian University Confederation (CUB) of the Local University Federations (FULES), as well as left-wing organisations, members of the ELN created by Che Guevara, peasants and revolutionary militants from Chile, Argentina and Peru. The initial guerrilla focus was located on the Andean slope north of La Paz, in the area of the Kaka and Tipuani Rivers, Teoponte region. The ELN 'General Staff' in Teoponte was made up of Osvaldo Peredo *aka* Chato, Tani Wilka Kolke *aka* Alejandro, Jorge Ruíz Paz *aka* Omar and Luis Barriga Luna *aka* Martin.

The guerrilla column of 67 men broke into the mining town of Teoponte, under the command of Chato Peredo. This small insurgent force was made up of 53 Bolivians, eight Chileans, two

Once again, troops were transported with TAM C-47s, Mustang fighters and Cessna U-17 liaison aircraft which were mobilised to locate the surviving guerrillas. (FAB via Jorge Cornejo).

Argentines, one Peruvian, one Brazilian, one Colombian, and one Spanish-American. In its ranks were professionals, workers and peasants.

The ELN combatants in 1970 were the following:

Bolivians:

Osvaldo Peredo *aka Chato* or *Nano,* Benito Mamani *aka Popi,* Néstor Paz Zamora *aka Francisco,* Darío Busch Barbery *aka Gregorio,* Álvaro Urquieta Paz *aka César,* Hugo Rodríguez Román *aka Ignacio,* Julio César Pérez López *aka Oscar,* Ricardo Justiniano *aka Loco Sergio,* Evaristo Bustos Araníbar *aka Dante,* Clemente Fernández *aka Nelson,* Enrique Farfán Maella *aka Chapaco,* Carlos Suárez Coimbra *aka Mamerto,* Javier Landívar Vilar *aka Quirito,* Benjamín Cordeiro *aka Casiano,* Hugo Bohórquez Fernández *aka Mauricio,* Pepe Arce Paravicini *aka Pedrito,* Raúl Ibarguen Coronel *aka Chaska,* Moisés Rueda Peña *aka Ringo,* Moisés Suárez Moreno *aka David,* Jorge Gustavo Ruiz Díaz *aka Omar,* Cancio Plaza Astrona *aka Santiago,* Edison Cegada Jurado *aka Jesús,* Ricardo Imakaki Vera *aka Marcos,* Rolando Araníbar Bustos *aka Sebas,* Adolfo Quiroga Bonadona *aka Gordo,* Adolfo Huici Alborta *aka Choco,* Antonio Figueroa *aka Toño,* Luis Letellier Araoz *aka Mauro,* Juan José Saavedra *aka Marco Antonio,* Alberto Revollo Olmos *aka Chaña,* Carlos Suárez Soto *aka Alfonso,* Carlos Antonio Cortés Rueda *aka Juanito,* Filiberto Parra *aka Jacobo,* Eloy Mollo Mamani *aka Dulio,* Herminio Vilka Kolke *aka Santos,* Mario Carvajal Ruiz *aka Carlos,* Efraín Lazarazu Cabrera *aka Mongol,* Alberto Caballero Medinacelli *aka Sergio,* Gonzalo Rojas Paredes *aka Jaime,* Francisco Imakaki Vera *aka Kolla,* Federico Argote *aka Ferte,* Estanislao Vilka Kolke *aka Alejandro,* Luis Barriga Luna *aka Martín,* Emilio Quiroga Bonadona *aka Napoleón,* Edgar Soria Galvarro *aka Pedro,* Carlos Navarro Lara *aka Luis,* Rafael Antezana *aka Changuito,* Delfín Mérida Vargas *aka Mario,* Lorgio Roca Parada *aka Aníbal,* Horacio Rueda Peña *aka José María,* Indalecio Nogales *aka Claudio* and Norberto Domínguez Silva *aka Jorgito.*

Chilean:

Guillermo Tirso Montiel Martínez *aka Pablo,* Julio Alfredo de la Cruz Olivares Romero *aka Cristian,* Calixto Pacheco González *aka Rogelio,* Guillermo Véliz González *aka Gastón,* José Miguel Arturo Celiz González *aka Alberto,* Carlos Brain Pizarro *aka Peruchin,* Hernán Ampuero Ferrada *aka Poropopó* and Julio E. Sambrano Acuña *aka Manuel*

Argentine:

Oscar Ricardo Puente *aka Diego* and Rubén Cerdal *aka Oswaldo.*

Peruvian:

Autero Callapiña Hurtado *aka Raúl.*

Brazilian:

Luis Renato Pires Almeida *aka Dippy.*

Colombian:

Fabián Barga *aka Chuma.*

Spanish-American:

Jorge D. Fernández Meana *aka Felipe.*

Once in Teoponte, the guerrillas started what they called Operación Ricardo Victoria. Later it spread to other towns in the province of Larecaja, north of La Paz, including Esperanza, Chocopani, Chimaque, and Pajonal Vivaque, in an area of 500 square kilometres. The objective after consolidating their presence in that area was to continue to the gold mining towns of Caranaví and Tipuani, but they did not reach the towns due to the rapid and forceful response of the armed forces. In the meantime, the guerrillas seized the facilities of the American mining company South American Placers, where they kidnapped two German technicians, Günter Lerch and Eugene Schulhauser. Their aim was to pressure the government to release 10 imprisoned guerrillas, and they also stole 50,000 Bolivian pesos.

Faced with this situation, the military government of General Ovando declared the provinces of Caupolicán, Larecaja and Nor Yungas in the Department of La Paz a military zone and established a State of Siege throughout the country. The government called on the guerrillas to put an end to their adventure and sent 10 guerrillas to Arica, Chile on a military plane. For their part, the guerrillas freed the two Germans they had kidnapped.

The Bolivian Army, with better preparation for the anti-subversive fight than in the fight against Guevara's 53 guerrillas in 1967, launched an effective campaign of extermination against Teoponte's column. Around 1,500 Army Rangers were deployed in the area. The military commanders faithfully complied with General Ovando's order: 'No wounded, no prisoners.' Thus, the insurgents who were not killed in combat were shot after being captured. The first armed clash between the army and the guerrillas took place at the end of July, where eight guerrillas and one soldier were killed.

Over 100 days, the guerrillas fell one by one, with isolated skirmishes, encirclements and fleeing in the jungle areas, while physical exhaustion, hunger and despair spread. Two of the combatants deserted, after stealing two cans of sardines, and were captured and executed by their own comrades.

In addition to being persecuted and harassed by army and police troops and enduring air raids by the Bolivian Air Force T-6Ds and P-51Ds using napalm, they had to endure terrible weather conditions in the jungle and mountains, extreme cold, food and weapons shortages because their logistics chain was abruptly cut. In just over 100 days, 58 guerrillas had been killed by the army, police and the air force and the fight finally ended in October of that year.

President General Juan José Torres. (Ejército Boliviano).

- **July** 1970: Eight in El Pajonal and two in Esperanza.
- **August** 1970: Three in Cholcaya and three in Hamburgo.
- **September** 1970: Three in Quebrada Quevedo, two in Hamburgo, two in Chimate, one in Culibrillana, three in La Noria, three in Vilaque, four in San Antonio, two in Mapiri and three in Santa Rosa.
- **October** 1970: Two in Hamburgo, seven in unknown places and five in San Jorge.

However, according to the version of the survivors, only nine or 10 died in combat, several died of starvation and the rest were captured alive and shot by the army. They recognised, however, that two guerrillas were shot by their comrades for having stolen food from the group.

Meanwhile General Juan José Torres assumed power through a popular uprising, with the participation of workers, peasant organisations, the university movement, and a sector of the military loyal to Torres on 7 October 1970, displacing General Alfredo Ovando from the presidency and establishing a military government of the national left.

The last eight guerrilla survivors, in miserable conditions, were rescued by gold miners on 26 October in the jungle area of Cotopampa. They convinced them to hand over their weapons and surrender. They went to the town of Tipuani on foot where they only arrived on 4 November. They were transferred on an air force aircraft to La Paz, accompanied by some miners and Catholic Church representatives. Luckily for them, Army General Juan José Torres was ruling. On this occasion, criminal proceedings were not opened against the subversives and two days later they were deported to Chile on the Air Force Douglas C-47 serial TAM-29 – this was another stroke of luck, since the socialist President Dr Salvador Allende had just taken office.

One of the survivors was Chato Peredo. In 1997, he joined Evo Morales's *Movimiento al Socialismo* (MAS/Movement to Socialism) and in 2011 he published a book on his guerrilla experience. He passed away on 12 January 2021 in Santa Cruz de la Sierra.

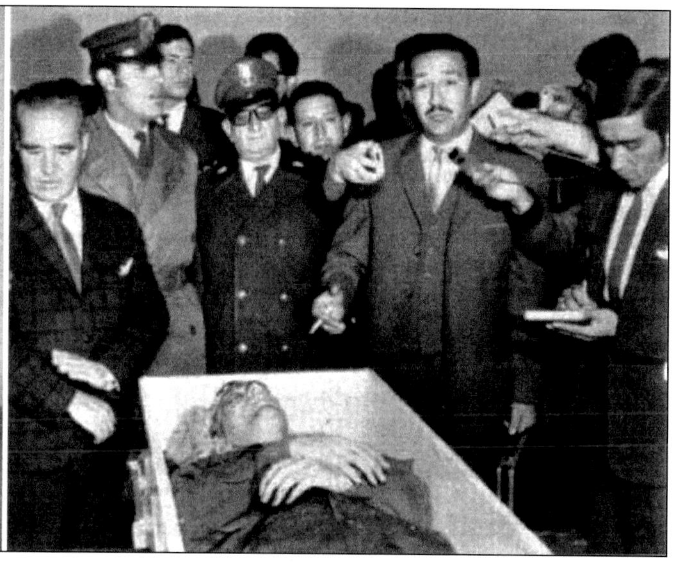

Guido Álvaro Peredo Leigue *aka* Inti (left). Colonel Quintanilla (second right) with some journalists and police officers next to Inti's coffin. (Policía Boliviana).

Very few ELN members could escape. The others were captured and most of them executed. The planning of that guerrilla force was lamentable; they looked like city hikers who were physically and militarily ill-prepared, with very poor logistics, who had to face a well-armed professional army that had already accumulated experience in the anti-guerrilla fight. Some so-called guerrillas could not bear the terrible conditions of the terrain and weather, and committed suicide.

According to Bolivian Army official records, the 53 guerrillas killed in action were the following:

EPILOGUE

After the revolutionary victory in Cuba in 1959, the policy of the new regime, which declared itself communist, was to export the revolution to all Latin America, strongly supporting the formation of the so-called 'National Liberation Armies'. In this context, the ELN led by Che Guevara arose, a subject widely covered in this volume.

Che's final adventure was a resounding failure and ended with his execution. Two more attempts by Marxist guerrillas arose in Bolivia that were quickly defeated by the Bolivian government security forces.

The question is now, why did Che's guerrilla uprising fail? According to the analysis carried out by retired Bolivian Army Major General Gary Prado Salmón, the reasons for the failure of the guerrillas were the following:

Firstly, Bolivia in 1967 had a constitutional government, elected in free elections with 61.81 percent of the votes. General Barrientos

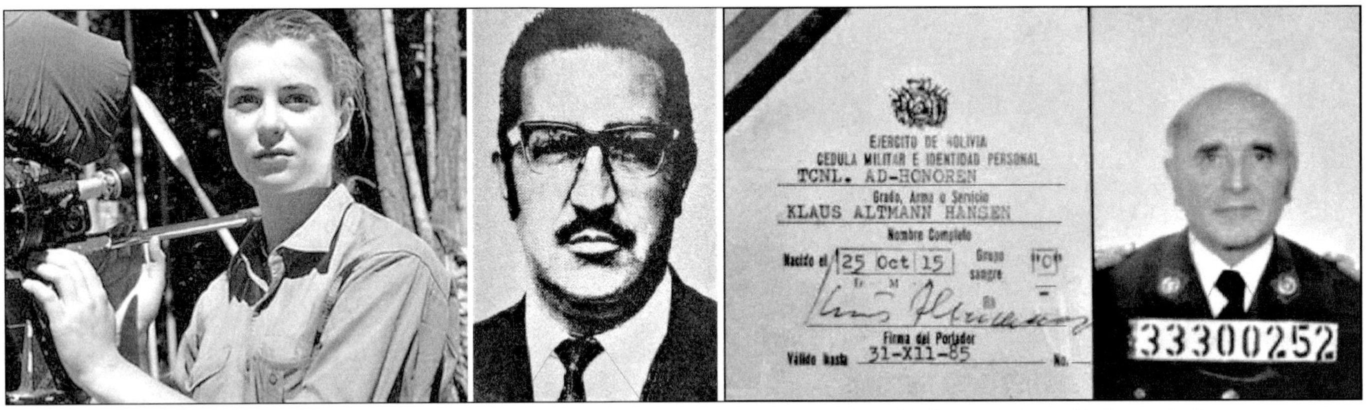

Monika Ertl *aka* Imilla, 'Che's avenger'. (left). Bolivian Consul in Hamburg, Colonel Roberto Quintanilla (centre). Klaus Barbie's military identification in Bolivia as Lieutenant Colonel Klaus Altmann Hansen (right). (Open source).

was highly appreciated by various sectors, especially the peasantry, and it was precisely the peasants who carried out important intelligence tasks by denouncing the guerrillas.

Chilean journalist Elmo Catalán Avilés *aka* Ricardo, one of the ELN leaders in 1970 (left). The General Staff of the ELN in 1970: from left to right, Estanislao Villca *aka* Alejandro, Jorge Fernández *aka* Felipe, Osvaldo Peredo *aka* Chato, Jorge Ruiz *aka* Omar and Luis Barriga *aka* Martín. (Open source).

Congress and all state institutions were fully functioning, there was freedom of the press and there were no political prisoners or exiles, although at the beginning of the conflict leftist leaders were arrested.

In addition, there had been important achievements for the civilian population such as the Agrarian Reform, and the rights to vote for women and indigenous people since the 1952 Revolution with the MNR.

The guerrillas had absolutely no popular support, not even from the mining and labour sectors, which questioned the Barrientos government. Nor did they have the support of the left-wing political parties.

The typical peasant mistrusted strangers in his area and especially if they were foreigners. The guerrillas were first met with the passivity of the peasants and later with hostility translated into immediate denunciation to the police and military authorities.

Che also did not believe that the American government would help a poor and distant country like Bolivia and although at the beginning of the conflict the army troops were poorly trained, the MTT mission of the US Army managed to alleviate this problem with the training of the Ranger-2 battalion which played an important role in the fight against the guerrillas.

Additionally, Che made several tactical errors. He never attacked military installations, staying almost always in the jungle or mountains and only raided some towns to buy food and medicine. The latter was a big mistake since their presence in the area was immediately reported to the military authorities.

Che repeatedly ignored opportunities to destroy the moral of Bolivian Army effectives. His continual habit of releasing army POWs, although humane, was really unparalleled in the history of guerrilla combat.

Che did not have formal military training but just guerrilla training, which was not enough. He did very well as a field commander in Sierra Maestra, Cuba, while carrying out orders from Fidel but it was a real disaster when he led his guerrillas in Bolivia when he did not even follow the principles established by himself in his writings and publications. He was a very poor strategist and his own guerrilla tactics were turned against him and his guerrillas when used by the Bolivian Army.

Elmo Catalán *aka* Ricardo (left) and Genny Köhler *aka* Victoria (right). (Open source).

Even within the organisational structure of Che's guerrillas, the Cubans were most trusted and held important positions, relegating Bolivians to menial tasks. This caused severe internal conflicts in the guerrillas.

The separation of the subversive forces into two columns weakened the guerrillas and made it easier for the army to destroy them.

The data provided by Regis Debray, Ciro Bustos and some other captured guerrillas to the Bolivian authorities, in order to save their own lives, contributed to the identification and capture of Che and his guerrillas. Furthermore, the 'carelessness' of the guerrilla Tania who left key documents abandoned in a Jeep meant that the Bolivian police were able to dismantle the guerrillas' logistical support network.

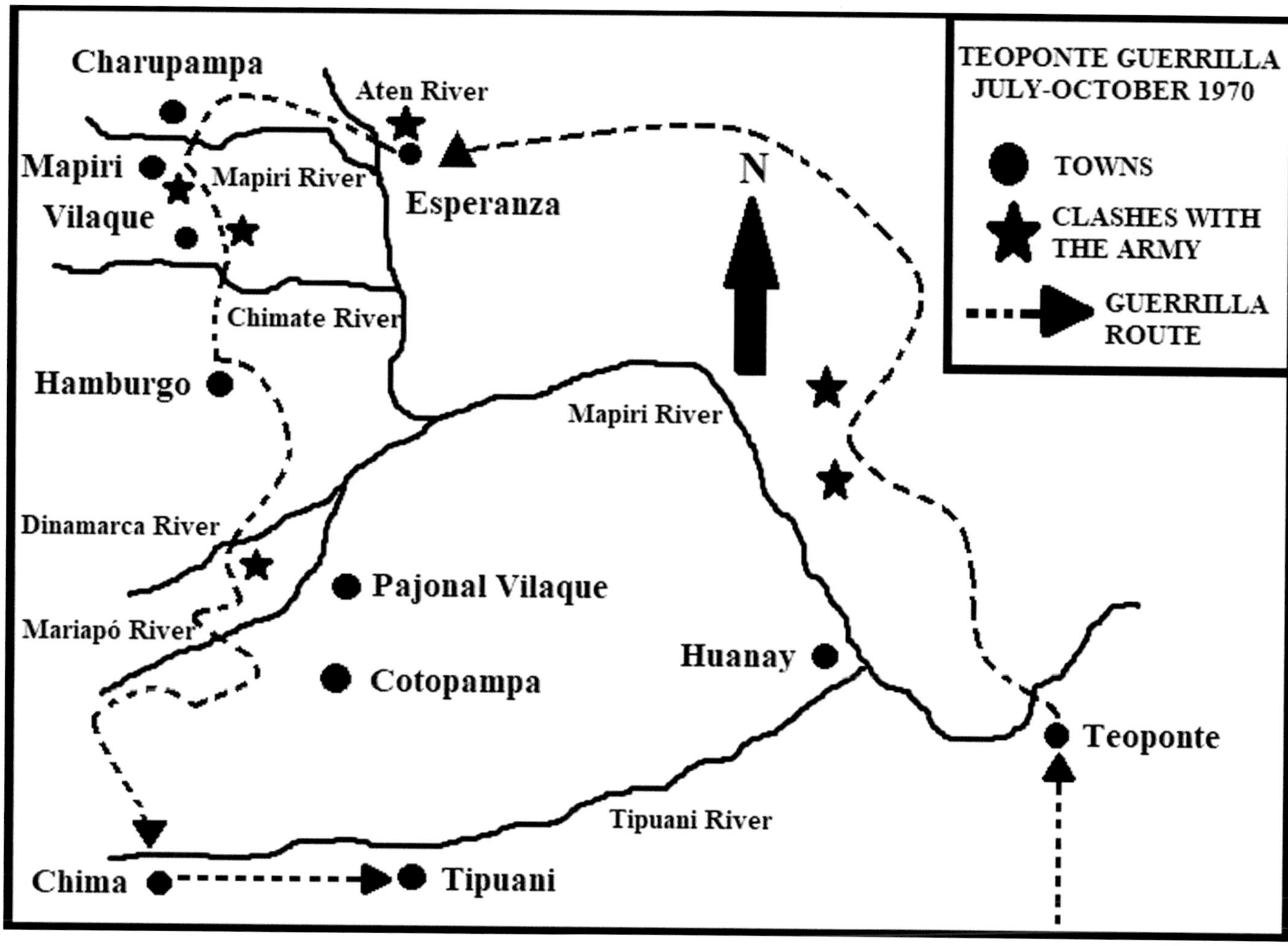

(Map by author)

The long-awaited Cuban help never arrived and their urban logistical support was discovered and suppressed, so they were left alone without any outside support.

Finally, Che's health deteriorated markedly during 1967, especially because he could not get medicine to alleviate his chronic asthma. Many times he had to be helped by his own comrades when he could not bear long walks. His destroyed health certainly seriously impaired his judgement.

Che's curse?

Several key personalities of the Bolivian government and armed forces ended their days tragically. Che's followers and admirers have stated that the tragic death of their leader has been avenged in some way.

- President General René Barrientos tragically died in a helicopter crash in 1969.
- The former Commander of the Armed Forces General Alfredo Ovando became very ill and died in 1982 and his family was the victim of a tragedy when his eldest son died in a plane crash on a FAB Cavalier TF-51D Mustang fighter in 1970 in Lake Titicaca.
- Former Army Chief of Staff and de facto President of Bolivia, General Juan José Torres, was assassinated by subversives according to one version, or by the ultra-right Triple A organisation according to another version, in Buenos Aires in 1976.
- The former Commander of the VIII Army Division, General Joaquín Zenteno Anaya, was murdered on a Paris street in 1976 by two French hitmen.
- Former Army Intelligence Chief Colonel Roberto Quintanilla was assassinated in his office at the Bolivian consulate in Hamburg in 1970 by the guerrilla Mónica Ertl.
- Former Ranger Regiment Commander Colonel Andrés Selich was assassinated in La Paz in 1973.
- In the case of Gary Prado, now a general, he was accidentally shot by one of his soldiers in 1981 during an occupation of an oil field and as a consequence he was paralysed from the waist down, living the rest of his life in a wheelchair.
- Eduardo Huerta, the sub-lieutenant of the army who commanded the Second Platoon of Company A which attacked Che's guerrillas, tragically died in a car accident on 9 October 1970.
- Honorato Rojas, the peasant who betrayed Joaquín's guerrilla column with vital information that led to the death of nine guerrillas in Vado del Yeso, was assassinated by a Bolivian communist two years later, on 15 July 1969, in his home near Santa Cruz.
- The former Minister of the Interior of the Barrientos government, the controversial Antonio Arguedas, first took refuge in Chile. Upon returning to Bolivia at the end of the 70s, he suffered two serious attacks, miraculously saving himself. He went into exile again, that time in Cuba. He died in Bolivia under strange circumstances when a bomb he carried with him exploded in the year 2000.

The President Army General Alfredo Ovando Candia (left). Army troops mobilised in the Teoponte area in 1970 (centre). General Juan José Torres who assumed the presidency on 7 October 1970. (Ejército Boliviano).

In 1967, several of the FAB's Cavalier TF-51D Mustangs received a new camouflage in two shades of green, with wingtips in tan, and a toned-down version of the shark mouth insignia. The Mustangs carried out raids with napalm bombs against the Teoponte guerrillas. (FAB via Jorge Cornejo).

A FAB P-51 fighter pilot runs to his plane for a sortie, symbolically encouraged by a condor. (FAB).

After the military regimes of Generals Alfredo Ovando (1969-70), Juan José Torres (1970–71), Hugo Bánzer (1971–78), Juan Pereda Asbún (1978) and David Padilla (1978–79), there was a brief lapse of civil government by Walter Guevara Arze of the MNR (1979). Another brief military government followed, that of General Alberto Natush Busch (1979) and then the first woman to become President of Bolivia, the MNR's Lydia Gueiler Tejada (1979–80). Between 1980 and 1982 the last three military governments took place, those of Generals Luis García Meza, Celso Torrelio Villa and finally Guido Vildoso Calderón. Since then and to date, there have been successive civilian presidents elected in democratic elections or constitutional presidential succession by resignation of the president: Hernán Siles Suazo (UDP/1982–1985), Víctor Paz Estenssoro (MNR/1985–1989), Jaime Paz Zamora (MIR/1989–1993), Gonzalo Sánchez de Losada (MNR/1993–1997), Hugo Bánzer (ADN/1997–2001), Jorge Quiroga (ADN/2001–2002), Gonzalo Sánchez de Losada once again (MNR/2002–2003), Carlos Mesa Gisbert (MNR/2003–2005) and Eduardo Rodríguez (Independent/2005–2006).

Until the advent of socialist governments, the Bolivian Armed Forces proudly remembered the victory over the Ñancahuazú *and Teoponte* guerrillas with public acts every year and they honoured those officers, non-commissioned officers and soldiers who fell in combat between 1967 and 1970, as well as the veterans of those campaigns.

From 2006 to 2019, socialism governed the country through the MAS with the president of indigenous origin, Evo Morales. He was forced to resign when a massive fraud was discovered in his fourth presidential election, and Jeanine Áñez Chávez (MDS) assumed the presidency until 2020. After a long time, during the brief period of the Añez government, a tribute was paid to officers, non-commissioned officers and soldiers of the Ñancahuazú Campaign of 1967. In the last elections, the MAS once again won the government in the figure of Luis Arce (MAS). The MAS socialist governments have remembered and honoured Che Guevara and his fellow guerrillas as national 'heroes', 'victims' of

In air operations, FAB Cessna U-17s were also used as FACs and for bomb raids against the guerrilla (left). (FAB via Jorge Cornejo).

the military, the CIA, the FBI and the 'Yankee Empire'. They even erected monuments to Che's memory: one big statue in El Alto and a huge bust and statue in La Higuera. The small school in La Higuera where Che was executed was converted to a sort of museum to his memory. Of course, the armed forces have stopped honouring and remembering their combatants as a way of 'pleasing' the socialist authorities on duty, and as a small sample of this, when Retired Major General Gary Prado Salmón died at the age of 84 on 6 May 2023, no military tribute was offered to that officer. And to end this story, Che Guevara's executioner, retired Bolivian Army Chief Warrant Officer Mario Terán Salazar, died at the age of 79 in Santa Cruz de la Sierra on 10 March 2022.

Just as the socialist governments in Bolivia remember and honour Che and his guerrillas, the Association of Veterans of the Army's operations in Ñancahuazú have been meeting every year to honour all their comrades who fell in combat in 1967.

Clockwise: FAB T-28 Trojan, F-51 Mustang, T-6D Texan and C-54 Liftmaster pilots. (FAB).

Top row, from left to right: Retired Major General Gary Prado Salmón, who passed away in 2023; retired NCO Mario Terán Salazar, who died in 2022, and former CIA Agent Félix Rodriguez, 82 years old at present. Bottom row, from left to right: former guerrillas Harry Antonio Villegas Tamayo *aka* Pombo, who passed away in 2019; Leonardo Tamayo Núñez, *aka* Urbano now 82, and Osvaldo Peredo *aka* Chato, who passed away in 2021. (Open source).

APPENDICES

Table 10: Staff of the IV & VIII Army Divisions[24]

			VIII Army Division
IV Army Division	March–May–1967	June–November 1967	June–December 1967
Commander:	Col. Humberto Rocha Urquieta	Col. Luís Reque Terán	Col. Joaquín Zenteno Anaya (*)
Chief of Staff:	Col. Juan Fernández Cálzaga	Col. Eladio Sánchez Gironda	Col. Ricardo Gonzáles Lock.
G-1: Personnel	Lt. Col. Vicente Antezana Arévalo	Capt. Humberto Cayoja Riart	Lt. Col. Hugo Ugalde
G-2: Intelligence	Lt. Col. Carlos Romero Arévalo	Maj. Hugo Echeverría Tardío	Maj. Arnaldo Saucedo Parada
G-3: Operations	Maj. Armando Reyes Villa	Maj. Víctor Castillo Suárez	Maj. Remberto Vilar
G-4: Logistics	Lt. Col. Carlos Klagges Strinford.	Lt. Col. Alberto Libera Cortéz	Lt. Col. Aldo Justiniano
Aide-de-camp:	-	-	Lt. Aguilar

(*) Col. Joaquín Zenteno Anaya replaced Col. Roberto Vargas Claros, Commander of the VIII Division from March to May 1967.

Table 11: Bolivian Army effectives and civilians killed by the ELN.[25]

Date	**Name**	**Army Unit**	**Place**
23 March 1967	Sub Lt. Rubén Amézaga Faure	IV Army Division	Ñancahuazú
23 March 1967	Private Juan Alvarado Romero	IV Army Division	Ñancahuazú
23 March 1967	Private Amador Armaza Castillo	IV Army Division	Ñancahuazú
23 March 1967	Private Santiago Gallardo Murillo	IV Army Division	Ñancahuazú
23 March 1967	Private Cecilio Márquez León	IV Army Division	Ñancahuazú
23 March 1967	Mr. Epifanio Vargas	Civilian guide	Ñancahuazú
23 March 1967	Mr. Pedro Romero García	Civilian guide	Ñancahuazú
10 April 1967	Lt. Jorge Ayala Chávez	Special Troops	Iripití
10 April 1967	Lt. Luis Saavedra Arambel	Special Troops	Iripití

Table 11 (continued): Bolivian Army effectives and civilians killed by the ELN.[25]			
10 April 1967	NCO Raúl Cornejo Campos	Special Troops	Iripití
10 April 1967	Private Marcelo Ávalos Pacaño	Infantry Reg. R.I.11	Iripití
10 April 1967	Private José Bigabriel Sánchez	Special Troops	Iripití
10 April 1967	Private Serapio Chavarría Arancibia	IV Army Division	Iripití
10 April 1967	Private Ángel Flores Caballero	Special Troops	Iripití
10 April 1967	Private Marcelo Maldonado Mita	Special Troops	Iripití
10 April 1967	Private Víctor Miranda Vidaurre	IV Army Division	Iripití
10 April 1967	Private Zenón Parada Mendieta	Special Troops	Iripití
10 April 1967	Private Jaime Sanabria Sandoval	Special Troops	Iripití
24 April 1967	Sgt. Guillermo Torres Martínez	Infantry Reg. RI.2	Taperillas
25 April 1967	Sgt. Villanueva Sánchez Cerro	Bolivian Police	El Mesón
25 April 1967	Mr. Luis Beltrán Roda	Civilian guide	El Mesón
26 April 1967	Private Miguel Espada Chumacero	Infantry Reg. RI.2	Taperillas
09 May 1967	Sub Lt. Henry Laredo Arce	NCO School	Ñancahuazú
09 May 1967	Corporal Alfredo Arroyo Pizarro	NCO School	Ñancahuazú
09 May 1967	Corporal Wilfredo Banegas Dorado	Infantry Reg. RI.24	El Espino
09 May 1967	Corporal Luis Peláez Alpiri	NCO School	Ñancahuazú
30 May 1967	Sub Lt. Eduardo Velarde Rodríguez	Infantry Reg. RI.24	El Espino
01 June 1967	Mr. Alejandro Saldías	Civilian guide	Muchiri
10 June 1967	Private Antonio Melgar Arteaga	Trinidad Company	El Cafetal
26 June 1967	Corporal Gerónimo Martínez Rivero	Mixed Company	Florida
26 June 1967	Private Mario Bautista Arnéz	VIII Army Division	Florida
26 June 1967	Private Augusto Córdova Arispe	VIII Army Division	Florida
06 July 1967	Private José Verazaín Llanos	Infantry Reg. RI.13	Samaipata
27 July 1967	Mr. J. Armando Cortez E.	Civilian guide	Corralones
30 July 1967	Private Rodolfo Mendía S.	Trinidad Company	Morocos
30 July 1967	Private Manuel Vejarano Vedía	Trinidad Company	Morocos
30 July 1967	Private Zenón Zabala Vellarde	Trinidad Company	Morocos
30 July 1967	Private Antonio Zabala Rapo	Trinidad Company	Morocos
31 August 1967	Private Antonio Vaca Céspedes	Infantry Reg. RI.12	Vado del Yeso
03 September 1967	Private Benito Velasco Gutiérrez	Infantry Reg. RI.13	Yajo Pampa
08 October 1967	Private Mario Characayo Mena	Rangers	El Churo
08 October 1967	Private Sabino Cossío Muriel	Rangers	El Churo
08 October 1967	Private Mario Lafuente Patiño	Rangers	El Churo
08 October 1967	Private Manuel Morales López	Rangers	El Churo
12 October 1967	Private Abel Callapa Cuéllar	Rangers	Naranjal
12 October 1967	Private Facundo Cruz Gutiérrez	Rangers	Naranjal
12 October 1967	Private Franz Muriel Castro	Rangers	Naranjal
12 October 1967	Mr. Daniel Calani Quispe	Civilian guide	Naranjal
12 October 1967	Mr. Ciro Robles Moscoso	Civilian guide	Naranjal
Total number of victims killed by the ELN: 42 Army effectives and 7 civilians.			
Total number of victims wounded in action: 35 Army effectives and 2 civilians.			

Table 12: Bolivian Armed Forces ranks (officers).[26]		
Bolivian Army	**Bolivian Navy**	**Bolivian Air Force**
General de Ejército (General of the Army)	Almirante (Admiral)	General de la Fuerza Aérea (Air Force General)
General de División (Major General)	Vicealmirante (Vice Admiral)	General de División Aérea (Air Division General)
General de Brigada (Brigadier General)	Contraalmirante (Rear Admiral)	General de Brigada Aérea (Air Brigade General)
Coronel (Colonel)	Capitán de Navío (Captain)	Coronel de Aviación (Air Force Colonel)
Teniente Coronel (Lieutenant Colonel)	Capitán de Fragata (Frigate Captain)	Teniente Coronel de Aviación (Air Force Lt. Col.)
Mayor (Major)	Capitán de Corbeta (Corvette Captain)	Mayor de Aviación (Air Force Major)
Capitán (Captain)	Teniente de Navío (Ship Lieutenant)	Capitán de Aviación (Air Force Captain)
Teniente (Lieutenant)	Teniente Primero (First Lieutenant)	Teniente de Aviación (Air Force Lieutenant)
Subteniente (Sub Lieutenant)	Teniente Segundo (Second Lieutenant.)	Sub Teniente de Aviación (Air Force Sub Lieutenant)
-	Alférez (Ensign)	-

Table 13: Bolivian Armed Forces ranks (NCOs).[27]		
Bolivian Army	**Bolivian Navy**	**Bolivian Air Force**
Sub Oficial Mayor (Chief Warrant Officer)	Maestro Técnico de Primera (1st Technical Master)	Sub Oficial Mayor (Chief Warrant Officer)
Sub Oficial Primero (1st Chief Officer)	Maestro Técnico de Segunda (2nd Technical Master)	Sub Oficial Primero (1st Chief Officer)
Sub Oficial Segundo (2nd Chief Officer)	Maestro de Primera (1st Class Master Chief)	Sub Oficial Segundo (2nd Chief Officer)
Sub Oficial Inicial (Initial Chief Officer)	Maestro de Segunda (2nd Class Master Chief)	Sub Oficial Inicial (Initial Chief Officer)
Sargento Primero (1st Sergeant)	Sargento Técnico de Primera (1st Technical Sgt.)	Sargento Primero (First Sergeant)
Sargento Segundo (2nd Sergeant)	Sargento Técnico de Segunda (2nd Technical Sgt.)	Sargento Segundo (Second Sergeant)
Sargento (Sergeant)	Cabo (Corporal)	Sargento (Sergeant)
Cabo (Corporal)	Marinero de Primera (1st Class Sailor)	Cabo (Corporal)
Soldado (Soldier)	Marinero (Sailor)	Dragoneante (Dragonling)
-	-	Soldado (Soldier)

Table 14: Bolivian Police ranks.[28]	
Officers	**NCOs**
General de Policía (Police General)	Suboficial Superior (Senior Chief Officer)
General Supervisor (Supervisor General)	Suboficial Mayor (Chief Officer)
General Superior (Senior General)	Suboficial Primero (First Chief Officer)
Coronel (Colonel)	Suboficial Segundo (Second Chief Officer)
Teniente Coronel (Lieutenant Colonel)	Sargento Mayor (Sergeant Major)
Mayor (Major)	Sargento Primero (First Sergeant)
Capitán (Captain)	Sargento Segundo (Second Sergeant)
Teniente (Lieutenant)	Sargento (Sergeant)
Sub Teniente (Sub Lieutenant)	Cabo (Corporal)
Officer Candidates (Police School)	Dragoneante (Dragonling)
Brigadier Mayor (Brigadier Major)	Agente de Policía (Police Agent)
Brigadier (Brigadier)	NCO Candidates
Subbrigadier (Deputy Brigadier)	Alumno (Student)
Cadete (Cadet)	-

Table 15: Che Guevara's ELN troops.[29]

Name	Nom de guerre	Nationality	Fate	Place and Date
Ernesto Guevara de la Serna (Commandant of the Cuban Revolutionary Army)	Che, Ramón, Fernando, Mongo or Tatu	Argentine-Cuban	Wounded in combat, captured and executed	La Higuera, 09.10.67
Jesús Suárez Gayol (Captain of the Cuban Revolutionary Army)	Felix or El Rubio	Cuban	KIA	Iripití River, 10.04.67
Eliseo Reyes Rodríguez (Captain of the Cuban Revolutionary Army)	Rolando or Capitán Luis	Cuban	KIA	El Mesón, 25.04.67
Antonio Sánchez Díaz (Commandant of the Cuban Revolutionary Army)	Marcos or Comandante Pinares	Cuban	KIA	Peña Colorada, 02.06.67
Carlos Coello (Lieutenant of the Cuban Revolutionary Army)	Tuma or Tumaini	Cuban	KIA	La Florida, 26.06.67
José María Martínez Tamayo (Captain of the Cuban Revolutionary Army)	Papi, Ricardo, Mbili or Taco	Cuban	KIA	Rosita River, 30.06.67
Juan Vitalio Acuña Núñez (Commandant of the Cuban Revolutionary Army)	Joaquín or Vilo	Cuban	KIA	Ambushed at Vado del Yeso 31.08.67
Ricardo Gustavo Machín Hoed de Beche (Commandant of the Cuban Revolutionary Army)	Alejandro	Cuban	KIA	Ambushed at Vado del Yeso 31.08.67
Israel Reyes Zayas (Lieutenant of the Cuban Revolutionary Army)	Braulio or Azi	Cuban	KIA	Ambushed at Vado del Yeso 31.08.67
Manuel Hernández Osorio (Captain of the Cuban Revolutionary Army)	Miguel or Manuel	Cuban	KIA	Quebrada de Batán, 26.09.67
René Martínez Tamayo (Lieutenant of the Cuban Revolutionary Army)	Arturo	Cuban	KIA	Quebrada del Yuro, 08.10.67
Orlando Pantoja Tamayo (Captain of the Cuban Revolutionary Army)	Olo or Antonio	Cuban	KIA	Quebrada del Yuro, 08.10.67
Alberto Fernández Montes de Oca (Captain of the Cuban Revolutionary Army)	Pacho or Pachungo	Cuban	KIA	Injured in the Yuro ravine, bled to death without medical assistance on 09.10.67
Octavio de la Concepción de la Pedraja (Medical Lieutenant of the Cuban Revolutionary Army)	Moro, Morogoro, El Médico or Munganga	Cuban	KIA	Cajones, 12.10.67
Harry Antonio Villegas Tamayo (Later Brigadier General of the Cuban Revolutionary Army)	Pombo or Carlos	Cuban	Survived	Later he was Brigadier General of the Cuban Army. He died in Havana on 29.12.2019
Dariel Alarcón Ramírez (Captain of the Cuban Revolutionary Army)	Benigno	Cuban	Survived	Later he became an opponent of the government of Fidel Castro. He died in exile in Paris in 2016.
Leonardo Tamayo Núñez (Captain of the Cuban Revolutionary Army)	Urbano	Cuban	Survived	Later he was Colonel of the Cuban Army. Lives in Havana

Table 15 (continued): Che Guevara's ELN troops.[29]				
Benjamín Coronado Córdova	Benjamín	Bolivian	Drowned	Grande River, 26.02.67
Lorgio Vaca Marchetti	Carlos	Bolivian	Drowned	Grande River, 16.03.67
Jorge Vázquez Viaña	Loro or Bigotes	Bolivian	Executed after being captured	Wounded in combat, admitted to the Choreti Hospital and kidnapped by the army to be assassinated on 22.04.67.
Casildo Condori Choque	Víctor	Bolivian	KIA	Peña Colorada, 02.06.67
Julio Velazco Montaño	Pepe	Bolivian	Deserted and later executed	Captured by the army and executed, 30.06.67
Serapio Aquino Tudela	Serapio or Serafín	Bolivian	KIA	Iquira River, 09.07.67
Raúl Quispaya Choque	Raúl or Ramón	Bolivian	KIA	Rosita River, 30.07.67
Eusebio Tapia Aruni	Eusebio	Bolivian	Survived	Arrested by the army on 25.07.67, tortured and sentenced to 30 years in prison. Amnestied in 1970. Lives in Bolivia.
Antonio Jiménez Tardío	Pedro or Pan Divino	Bolivian	KIA	Ambushed in the Iñao Mountain Range, 09.08.67
Apolinar Aquino Quispe	Polo	Bolivian	KIA	Ambushed at Vado del Yeso 31.08.67
Walter Arencibia Ayala	Walter or Abel	Bolivian	KIA	Ambushed at Vado del Yeso 31.08.67
Moisés Guevara Rodríguez	Moisés, Armando or Tocayo	Bolivian	KIA	Ambushed at Vado del Yeso 31.08.67
Freddy Ernesto Maymura Hurtado	Freddy, El Médico or Ernesto	Bolivian	Executed after being captured	Captured on 31.08.67 in Puerto Mauricio. Killed hours later.
José Castillo Chávez	Paco or Paquito	Bolivian	Survived	Sole survivor of Vado del Yeso. Captured on 31.08.67
Mario Gutiérrez Ardaya	Julio	Bolivian	KIA	Quebrada de Batán, 26.09.67
Roberto Peredo Leigue	Coco	Bolivian	KIA	Quebrada de Batán, 26.09.67
Antonio Domínguez Flores	León	Bolivian	Survived	Surrendered to the army on 27.09.67
Orlando Jiménez Bazán	Camba	Bolivian	Survived	Captured by the army on 30.09.67, tortured and sentenced to 30 years in prison. Amnestied in 1970. Died in Sweden in 1994.
Aniceto Reinaga Gordillo	Aniceto	Bolivian	KIA	Quebrada del Yuro, 08.10.67
Simeón Cuba Sarabia	Willy	Bolivian	Captured and later executed	La Higuera, 09.10.67
Jaime Arana Campero	Chapaco	Bolivian	Captured and later executed	Wounded and killed in Cajones, 12.10.67
Francisco Huanca Flores	Pablo	Bolivian	Captured and later executed	Wounded and killed in Cajones, 12.10.67
Julio Luis Méndez Korne	Ñato	Bolivian	KIA	Mataral, 15.11.67
Hugo Choque Silva	Chingolo	Bolivian	Deserted and later captured	July 67
Guido Álvaro Peredo Leigue	Inti	Bolivian	Survived	In 1969 he reorganised the ELN. Captured in La Paz, and assassinated on 09.09.69
David Adriazola Veizaga	Darío	Bolivian	Survived	In 1969 he joined the ELN again. Assassinated in La Paz on 31.12.69

Table 15 (continued): Che Guevara's ELN troops.[29]				
Salustino Choque Choque	Salustio	Bolivian	Survived	Arrested by the army, tortured and sentenced to 30 years in prison. Amnestied in 1970.
Vicente Rocabado Terrazas	Orlando	Bolivian	Survived	Captured by the army on 14.03.67, tortured and sentenced to 30 years in prison. Amnestied in 1970.
Pastor Barrera Quintana	Daniel	Bolivian	Survived	Captured by the army on 14.03.67, tortured and sentenced to 30 years in prison. Amnestied in 1970.
Juan Pablo Chang Navarro	El Chino, Francisco or Emilio	Peruvian	Captured and later executed	La Higuera, 09.10.67
Restituto José Cabrera Flores	El Negro	Peruvian	Executed after being captured	Survivor of the ambush in Puerto Mauricio on 31.08.67. Captured and killed on 04.09 in Palmarito River.
Lucio Edilberto Galván Hidalgo	Eustaquio	Peruvian	Captured and later executed	Wounded and killed in Cajones, 12.10.67
Ciro Roberto Bustos (*)	Carlos, El Pelao, Mauricio or Laureano	Argentine	Survived	Arrested by the army on 20.04.67, tortured, and sentenced to 30 years. Amnestied in 1970. Died in Sweden on 01.01.2017
Haydée Tamara Bunke Bider (+)	Tania or María	Argentine-East German	KIA	Ambushed at Vado del Yeso 31.08.67
Jules Régis Debray (*)	Danton or El Francés	French	Survived	Arrested by the army on 20.04.67, tortured, and sentenced to 30 years in prison. Amnestied in 1970. Lives in Paris.
Total guerrilla troops: 52. Killed: 37. Survived: 15.				
(*) Both Debray and Bustos have been considered 'visitors' and not combatants by many authors.				
(+) Tania was not a combatant but remained with the guerrillas at Ñancahuazú.				

Table 16: The guerrilla columns on 20 April 1967.[30]		
Che's column		**Joaquín's column**
Che	Víctor	Joaquín
Aniceto	Willy	Tania
Chingolo	Eustaquio	Ernesto
Coco	El Chino	Walter
Darío	Antonio	Moisés
Eusebio	Arturo	Negro
Inti	Benigno	Alejandro
Julio	Marcos	Paco
León	Miguel	Polo
Loro	Moro	Braulio
Luis	Pacho	-
Ñato	Pombo	-
Pablo	Ricardo	-
Pedro	Rolando	-
Pepe	Tuma	-
Raúl	Urbano	-
Serapio	Cambá	-

Table 17: ELN Urban Logistics Organisation.[31]		
Name	**Nom de guerre**	**Notes**
Dr. Walter Pareja Fernández	Pareja	Physician. Head of the Urban Organisation.
Rodolfo Saldaña	Rodolfo	Operational Head of the Urban Organisation.
Dr. Hugo Bleichner Taboada	Bleincher	Physician. Member of the Urban General Staff.
Dr. Humberto Rhea Clavijo	Humberto	Physician in charge of medicines, drugs, surgical supplies. Member of the Urban General Staff.
Norberta Aguilar	Norberta	Member of the Urban General Staff.
Renán Elías	Renán	Member of the Urban General Staff.
Luis Tellería Murillo	Facundo	PCB. La Paz supply chief.
Julio Dagnino Pacheco	Sánchez	Peruvian. In charged of funds received from Havanna.
Félix Arrancibia Berrera	Arrancibia	Member of the Urban Organisation.
Héctor Bejar	Bejar	Member of the Urban Organisation.
Humberto Vásquez Machicado	Humberto	Member of the Urban Organisation. Loro's brother.
Loyola Guzmán Lara	La Loyo	PCB. Visited Ñancahuazú. Member of the Urban Organisation.
Dr. Antonio Lozano	Lozano	Dentist. Member of the Urban Organisation.
Roberto Moreyra Montesinos	Moreyra	Member of the Urban Organisation.
Paca Bernal Leyton	Paquita	Member of Urban Organisation.
Casildo Condori Vargas	Víctor	Member of the Urban Organization.

SOURCES

Books

Anderson, Jon Lee, *Che Guevara: una vida revolucionaria* (Barcelona: Editorial Anagrama, 1997)

Andrade, John M., *Latin-American Military Aviation* (Leicester: Midland Counties Publications, 1982)

Assmann, Hugo, *Teoponte. Una experiencia guerrillera* (Oruro: Centro de Desarrollo Integral-CEDI, 1971)

Butler, Phil & Dan Hagedorn, *Air Arsenal North America. Aircraft for the Allies 1938–1945. Purchases and Lend-Lease* (Hinckley, UK: Midland Publishing, 2004)

Chávez Moruno, Germán, Ñancahuazú, *Bolivia 1967 Mi contribución para esclarecer la realidad histórica* (Kindle edition in Spanish, 2022)

Cornejo, Jorge Arturo, *Operaciones de la Fuerza Aérea Boliviana durante la Campaña Antiguerrillera en* Ñancahuazú, *Año 1967* (La Paz: Author's edition, 2023)

Cupull Reyes, Adys & Froilán González García, *Huellas de Tania* (La Habana: Casa Editorial Verde Olivo, 2022)

De Mesa, José; Gisbert, Teresa & Mesa, Carlos, *Historia de Bolivia* (La Paz: Editorial Gisbert y Cia., 2008)

Dienst, John & Dan Hagedorn, *North American F-51Mustang in Latin American Air Forces Service* (Arlington: Aerofax, Inc, 1985)

Diez de Medina, Fernando, *El General del Pueblo. René Barrientos Ortuño, Caudillo Mayor de la Revolución Boliviana* (La Paz: Author's edition. 2005)

Fuerza Aérea Boliviana, *Resumen Histórico de las Brigadas Aéreas, Institutos y Unidades de la Aviación Militar* (La Paz: Editorial Aeronáutica, 2001)

González, Froilán & Adys Cupull, *De la Higuera a Chile: El Rescate. Testimonio de los sobrevivientes de la Guerrilla del Che y de los que participaron en el salvamento* (Ituzaingó: Editorial Cienflores, 2020)

Guevara Lynch, Ernesto, *Mi hijo el Che* (La Habana: Editorial Arte y Literatura, 1988)

Hagedorn, Dan & Mario Overall, *Douglas DC-3/C-47 in Latin American Military Service* (Manchester: Crécy Publishing Ltd. 2021)

Hagedorn, Dan, *P-38 in Latin America* (Aviation Art & History, 2022)

Hagedorn, Dan, *Che Guevara in Bolivia*. Downloaded text for *Latin American Air Wars* (Hikoki Publications, 2006)

Hagedorn, Dan, *Texans and Harvards in Latin America* (West Sussex, UK: Air Britain Historians Ltd. 2009)

James, Daniel, *The Complete Bolivian Diaries of Ché Guevara and Other Captured Documents* (New York: Cooper Square Press, 2000)

Klein, Herbert S., *A Concise History of Bolivia* (Cambridge: Cambridge University Press, 2021)

Llosa, José Antonio, *René Barrientos Ortuño, Paladín de la Bolivianidad* (La Paz: Empresa Editora Novedades, 1966)

Loza, Francisco Xavier, *El Vuelo del Marihuí y del Cóndor. Ciento y años de la Aviación en Bolivia* (La Paz: Editoria Presencia, 2020)

Márquez, Nicolás, *La Máquina de Matar: Biografía definitiva del Che Guevara a 50 años de su muerte* (Buenos Aires: Editorial Grupo Unión, 2015)

Ministerio de Defensa de la República de Bolivia, *Libro Blanco de Defensa de la República de Bolivia* (La Paz: Instituto Geográfico Militar, 2004)

Prado Salmón, General Gary, *La Guerrilla Inmolada. La campaña del Che en Bolivia. Testimonio y análisis de un protagonista* (Santa Cruz de la Sierra: Editorial Punto y Coma S.R.L., 1988)

Ratner, Michael & Michael Steven Smith, *How the CIA killed Che. The Murder of a Revolutionary* (New York: Skyhorse Publishing, Inc, 2016)

Rodriguez, Félix I. & John Weisman, *Shadow Warrior. The CIA Hero of a Hundred Unknown Battles* (New York: Simon & Schuster. 1989)

Sapienza Fracchia, Antonio Luis, *The Chaco Air War 1932–1935* (Warwick: Helion Publishing Co. 2018)

Sapienza, Antonio Luis & José Luis Martínez Peláez, *The Chaco War 1932–1935. Fighting in the Green Hell* (Warwick: Helion Publishing Co. 2020)

Soria Galvarro, Carlos, *Andares del Che en Bolivia* (Ituzaingó: Editorial Cienflores, 2020)

Soria Galvarro, Carlos, *El Che en Bolivia. Documentos y Testimonios. Su Diario de Campaña* (La Paz: Editorial La Razón, 2005)

Soria Galvarro, Carlos, *El Che en Bolivia. Documentos y Testimonios. Los otros diarios y papeles* (La Paz: Editorial La Razón, 2005)

Soria Galvarro, Carlos, *El Che en Bolivia. Documentos y Testimonios. Su último combate* (La Paz: Editorial La Razón, 2005)

Soria Galvarro, Carlos, *El Che en Bolivia. Documentos y Testimonios. ¿Traición del PCB?* (La Paz: Editorial La Razón, 2005)

Soria Galvarro, Carlos, *El Che en Bolivia. Documentos y Testimonios. Pensamiento Boliviano* (La Paz: Editorial La Razón, 2005)

Taibo II, Paco Ignacio, *Ernesto Guevara, también conocido como El Che* (México: Editorial Planeta-Joaquín Mortiz, 1996)

Vargas Valenzuela, Capitán de Navío José, *Tradición Naval del Pueblo de Bolivia* (La Paz: Editorial Los Amigos del Libro, 1974)

Vazquez Díaz, Rubén, *Bolivia a la hora del Che* (Mexico, DF: Editorial Siglo XXI. 1978)

Villa de la Tapia, Cnel. Av. Amalia, *Alas de Bolivia. Síntesis Histórica de la Aviación Nacional* (La Paz: Editorial Aeronáutica, 1983)

Weiss, Mitch & Kevin Maurer, *Hunting Che. How a US Special Forces Team Helped Capture the World's Most Famous Revolutionary* (New York: The Berkley Publishing Group, 2013)

Articles

Arrien Sueldo, Coronel DAEN S.P. Guido, 'Historia del P-51 en la Fuerza Aérea Bolivana' in *Revista Aeronáutica*, Año XXXVI, No. 41 (La Paz: Órgano Oficial de la Fuerza Aérea Boliviana, October 1992)

Fuerza Aérea Boliviana, 'Del Acervo Histórico de la Fuerza Aérea Boliviana' in *Actualidad Aeronáutica*, No. 74. (La Paz: Fuerza Aérea Boliviana, 1992)

Gildner, R. Matthew, 'La historia como liberación nacional: creando un pasado útil para la Bolivia post revolucionaria' in *Ciencia y Cultura*, Nro. 29 (La Paz: Universidad Católica Boliviana, 2012)

Reque Terán, General (Ret) Luis Antonio, 'Ñancahuazú. La lucha contra el "Che" Guevara' in *Air Power Journal*, Spanish Edition, Spring 1993

Rodriguez Ostria, Gustavo; 'El legado del Che. Del Ejército de Liberación Nacional al Partido Revolucionario de los Trabajadores en Bolivia, 1967–1977. Dossier Guevarismo en América Latina' in *Políticas de la Memoria*, Nro. 18, verano 2018–2019, La Paz

Murillo Bernardis, Lic. Diego, 'Historia de Bolivia. Curso Pre Facultativo Gestión 2011. Carrera de Ciencia Política y Gestión Pública. Facultad de Derecho y Ciencias Políticas' (La Paz: Universidad Mayor San Andrés. 2011)

Sandoval, Rolando, 'Ñancahuazú *una experiencia inolvidable*' in *Revista Aeronáutica* No. 49 (La Paz: Editorial Aeronáutica, 2003)

University Thesis

Behoteguy Chávez, Gabriela, *Memorias de Pacto y Terror. Historias del General René Barrientos Ortuño en Bolivia (1959–1969).* Thesis presented to obtain the Master's degree in History and Memory. (La Plata: Facultad de Humanidades. Maestría en Historia y Memoria, Universidad Nacional de La Plata, 2023)

Web pages

Bolivian Naval Force at <https://www.histarmar.com.ar/ArmadasExtranjeras/Bolivia/ArmadaBolivia-1.htm>

Bolivian Police at <www.policia.bo> and <https://es.wikipedia.org/wiki/Policia_Nacional_de_Bolivia>

Bolivian tanks and armoured vehicles at <https://tanks-encyclopedia.com/bolivian-armor/>

Briscoe, Charles H., *The Special Forces Mission to Cochabamba, Bolivia 1967. Special Forces History, Veritas, Vol. 4, No. 4, 2008* at <https://arsof-history.org/articles/v4n4 _1.html>

El agente de la CIA que atrapó al Che Guevara: Fidel Castro lo mandó a la muerte en Bolivia at <https://www.abc.es/internacional/abci-agente-cia-atrapo-che-guevara-bolivia_noticia.html>

Finlayson, Kenneth, *The Haves and Have Nots. US & Bolivian Order of Battle. Special Forces History, Veritas, Vol. 4, No. 4, 2008* at <https://arsof-history.org/articles/v4n4_have_and_have_nots_page_1.html>

Jones Jr., Robert W., *Che's Posse: Divided, Attritred and Trapped. Special Forces History, Veritas, Vol. 4, No. 4, 2008* at <https://arsof-history.org/articles/v4n4 _1.html>

Ley Orgánica de las Fuerzas Armadas Bolivianas, 20 de diciembre 1963 (Bolivian Armed Forces Law, 20 December 1963) at <http://www.vicepresidencia.gob.bo/Inicio/tabid/36/ctl/wsqverbusqueda/mid/435/Default.aspx?id_base=2&id_busca=280>

Mesa Gisbert, Carlos D., *Bajas del Ejército Boliviano y Civiles en combate durante la Campaña de* Ñancahuazú *en 1967* at <https://carlosdmesa.com/2017/10/08/homenaje-a-los-bolivianos-militares-y-civiles-que-murieron-en-la-guerrilla-de-nancahuazu/>

Olguin, Jonathan, *Bolivian Air Force operations during the* Ñancahuazú *Counterinsurgency Campaign 1967* at <www.laahs.com>

Sacquety, Troy J., *The Aftermath: Che, the Late 1960s, and the Bolivian Mission. Special Forces History, Veritas, Vol. 4, No. 4, 2008* at <https://arsof-history.org/articles/v4n4 _1.html>

Teoponte Guerrilla at <http://movguevaristabolivia.blogspot.com/2015/07/la-guerrilla-de-teoponte-expresion-de.html> and also at <https://www.meer.com/es/66996-teoponte-la-guerrilla-tragica>

Yofre, Juan Bautista Tata, *Una vida al límite: la joven alemana que mató al militar que cortó las manos del Che Guevara y murió delatada por el nazi Klaus Barbie*. Article published in <www.infobae.com> on 6 July 2023.

NOTES

1. José De Mesa, Teresa Gisbert and Carlos Mesa, *Historia de Bolivia* (La Paz: Editorial Gisbert y Cia., 2008).
2. See <https://es.wikipedia.org/wiki/Historia_territorial_de_Bolivia>
3. Antonio Luis Sapienza & José Luis Martínez Peláez, *The Chaco War 1932–1935. Fighting in the Green Hell* (Warwick, Helion: 2020).
4. Although Bolivia considered the whole Chaco region as its territory (250,150 km^2), it only occupied 43,450 km^2 between 1905 and 1932. Besides this, Paraguay also considered the whole Chaco as its territory.
5. Nicolás Márquez, *La Máquina de Matar: Biografía definitiva del Che Guevara a 50 años de su Muerte* (Buenos Aires: Editorial Grupo Unión, 2015).
6. Márquez, *La Máquina de Matar.*
7. From <https://tanks-encyclopedia.com/bolivian-armor/>
8. See <https://es.wikipedia.org/wiki/Ejercito_de_Bolivia>.
9. See <https://es.wikipedia.org/wiki/Anexo:Divisiones_militares_de_Bolivia>.
10. Antonio Luis Sapienza Fracchia, *The Chaco Air War 1932–1935* (Warwick, UK: Helion Publishing, 2018).
11. Phil Butler & Dan Hagedorn, *Air Arsenal North America. Aircraft for the Allies 1938–1945. Purchases and Lend-Lease.* (Hinckley, UK: Midland Publishing, 2004).
12. *Fuerza Aérea Boliviana: Resumen Histórico de las Brigadas Aéreas, Institutos y Unidades de la Aviación Militar* (La Paz: Editorial Aeronáutica, 2001).
13. See <https://es.wikipedia.org/wiki/Anexo:Aeronaves_historicas_de_la_Fuerza_Aérea_Boliviana>.
14. See < https://www.histarmar.com.ar/ArmadasExtranjeras/Bolivia/ArmadaBolivia-1.htm> and Vargas Valenzuela, Capitán de Navío José: *Tradición Naval del Pueblo de Bolivia* (La Paz: Editorial Los Amigos del Libro, 1974).
15. Mitch Weiss & Kevin Maurer, *Hunting Che. How a US Special Forces Team Helped Capture the World's Most Famous Revolutionary* (New York: The Berkley Publishing Group, 2013).

16. General Gary Prado Salmón, *La Guerrilla Inmolada. La Campaña del Che en Bolivia. Testimonio y Análisis de un Protagonista* (Santa Cruz de la Sierra: Editorial Punto y Coma S.R.L., 1988).
17. Daniel James, *The Complete Bolivian Diaries of Ché Guevara and Other Captured Documents* (New York: Cooper Square Press, 2000).
18. 'Hammer and anvil' is a military tactic involving the use of two primary forces, one to pin down an enemy, and the other to smash or defeat the opponent with an encirclement manoeuvre.
19. Daniel James, *The Complete Bolivian Diaries of Ché Guevara and Other Captured Documents* (New York: Cooper Square Press, 2000).
20. General Gary Prado Salmón, *La Guerrilla Inmolada. La Campaña del Che en Bolivia. Testimonio y Análisis de un Protagonista* (Santa Cruz de la Sierra: Editorial Punto y Coma S.R.L., 1988).
21. General Gary Prado Salmón, *La Guerrilla Inmolada. La Campaña del Che en Bolivia. Testimonio y Análisis de un Protagonista* (Santa Cruz de la Sierra: Editorial Punto y Coma S.R.L., 1988).
22. Félix I. Rodriguez & John Weisman, *Shadow Warrior. The CIA Hero of a Hundred Unknown Battles* (New York: Simon & Schuster, 1989).
23. Rodriguez & Weisman, *Shadow Warrior.*
24. Nicolás Márquez, *La Máquina de Matar: Biografía Definitiva del Che Guevara a 50 Años de su Muerte* (Buenos Aires: Editorial Grupo Unión, 2015).
25. Mitch Weiss & Kevin Maurer, *Hunting Che. How a US Special Forces Team Helped Capture the World's Most Famous Revolutionary* (New York: The Berkley Publishing Group, 2013).
26. Weiss & Maurer, *Hunting Che.*
27. Weiss & Maurer, *Hunting Che.*
28. Weiss & Maurer, *Hunting Che.*
29. Rodriguez & Weisman, *Shadow Warrior.*
30. Froilán González & Adys Cupull, *De la Higuera a Chile: El Rescate. Testimonio de los Sobrevivientes de la Guerrilla del Che y de los que Participaron en el Salvamento* (Ituzaingó: Editorial Cienflores, 2020).
31. Bolivian Army Archives, year 1967.
32. See <https://carlosdmesa.com/2017/10/08/homenaje-a-los-bolivianos-militares-y-civiles-que-murieron-en-la-guerrilla-de-nancahuazu/>
33. Bolivian Armed Forces Law, 20 December 1963 at <http://www.vicepresidencia.gob.bo>.
34. Bolivian Armed Forces Law, 20 December 1963 at <http://www.vicepresidencia.gob.bo>.
35. Organic Law of the Bolivian Police, 18 December 1961 at <https://www.lexivox.org/norms/BO-L-153.html>.
36. General Gary Prado Salmón, *La Guerrilla Inmolada. La Campaña del Che en Bolivia. Testimonio y Análisis de un Protagonista* (Santa Cruz de la Sierra: Editorial Punto y Coma S.R.L., 1988).
37. Daniel James, *The Complete Bolivian Diaries of Ché Guevara and Other Captured* Documents (New York: Cooper Square Press, 2000).
38. Daniel James, *The Complete Bolivian Diaries of Ché Guevara and Other Captured* Documents (New York: Cooper Square Press, 2000).

ABOUT THE AUTHOR

Antonio Luis Sapienza Fracchia was born in Asunción, Paraguay on 14 May 1960. He graduated from the Catholic University of Asunción where he got a BA in Clinical Psychology. He also took specialised English courses at Tulane University of New Orleans, Louisiana, and teaching methodology at San Diego State University in California. He is now retired but worked for nearly 40 years as an English teacher and one of the Academic Coordinators at the *Centro Cultural Paraguayo-Americano* (CCPA), a binational institute in Asunción. Married with two children, he resides in the capital. He is an Aviation Historian who wrote more than 500 articles in specialised magazines and web pages on the Paraguayan Aviation history and has given numerous lectures in schools, universities, institutes, military and civil institutions in Paraguay and abroad. Since 2010, he has been an aviation history professor in the Paraguayan Air Force (FAP). In August 2023, he was appointed Corresponding Academician of the Paraguayan Academy of History. He has published twenty-six books since 1996, with this one being his thirteenth with Helion. He received a total of seven decorations for his academic merits, two from Argentina, one from Brazil and four from his own country, Paraguay, two from the Air Force, one from the Naval Aviation and one from the Civil Aviation Authority DINAC.